The Jewish Paradox

The incredible, ironic, bizarre, funny, and provocative in the image of the Jews

Revised Edition

M. HIRSH GOLDBERG

SCARBOROUGH HOUSE

To My Family

Scarborough House
Lanham, MD 20706

FIRST SCARBOROUGH HOUSE EDITION 1993

Copyright © 1979, 1993 by M. Hirsh Goldberg
All rights reserved
Printed in the United States of America

The Jewish Paradox was originally published as *Just Because They're Jewish* by Stein and Day Publishers in 1979.

Library of Congress Cataloging-in-Publication Data

Goldberg, M. Hirsh.
The Jewish paradox : the incredible, ironic, bizarre, funny, and provocative in the image of the Jews / M. Hirsh Goldberg. — 1st Scarborough House ed.
p. cm.
Rev. ed. of: Just because they're Jewish. 1979.
Includes bibliographical references and index.
1. Jews—History. 2. Jews—Anecdotes. 3. Jews—Public opinion. I. Goldberg, M. Hirsh. Just because they're Jewish. II. Title.
DS118.G565   1993
909'.04924—dc20   93–13216 CIP

ISBN 0–8128–8544–9 (pbk. : alk. paper)

"The trouble with most people is not that they don't know much, but that they know so much that isn't true."
—Will Rogers

Contents

Preface to Revised Edition   vii

I   THE INFLUENCE OF THE IGNORANCE FACTOR   1
How a myth murdered millions
    Exhibit A: The Inquisition and the Jews

II   THE JEWS IN STEREOTYPE   19
Misconceptions about the Jews as a people
    Exhibit B: The Jewish "Look"

III   ABOUT THAT RELIGION WHICH BROUGHT YOU THE TEN COMMANDMENTS   43
Misconceptions about the faith of the Jews
    Exhibit C: The Ten Commandments

IV   PRAISE THE LORD AND PASS THE AMMUNITION   73
A study of the most dangerous Jewish stereotype
    Exhibit D: The twelve-year-old Jewish Soldier

V   "A JEW, I PRESUME?"   101
A gallery of Jews who shatter the stereotypes
    Exhibit E: Jewish Landownership

VI   PRAISE THE LORD AND PASS THE BASEBALLS, FOOTBALLS, AND BASKETBALLS, TOO   129
More Jews where you'd least expect them
    Exhibit F: Jewish Popularity

VII   WHAT ABOUT MRS. PORTNOY'S COMPLAINT?   153
The truth about the Jewish mother
    Exhibit G: Jewish Prayer Services

| VIII | STICKS AND STONES MAY BREAK YOUR BONES, BUT NAMES CAN KILL YOU | 173 |

Warning: Mankind has shown that false images can be dangerous to life
Exhibit H: The Blood Accusation

| IX | TO HELL WITH HITLER: A JOURNEY INSIDE THE HOLOCAUST | 199 |

The culmination of ignorance
Exhibit I: Toleration

| X | HATH A JEW EYES? | 227 |

In conclusion . . .

Chapter Sources	241
Acknowledgments	255
Index	257

Preface to Revised Edition

My first book, *The Jewish Connection*, presents the many unusual aspects of Jewish history and the largely unknown contributions of the Jewish people to the world at large. This, my second book, is intended to show the 'other side' of the *Jewish Connection*—what people think they know about the Jews but is not true . . . the myths, the misconceptions, the stereotypes.

And whereas my first book dealt with the incredible, believe-it-or-not aspects of the story of the Jews, this one deals with the incredible, believe-it-or-not aspects of the image of the Jews.

As a result, you have in your hands the second of what is really a two-volume exploration of little-known or misunderstood facets of the Jewish experience over the past 3,000 years.

When originally published, this work carried a title given to it by the publisher—*Just Because They're Jewish*. But I always felt such a title sounded too defensive and was too easily dismissive of the many cross-currents of history that had gone into creating the numerous misconceptions that had warped the Jewish image throughout the ages. The title also neglected to touch on something else that had intrigued and bewildered me throughout the seven years of research and writing that had gone into these two books.

What had astonished me was a strange paradox—how could a people such as the Jews, who have been on the world scene for 3,000 years, who have a history and literature (the Bible) well known throughout the globe, who had their own homeland and then lived openly among other nations for centuries, be so misrepresented, so misunderstood, and so stereotyped in the minds of so many for so long?

No other people have been in contact with such a diversity of countries. No other religion has had such an influence in the world as to spawn two additional major religions with more than a billion adherents. No other nation's literature has influenced world thinking and been as widely read as has the Hebrew Bible.

And yet no other people, no other religion, no other literature have been so villified and misconstrued, with the result often being oppression, discrimination and devastation for Jews. It is one of the great paradoxes of history. It is *the* paradox of Jewish history.

According to the dictionary paradox derives from *para* ("beyond") and *doxa* ("opinion"). The word *paradox*, then, captures much of the mindless virulence of anti-Semitism. In this regard, this book seeks not only to demonstrate the continuing presence of paradox affecting and afflicting the Jewish condition, but by doing so, it is hoped, help lessen if not prevent future assaults on the Jewish image.

Thus, I believe the title *The Jewish Paradox* better captures the essence of this book and makes its relationship with its predecessor, *The Jewish Connection*, more apparent. Although each book stands on its own, I think a reading of the two provides a different perspective on a people with a unique history.

M. Hirsh Goldberg

January 25, 1993
Baltimore, Maryland

I
The Influence of the Ignorance Factor

*How a myth
murdered millions*

FACT: The Aryan myth that Hitler used against the Jews was originally founded by a man who had campaigned for Jewish emancipation in Germany—and had married a Jew.

FACT: The racial aspects of the Aryan myth were popularized by a scholar who later openly rejected the existence of an Aryan race.

FACT: A Germanic legend prevalent for centuries said that Adam spoke German.

FACT: According to theories advanced during the nineteenth century, India had cultivated the West—and such biblical figures as Abraham, Sarah, and Moses were Indians.

FACT: In 1887, two years before Hitler was born, a Frenchman predicted the eventual Holocaust.

> I keep reading between the lies.
> —Goodman Ace

WE ALL SHARE one thing in common—we are all born ignorant.

No matter who we are or what our background, we come into this world without knowledge. As the Book of Job says, "Man is born a wild ass."

Life, then, is a process of learning; learning about ourselves, learning about other selves.

The problem is that learning takes effort, and we do not always learn correctly. We do not automatically replace our ignorance with truth. This is especially the case in the way we acquire information about people of other races and religions. We tend to adopt the easy stereotype, accept the erroneous myth, endorse the half-truth, even embrace the whole lie. The result is that we live in a world oddly divided between the true and the false, between those who are rooted in reality and those who are, to put it mildly, way-off.

The resulting spread of misinformation, misconceptions, inaccuracies, distortions, and outright untruths has shaped our lives to a far greater extent than we generally realize. Fear, hatred, and envy can explain much of the racial and religious animosity on our planet, but a key force feeding these impulses is the persistent incorrect knowledge we have about each other. If we are to understand much that makes our history happen, we must factor in the element of ignorance.

This book, then, is a study of what I call the Ignorance Factor.[1]

---

[1] I am using "ignorance" in its dictionary meaning of "lack of knowledge, uninformed, unaware." This should not be confused, as it often is, with stupidity, which according to the dictionary, "implies lack of normal intelligence." The stupid person may pose a problem because he doesn't know *what* he is doing, but the ignorant person is the real problem because he doesn't know *why* he does *what* he is doing.

[4]

Here will be presented the many unusual ways in which ignorance, mistakes, and misconceptions have affected our world—from filling our libraries with errors to filling our minds with erroneous conceptions about others. And since ignorance can be dangerous—leading to stereotyped thinking, prejudice between peoples, and discrimination against minorities—this book will show how one minority group, the Jews, has been particularly misunderstood.

The need for such an exposure of our ignorance has become increasingly vital. We live in a century that prides itself on the accumulation and use of knowledge, yet we have witnessed in this same time span a dramatic increase in the misconceptions and misunderstandings among peoples. Adolf Hitler was able to rise to power, lead a nation, and plunge a world into war through the artful weaving of distortions and myths. And many of these untruths continue to be mouthed, if with different intensity, by various levels of people—from the viciously anti-Semitic to the uninformed, from our leaders to their followers, thereby filling our world with sound and fury signifying ignorance.

I first began to notice the existence and impact of the Ignorance Factor during research for my first book, *The Jewish Connection*. While delving into the nooks and crannies of history in my desire to search out the obscured ironies and incredible facts of the Jewish experience, I began to see how widespread is mankind's basic ignorance about his world. In my desire to secure at least two and often three or more supporting authorities to confirm any information I presented, I discovered that our most respected scholars and reference works are either uncertain or in conflict about so much in the past. I especially noticed during my cross-checking how even simple facts are many times disputed.

During this research, I also began to realize how much the Jewish people and religion have been misunderstood, distorted, and erroneously stereotyped—usually not so much by anti-Semitism, as from ignorance. The non-Jew, it seems, has too often learned about the Jew through bits and pieces of information that have been incorrectly understood and inaccurately transmitted. Another surprise I encountered was that Jews, too, have erroneous information about their own people and religious heritage. Such is the pervasiveness of the Ignorance Factor, which not only affects all religions and races, but afflicts them as well.

This book will explore how a great many of the myths, mix-ups, and misconceptions about the Jews have arisen—and what the truth is as revealed by intensive research. In many instances, the disparity between popular perceptions and actual truths has been surprising, even shocking. And what is especially shocking is to learn how throughout history injustice has flowed from ignorance to engulf the Jewish people.

Before looking in detail into the many unusual, ironic and bizarre ways the world has been mistaken about the Jews, let us consider how one specific misconception about Jews could arise, flower, and lead to death and destruction not just for Jews, but for millions of non-Jews. Indeed, this was a myth, directed at world Jewry, that gained the widespread, enthusiastic support of a cultured nation, received the full backing of a government, and dominated a continent to such an extent that the very core of civilization was threatened. And exploiting the madness of this myth was Adolf Hitler.

It was on Monday, January 30, 1933, shortly before noon, that German President Hindenburg, acting according to the constitution, entrusted the chancellorship of Germany to Adolf Hitler. At 5:00 P.M., Hitler held his first cabinet meeting, and that evening he greeted the German people as their new leader. The Third Reich had begun.

The night was cold and wintry as the new chancellor—his body rigid, his face radiant—stood at an upper window of the chancellery and watched a massive torchlight parade in his honor. While a spotlight was kept trained on Hitler, twenty five thousand storm troopers marched by in disciplined columns, shouting fight songs and carrying flaming torches—the smell of smoke twisting out over the city, the dancing lights illuminating the mesmerized faces along the streets. In a procession that went on for hours, Berlin was filled with the incessant throb of drums, the crash of boots, the cry of "Sieg Heil!" The sign of the swastika was everywhere, appearing for the first time on the sleeves of some of the regular policemen, dominating the blood-red Nazi flags that coiled and uncoiled in the chill air. Germans of all ages thronged the sidewalks to watch. Youngsters climbed into trees and clung to the iron fences. Women cheered. Middle-aged men gave the Nazi salute. Caught up in what has been termed one of the greatest demonstrations of enthusiasm under Hitler, the crowd repeatedly sang *Deutschland, Deutschland über Alles.*

And above the mass of people, for hour after hour, stood Adolf Hitler, basking in the glow of the fires and the spotlight.

What had been the galvanizing idea used to propel to such immense power a man who had never graduated from high school, who had failed in his first chosen field, art, who had never held an official position higher than lance corporal?

Above all else, it had been his passionate espousal of the myth of the Aryan race—that Germany's superior Aryan heritage was being threatened by the influence of the inferior Jew. He had talked of uplifting the German people from the quagmire of defeat and destitution by building a racially pure Aryan nation. The noble, mighty Aryan was destined for great things, he had been telling them, if only they would guard against the introduction into their race of the impure blood of the Jews.

Racial impurity had plagued them before, said Hitler. "The Aryan gave up the purity of his blood, and therefore, lost his sojourn in the paradise which he had made for himself," Hitler had written in *Mein Kampf.* What must be done to regain this superiority was clear to Hitler: "It is no accident that the first cultures arose in places where the Aryan, in his encounters with lower peoples, subjugated them and bent them to his will."

"We see before us the Aryan race which is manifestly the bearer of all culture," he had repeated in various forms in countless speeches and statements. "Take away the Nordic Germans and nothing remains but the dance of Apes."

The Germans were the modern Aryans and thus the Master Race, he had exhorted them, "the highest species of humanity on this earth."

Where had Hitler gotten his racial theory that there was only one truly creative force in history—the Aryan race? How had he found such support among the German people for his talk of an Aryan race? And why had he written in *Mein Kampf,* "The mightiest counterpart to the Aryan is represented by the Jews"?

We must go back almost 150 years before Hitler took office that January day in 1933, to a simple passage in an article on an ancient language virtually no one spoke and few could read with understanding—to an article on Sanskrit.

The incredible truth is, as we shall see, that the myth that Hitler had seized on and that eventually led to the Holocaust began not with talk of race, but linguistics. It started with a passage written not by a German, but an Englishman, had as its model of superiority not Germany, but India, and was never endorsed in its eventual racial form by two of its leading early advocates. In fact, one of them strongly repudiated the concept of an Aryan race.

It all began innocently enough. In 1788, William Jones, an English poet and jurist who had been appointed a Justice of the High Court of Bengal, wrote an article about his recent study of Sanskrit and his realization that this language had strong affinities with Greek and Latin. In a key passage, he declared that "the roots of verbs" and "the forms of grammar" bore such strong affinity to these languages that "no philosopher could examine them all three without believing them to have sprung from some common source which, perhaps, no longer exists."

This innocuous-sounding statement has been said to mark the discovery that the languages seen in much of Europe originated in India and Iran; that Sanskrit, Persian, and such European languages as German, French, Russian, etc., form what is called the Indo-European family of languages.

Not all linguists agreed with Jones's discovery. One noted German grammarian, Adelung, in fact, continued to support the theory that language had one common origin: it had begun with the beginning of the human race—in Kashmir, the site, he said, of the Garden of Eden.[2]

But most authorities in Eastern culture did support Jones's findings. Enter Karl Wilhelm Friedrich von Schlegel (1772–1829), who is named by Leon Poliakov in his comprehensive study, *The*

---

[2] Although the Biblical account of mankind's descent from Adam had been widely accepted in Europe for centuries, the language he had spoken was the subject of debate. Starting in the Middle Ages, one legend prevalent in the Germanic countries was that Adam spoke—what else?—German.

Aryan Myth, as the real founder of the Aryan myth. This German philosopher, poet, critic, diplomat, historian, and even novelist was also a student of Sanskrit. In a series of lectures on history which he began giving in 1805 at the University of Cologne, and in writings beginning in 1808, he gave impetus to Jones's thoughts by linking the concept of language with race.

Schlegel eventually advanced the theory that these interrelated languages derived not only from a common ancestor tongue, which he eventually called "Aryan," but from a specific people called Aryans who spoke this language and lived in a land called Aryana. Of course, no trace existed of such a people, their language, or their land. As one writer has noted, "Not a line of Indo-European (Aryan) literature has been preserved, and not a single skeleton, inscription, weapon, or other object has been identified as Indo-European."

Schlegel proposed that eventually the Aryan people and tongue emerged on the world scene out of India. "Everything, absolutely everything, is of Indian origin," he once wrote. In what must rank as one of history's greatest flights of fancy, Schlegel offered that even Egyptian civilization was the result of the efforts of missionaries from India, and that the Egyptians, influenced by the Indians, "founded a civilizing colony in Judaea; but the 'Tartar' nation of Moses was only partially indoctrinated with the Indian truths, since it was ignorant of metempsychosis and especially of the immortality of the soul." [3]

Schlegel went on to elaborate on this theory in his important *Essay on the Language and Wisdom of the Indians* written in 1808. It was in the third section of this book, after discussing the beauty of Sanskrit and its expressiveness, that Schlegel turned anthropologist. Here he wrote of a new people formed in northern India who had swept westward, in marching columns of masterful men, to found empires and civilize the West. The superiority of this people could be seen, said Schlegal, in "the gigantic grandeur and durability of Egyptian and Indian architecture in contradistinction to the fragile littleness of modern building."

---

[3] This India Connection was widespread among intellectuals in those days. The great philosopher Voltaire had previously written that Adam had taken everything, including his name, from the Indians, and an English writer held that Moses was an Indian renegade.

And then Schlegel makes the statement that will propel the Aryan idea into seeming fact: "This consideration will enable us by analogy to grasp the idea ... that all these famous nations sprang from one stock, and that their colonies were all one people directly or indirectly, of Indian origin...."

At this point, Schlegel had not yet used the word "Aryan" (he endorsed its use, for linguistic reasons, in 1819), and he backed off from any more speculation about the origins of man. He noted, for instance, that he was referring to "facts which preceded history" and concluded, most interestingly in the light of future events: "It is not suitable here to pursue this enquiry any further, important though it is for the history of our country."

But in those times of nationalistic fervor among Germans, Schlegel's thoughts and theories were enough to fuel an intellectual bonfire. His own brother, August Wilhelm, also a poet and critic (he translated Shakespeare into German), was the first to spread these ideas as a way to promote German nationalism: "If the regeneration of the human species started in the East, Germany must be considered the Orient of Europe." Some surprising ironies soon followed. One theorist described future Aryans as "Semites of the Far East." Another ascribed Judaism to a primitive Brahmanism, with Abraham-Brahma and Sara-Sarasvadi being Brahmins. Soon there were learned discussions and treatises on *Indo-Europeans* or, as obviously preferred by many in Germany, *Indo-Germans*.

By the 1820s—a hundred years before Hitler's entry on the German scene—"the authentic and useful science of linguistics became absorbed in the crazy doctrine of 'racial anthropology,'" writes Poliakov. "Worse still, political passions influenced the course taken by these anthropological distortions. Moreover, it was at the time when these new words and new theories began to abound that the Jewish question was being discussed with special fury."

Full emancipation for the Jews had come to Germany only after the Germans had been defeated by France and were still under French occupation, a fact that fed German anti-Semitism and made it ripe for the new thinking about Aryans. Since thinkers like Schlegel had said the languages of the world were divided between the Aryan and the Semitic languages, talk began to grow about other possible differences between the Aryans and the Semitic Jews. Now, concepts and discussions were far afield from linguistics.

Enter Professor Friedrich Max Müller (1823–1900), the outstanding German-born, but English-raised, philologist and mythologist. Poliakov calls him "the leading Sanskrit scholar of the nineteenth century." Based on his early linguistic work, Müller assumed that since an Indo-European or Aryan mother tongue had existed, there must also have existed an Aryan race that had employed such a language. Because of his stature in the scholarly world of the time, his assertions about an Aryan race helped spread the racial idea both among intellectuals and the public. He is therefore considered to be key to the popularization of the myth of an Aryan race, so much so that he has been termed the Aryan myth's "distinguished godfather."

After the middle of the century, works on the race theme began to attract a wide audience. For example, *Essay on the Inequality of the Human Race* by Count Joseph Arthur de Gobineau, a French diplomat. He wrote in this 4-volume study (1853–55) that the white race—of which the jewel was the Aryan, especially the Aryan German—is superior to the yellow and black races in intellect and spirituality and implied that the Aryan race was superior to the Jewish "mongrel race." Another Frenchman, the scholar Ernest Renan, who was not considered anti-Jewish, wrote in a very influential work, *Studies of Religious History* (1856), that the "Semites" were an "incomplete race" while the Indo-European race had brought about "all the great military, political, and intellectual movements."

But Müller eventually realized that peoples of different races could have employed the same Aryan language, and later in his career he actually tried to correct any misunderstandings about this. In explaining why, when he referred to "Aryan" he meant not race, but language, Müller wrote:

> I have declared again and again that if I say Aryans I mean neither blood nor bones, nor hair nor skull; I mean simply those

who speak an Aryan language. . . . To me an ethnologist who speaks of Aryan race, Aryan blood, Aryan eyes and hair, is as great a sinner as a linguist who speaks of a dolichocephalic dictionary or a brachycephalic grammar. It is worse than a Babylonian confusion of tongues—it is downright theft. We have made our own terminology for the classification of languages; let ethnologists make their own for the classification of skulls, and hair, and blood.

But few seemed to be listening. Müller's retractions never received the notoriety his earlier works had. In a demonstration of how, as we will see, the Ignorance Factor is prevalent even in our most respected sources, *The Aryan Myth* states, "The textbooks and encyclopedias continued to quote the Max Müller of the earlier period."

Thus, Müller, and Schlegel before him, could do little to halt the use of their ideas for racial ends. "What matters is who uses the words, and it is common knowledge that, once in circulation, they quickly escape the control of the linguists who coined them," writes Poliakov.[4]

During the following decades, anti-Semites simply went ahead building on what was now developing into accepted fact—that a race of white people called Aryans had founded the best aspects of western civilization and were superior to the Semitic Jew, who was seen as a threat of impurity to Aryans. Thus was the centuries-old religious basis for anti-Jewish hatred replaced by a racial basis.

The very term anti-Semitism was coined at this time (1873) by William Marr, an avowed believer in the superiority of the Aryans. In a pamphlet entitled *Victory of Judaism over Germandom*, published in Germany and so popular it went through twelve editions in six years, Marr called for the prevention by physical means of the "Jewification of society." He also told the German people that the "Jewish problem" was not religious, but racial. His

---

[4] Another scholar to whom this happened was Ernest Renan, who was also important to the popularization of the Aryan myth, especially in France. He, too, later tried without much success to prevent his work from being used by those promoting racialism.

success led him in 1879 to found the first group in any country to use the title, "The Anti-Semitic League." [5]

The composer Richard Wagner also wrote an anti-Jewish pamphlet that received wide attention around this time. First issued in 1869 and then reissued in a slightly revised edition twenty years later, *Judaism in Music* promoted Wagner's thesis that "Jewish blood" was so inferior that it could not produce anything truly creative in the arts or in thought, a concept Hitler later enthusiastically supported.

By 1886, a French writer—Edouard Drumont—could achieve great popular success with a 1,000-plus page book *(La France Juive* or *Jewish France)* that declared modern France's most treacherous foe to be the Jews, who had no sense of justice, carried disease, were born criminals and traitors, and could be recognized by their "crooked nose, the eager fingers, the unpleasant odor." The book went through more than 100 editions and unleashed a wave of anti-Semitism in France that carried over into the Dreyfus Affair.

By 1899, the son-in-law of composer Richard Wagner, Houston Stewart Chamberlain, could write a vitriolic attack on the Jews that would eventually sell almost 1,000,000 copies and be enthusiastically received by Kaiser Wilhelm II. Entitled *Foundations of the Nineteenth Century*, the 1500-page book offered such choice declarations as this one: "The Jewish race is altogether bastardized, and its existence is a crime against the holy laws of life."

By 1904, a French thinker Jean Finot could write that "today, out of 1,000 educated Europeans, 999 are convinced of the authenticity of their Aryan origins."

By 1914, a novel on an anti-Semitic racial theme could become a big bestseller, with nearly a million copies in print as of 1933. Entitled *Die Sunde wider das Blut* by Arthur Dinter, the book's main theme was *telegony*—the concept that "an Aryan woman, if only once soiled by a Jew, was destined to breed only Jewish [or Hebroid] children."

---

[5] The coining of the word "anti-Semitism" in the 1870s by a German hater of Jews is a reminder that the pro-Aryan was proud to be called an anti-Semite. In fact, not only is the continued use of the word anti-Semitism inaccurate because it literally embraces non-Jewish Arabs who are also Semites, but it is also an unconscious perpetuation of Aryanism since it emphasizes the Semitic-Aryan schism.

By the 1920s, Hitler was basing his political career on the bogus principle of Aryan superiority, the inferiority of the Jew, and the threat of the "Jewish peril." Seizing on this racial myth as a way to build German pride, Hitler preached that the Germans represented the true descendants of the Aryans and that "subhuman" Jews, who were contaminating the Aryan race, must be "eliminated."

By the 1930s, people were living or dying simply because they could be classed as "Aryan" or "Semite."

Thus is ignorance perverted. Our lack of knowledge is not always replaced with truth; ignorance can be and often is replaced simply by ignorance of a different kind. And in the case of Friedrich von Schlegel, the misapplication of his ideas in the cause of anti-Semitism has a special bitter irony. For Schlegel, the founder of the Aryan myth, was himself not only an advocate of complete emancipation of the Jews, but campaigned for it—and married the daughter of the Jewish philosopher Moses Mendelssohn.

Thus, the origin and development of the Aryan race myth, over nearly a century and a half, is a case in point of the force of the Ignorance Factor.

There is one other lesson here. The whole sorry story of the Aryan race myth is evidence that replacing our ignorance with correct information is so difficult that our leading minds are often no better at it than the average person. After all, the theory that had captivated much of Europe for so long and engaged brilliant people in earnest debate and study now sits in intellectual ruins. Today, nearly 175 years after Friedrich von Schlegel first discussed it, less than a half century after Hitler rose to power and began putting it into practice, the Aryan myth is dismissed by scholars and the general public alike. (When was the last time you heard anyone, except racial die-hards, seriously advance the idea of a superior Aryan race?) *The Encyclopaedia Britannica*, in its entry on Aryan, notes that in modern times the term has become "almost useless" and that "even in the purely linguistic meaning common in the 19th century, it has been abandoned." *Webster's New World Dictionary* says that "Aryan has no validity as a racial term." And the *World Book Encyclopedia* states flatly, "There is no such thing as an Aryan *race.*"

In fact, the legal aspect of the term "Aryan" was even rejected by the U.S. Supreme Court [United States vs. Bhagat Sing Thind]. While ruling on the request of a high caste Hindu from India to be classified as a white person under U.S. immigration law, the Supreme Court noted that "the eligibility of this applicant for citizenship is based on the sole fact that he is of high caste Hindu stock, born in Punjab, one of the extreme northwestern districts of India, and classified by certain scientific authorities as of the Caucasian or Aryan race." But the Court went on to discuss the Aryan theory and repudiated it, as follows:

> The Aryan theory as a racial basis seems to be discredited by most, if not all, modern writers on the subject of ethnology. A review of their contentions would serve no useful purpose. It is enough to refer to the works of Deniker *(Races of Man,* 317), Keane *(Man: Past and Present,* 445-6), Huxley *(Man's Place in Nature,* 278), and to the *Dictionary of Races, Senate Document* 662, 61st Congress, 3d Sess., 1910-1911, page 17.
>
> The term "Aryan" has to do with linguistic, and not at all with physical characteristics, and it would seem reasonably clear that mere resemblance in language, indicating a common linguistic root buried in remotely ancient soil, is altogether inadequate to prove common racial origin. There is, and can be, no assurance that the so-called Aryan language was not spoken by a variety of races living in proximity to one another. Our own history has witnessed the adoption of the English tongue by millions of negroes, whose descendants can never be classified racially with the descendants of white persons, notwithstanding both may speak a common root language.

The Supreme Court decision in which this appears was handed down on February 19, 1923, about the very time Hitler was first making his mark in politics and fulminating about the Aryan race and the Jewish threat to its purity, but too many people preferred to ignore the evidence and follow their emotions. The Ignorance Factor had taken over.

When Hitler stood at his window that night in 1933, welcomed by a people consumed in a wave of emotion, the stage was set for what eventually would lead, step by jackbooted step, not only to the deaths of 6,000,000 Jews but to the loss of 3,500,000 Germans in a war that would kill close to 50,000,000. And it would all be largely fueled by misguided belief in a mistaken myth of racial superiority.

Thus, an eerie prediction made the century before was to come thunderously true. In 1887, two years before Hitler was born, a Frenchman who had been infatuated with the Aryan concept (he had once said that the Aryans "made France great") had a vision of what this emphasis on race could lead to. Wrote Georges Vacher de Lapouge: "I am convinced that in the next century people will slaughter each other by the million because of a difference of a degree or two in the cephalic index. It is by this sign ... that men will be identified ... and the last sentimentalists will be able to witness the most massive exterminations of peoples."

INTRODUCING GOLDBERG'S LAW

If anything can be misconstrued about the Jews, it will be ... and has been.

Exhibit A: THE INQUISITION AND THE JEWS

THE INQUISITION WAS NOT DESIGNED TO PERSECUTE THE JEWS— AND AFFECTED JEWS ONLY BECAUSE IT WAS REALLY MEANT TO PUNISH CHRISTIANS

That Jews and their history are often misunderstood can be seen by looking at another period of great upheaval for the Jews—the Inquisition. During that time, the Jews became the unwitting victims of a campaign actually directed at Christians. Also, contrary to popular belief, Jews who openly remained Jews were not tortured or killed as part of the inquisition proceedings.

The Inquisition was specifically authorized by the Church to root out heresy among Catholics, so only heretical Christians and Jewish converts to Christianity accused of secretly reverting to Judaism were prosecuted. Unbaptized Jews living openly as Jews continued to observe their own religion, free of the accusation of heresy. In fact, the prosecution of Jews was strictly forbidden to the Inquisition and outside its ecclesiastically given authority. This, however, did not stop leaders of the Inquisition from putting pressure on individual Jews and Jewish communities to convert or leave a country, because it was feared that the presence of Jews would encourage heresy among Christians: Jews might entice Christians to convert to Judaism or lure Jewish converts to Christianity back to their original faith. The Jews were expelled from Spain in 1492—even though the Pope objected—because of pressure from the Inquisition on King Ferdinand and Queen Isabella to protect the country from Christian heresy. Thus, even though the Inquisition was not supposed to interfere with the practice of Judaism by Jews, it wound up doing precisely that for the wrong reason.

II
The Jews in Stereotype

*Misconceptions about
the Jews as a people*

FACT: The German leader Bismarck once advocated that to improve their race, Germany's male aristocrats should marry Jewish women.

FACT: Jews were once thought to have a distinct odor that suddenly disappeared if they converted.

FACT: Jewish law is more lenient about who is a full Jew than Nazi law was.

FACT: A scientific study found that the majority of Jews do not have a "Jewish nose," but a "Greek nose."

> I am free of all prejudices.
> I hate everyone equally.
> —W.C. Fields

"There are more misconceptions in circulation about the Jews than about any other people," wrote Theodor Herzl in 1895 in *The Jewish State*, the document that launched Herzl's campaign to restore the Jews to their homeland.

When he wrote this, Herzl was an assimilated Jew ignorant about much in Jewish life, yet during his previous career as playwright and foreign correspondent he had obviously sensed one of the most significant problems about the Jewish experience: the Jews have encountered—and continue to encounter—a complexity of misconceptions and stereotypes that far outnumber those held about other ethnic groups. While one can probably list on one hand the stereotypes held about Blacks or Puerto Ricans or Chicanos or Irish or any other minority that has experienced discrimination, the Jews face a bewildering array of misunderstandings, distortions, and outright fictions—many, as we will see, incredible, ironic, bizarre, and even contradictory.

Misconceptions about the Jews are literally as old as Biblical times and as recent as today's headlines. "Behold, the people of the children of Israel are too many and too mighty for us; come, let us deal wisely with them, lest they multiply, and it come to pass, that, when there happens any war, they will join our enemies, and fight against us." The speaker was not Adolf Hitler railing about supposed Jewish treachery or a Czar or Josef Stalin whipping up the Russian masses to turn on the Jews. It was Pharaoh offering his reasons for enslaving the Jews (Exodus I, 9–10).

"There is a certain people scattered abroad and dispersed among the people in all the provinces ... and their laws are diverse from those of every people; neither keep they the king's laws; therefore it profiteth not the king to suffer them." The speaker was not a king or prince in medieval Europe preparing the way to expel the Jewish population. It was Haman, the arch villain of Purim, explaining to the king of Persia why the Jews should be annihilated (Esther III, 8).

These incidents, so often repeated in Jewish history, provide an insight into why Jews have been misunderstood and unfairly stereotyped. In each of these Biblical stories, the Jews were a minority in another land. This is of more than passing coincidence, for to be in the minority in any country is to be, by definition, weaker and more vulnerable than those in the majority—and therefore more susceptible to the dangers of falsehoods.

This, though, should be of concern to everyone, for each human being is in reality the member of some minority. Yes, even that celebrated member of the American ruling class, the white Anglo-Saxon Protestant, is a minority. I have often thought it more than symbolic that the WASP is known by the name of such a small insect, for in reality not one aspect that characterizes him/her is in the majority in the world. As opposed to the WASP's white race, Protestant religion, English language, and place of national origin in the Western world, the race with the most members is the oriental, the religion with the most adherents is Catholicism, the language spoken by the most people is a dialect of Chinese known as North Mandarin, the largest nation in terms of size is Russia, and the country with the largest population is China.

We are, then, all members of some minority, and as such we run the risk at some time of being caught up in someone else's misbelief about ourselves. And little in life can be as terrorizing for the individual as to be in the vulnerable position of one among many. We have such a built-in psychological problem with minorities that we often equate the member of a minority with the strange and mysterious. Notice that we refer to the foreigner as an "alien"—the very name we use in science fiction for a being from outer space and another world.

This is why one of the most beloved sentiments in American history is undoubtedly the one attributed to American humorist and common-sense philosopher Will Rogers:

"I never met a man I didn't like."

Prejudice is so rampant in our world that we are at first disarmed, then refreshed, to find someone so untainted by personal bias that he was willing to accept—and like—everyone he ever met. We marvel that Will Rogers, himself the member of a minority group (he was part Indian), could overcome the friction and animosity that often arise in individual human relationships and between groups of people.

And marvel we should, because the sorriest chapter of human history is how the world's many races, religions, and nations have failed to live amicably together. We live in a world in which, all too often, unfounded myths and fears have caused so many to dislike so many others they never met.

As evidence, I offer into the record a reminder of some great national proverbs from out of Europe's past. "No Russian is any good unless he is first beaten" is a German proverb, while according to a Russian proverb, "The German may be a good fellow, but it is better to hang him." The French have a saying that "England is a good land with a bad people," yet a Spanish proverb declares, "The Frenchman is a scoundrel." And then there is the Italian proverb of long ago which one might say proved true in World War II: "Wherever Germans are, it is unhealthy for Italians."

The most abrasive relationships appear to develop between the religious of differing faiths. The Jews are not alone in feeling the scorn of a rival religion; Christian faithful have argued and fought among themselves in a veritable battle of the sects. An English proverb of the seventeenth century offered a four-word poem of religious venom: "A friar, a liar." And then there is the curse to end all curses. Around 1536, Scottish priests read the following curse on the English for the closing of religious houses:

> I curse their head and all the hairs of their head. I curse their face, their eyes, their mouth, their nose, their tongue, their teeth, their shoulders, their back, and their heart, their arms, their legs, their hands, their feet, and every part of their body from the top of their head to the soles of their feet, before and behind, within and without . . . I curse them walking and I curse

them riding. I curse them eating, and I curse them drinking. I curse them within the house, and I curse them without the house. I curse their wives, their barns and their servants.... I curse their cattle, their wool, their sheep, their horses, their swine, their geese, and their hens. I curse their halls, their chambers, their stables, and their barns....

That prejudice can be unthinking and widespread can also be seen in a study on prejudice conducted in the 1920s in the United States. An article about the results—"Where Do We Get Our Prejudices?"—was published by *Harper's Magazine* in September, 1926, and reprinted in a widely disseminated college textbook entitled *Contemporary Thought*. The report surveyed a thousand persons who were selected "from groups who already happened to be interested in the discussion of public questions." Robert L. Duffus, author of the article, noted that the respondents to survey questions "were above the average in education and intelligence. ... This is important to remember. We are not dealing with the ignorant or the subnormal, but ... with ourselves."

Among the sentiments expressed in written replies was the one by a Protestant woman who wrote how she still held prejudices against Catholics because of what she had been told as a child:

When I was a little girl just starting to school, someone told me that in all the Catholic churches the Catholics kept weapons and ammunition in the basements, all ready at the slightest provocation to make war on the Protestants and kill them. The same person told me that she knew a Catholic lady who had said that she could wade in Protestants' blood up to her knees with a smile on her face. I have had Catholic girl friends since then, some of the best friends I have known, but I could never get rid of my first impressions.

She was not the only Protestant quoted with a prejudicial fear of Catholic war-making. "Another correspondent," wrote Duffus, "a college student, found it hard to eliminate the picture of a Catholic as one who 'hoped to wade knee-deep in Protestant blood in a religious war.'"

[25]

Another respondent disliked Spaniards "because he had read of Spanish cruelties in the conquest of America." A grown man said he "feels a natural repugnance whenever I see or hear the word 'Mexican'" because as a twelve-year-old he had tied a can to the tail of a dog only to be frightened by its angry Mexican owner who chased him. A woman, who as a child had been told a story about a white girl kidnapped by two blacks, admitted that she still harbored "a rather decided prejudice against the negro" because of the account.

The Jews, of course, did not escape being the object of dislike. One man reported that his hatred for Jews dated from the day as a youngster he broke a white milk pitcher while playing in the home of his Jewish friend and became frightened when his friend admonished him. "From that day I never played with Henry again, for I both hated him and at the same time was afraid of him." Although this man noted that he had had "many pleasant dealings" with Jews since his childhood, "yet when one mentions the name 'Jew' I am liable to grow very angry or condemn the Jewish race in a terrible manner, for then . . . the recollection of my childhood experience comes to mind."

Prejudice is so pervasive that it can be found not only in the average person as seen in this study, but even in a President of the United States. "The Italians . . . you can't find one who is honest." The speaker was Richard M. Nixon, overheard on his White House tapes. But there is a special irony here. The termination of Nixon's presidency demonstrated the very falsehood of this statement. For the man who presided over much of the Watergate trials and showed himself to be so staunchly honest and rigidly impartial was Judge John Sirica, who is of Italian background.

Nixon had finally found his honest Italian.

So much for the veracity of prejudice.

In all this, however, one minority stands out in special need of truth and understanding—the Jew. If all those sovereign nations of Europe could harbor such ill will toward each other during the course of history, if the various sects within Christianity could believe in ignorant myths about each other, then what can we expect to find in public attitudes toward a minority like the Jews?

Indeed, the Jews have been the eternal minority in the world these past two thousand years, many times the sole significant minority within a country. Only in relatively recent history have other groups been uprooted or migrated to new lands and become a minority in that land. Blacks, Puerto Ricans, Mexicans, Chinese, Italians, Irish, Germans, Poles—all are minorities in America, but all enjoy majority status in their own lands. Only since 1948 could Jews point to another homeland, as every other ethnic group in America or elsewhere could always do.

The Jew, then, has suffered as much if not more than anyone else from the Ignorance Factor. In fact, Jewish suffering has arisen not so much at the hands of the true anti-Semite, for the blind hater is small in number. The potential for Jewish problems has rested with the vast majority of people who are indifferent about Jews and for whom the presence or absence of correct information about the Jewish people has been the critical turning point. The Nazis used heavy and continuous doses of propaganda against the Jews because, except for pockets of true hatred, they had to. But when the Holocaust came it showed how much mankind's ignorance could be manipulated to distort the real Judaism and the true Jew.

Indeed, while prejudice exists in one form or another between all peoples—and Jews can feel consoled they have not been alone in being distrusted or discriminated against—nothing in history quite matches the myths, misconceptions, and misinformation that have swirled and continue to swirl around the Jews. Because they have come into contact with such a wide assortment of people in a myriad of situations over an especially long history, the Jewish people have experienced the full blast of the ignorance of prejudice. As a result, the animosity that has arisen against the Jew is often based on the most ludicrous of reasons, the most inept logic, the most indecent perversion of the truth, the blindest and wildest of thinking. The Ignorance Factor has been so massive in regard to the Jews that the real truths about this people have been obscured beneath the debris of centuries of misunderstanding.

Thus, the story of the Jews, seemingly so widely told, in reality has not been told fully, or, if related, has invariably been distorted through the mind of a mankind cluttered with half truths and whole lies.

So prevalent does this tendency to misunderstand the Jews seem to be—and so often has this misunderstanding occurred and reoccurred in history—that it has led me to develop a theory about the nature of the Jewish experience. I call it Goldberg's Law, which stated simply is: *if anything can be misconstrued about the Jews, it will be ... and has been.*[1]

Consider the odd range of stereotypes held about the Jews, especially in light of non-Jewish actions in face of those stereotypes:

The Jew was said to be clannish, yet Europe made its Jews live apart in ghettos.

The Jew was scorned because he dressed differently and would not assimilate, but popes and rulers periodically decreed Jews should wear identifying patches, clothes, hats, or badges to set them off from the general populace.

The Gentiles took exception that Jewish law did not permit Jews to eat with others, yet the edicts of the Lateran Council in 1215 (and a host of other exclusionary laws down through the ages) invariably prohibited Christians from dining or socializing with Jews.

The Jew was accused of wanting to avoid work with his hands and preferring to live in the cities; many European countries, however, did not permit Jews to work a farm, own land, or live outside of ghettos until the nineteenth century.

Jews were said to have accumulated much wealth and money, yet were also charged with being a burden on a country because of their poverty.

The Yankee peddler was an esteemed figure in early America for his business shrewdness and initiative, but the Jewish peddler was scorned for his business shrewdness and initiative.

The Jew was denigrated for being too aggressive and pushy, and then just as often labeled a "parasite" for not contributing enough to a country.

---

[1] I offer Goldberg's Law with all due respect to the fabled Murphy's Law, which says: if anything can go wrong, it will. Obviously, Murphy had some Jewish blood in him.

While some said Jews were too interested in money and business, others said he was too immersed in religious learning and studying old books that had no mercantile value.

The Jews have been accused of being communists in Western countries and capitalists in communist countries.

When the Nazis declared that Jews were inferior and warned everyone about a Jewish plot to rule the world, no one stopped to explain how inferior people could accomplish so much or why the superior German should be afraid of the inferior Jew.

Josef Stalin thought his Jewish doctors were trying to poison him. Adolf Hitler thought the Jews were trying to poison the Germans' blood. Medieval Christians thought the Jews were trying to poison their wells.

And so it goes. Up and down through history. The Jews are vilified, ostracized, criticized—a result, it seems, when you consider the illogic of the paradoxes inherent in Jewish history.

Significantly, many of the stereotypes about the Jew have reoccurred over the centuries. In fact, so persistent are the images of the Jew that a survey of public opinion polls taken between 1937 and 1962 about American attitudes toward Jews—and reported on in *Jews in the Mind of America*—revealed that there was "a strongly traditional character" to the images expressed by those polled: "None is new or original; most if not all date back hundreds or even thousands of years."

All of which is clear proof of Goldberg's Law and its age-old corollary about being damned if you do and damned if you don't. The Jews have often been damned no matter what they did ... or didn't do.

In considering the unusual scope of ignorance which the Jews have encountered, let us first begin with beliefs held about Jewish physical characteristics. Like the centuries-old concept that a Jew has such quaint accouterments as horns, a tail, a special body smell, and a particular size and style of nose.

That Jews had horns and a tail emanated from the Christian belief that since the Jews killed Christ they either were in league with the devil or were incarnations of the devil himself, complete therefore with Satan's horns and tail. Medieval folklore is heavy with stories of Jews with horns. What might have helped was one of those mistranslations of the Bible. The first time the Bible was translated from Hebrew into Greek a mistake was made in the description of Moses coming down from Mount Sinai with the Ten Commandments. In the Hebrew, Moses is said to have *karan*, a "ray of light" shining from his forehead. In the Greek, this read *keren*, or that "horns" were coming from his head. The mistranslation was further propelled into the consciousness of western man when Michelangelo, sculpting Moses the Lawgiver, gave the leader of the Jews two beautiful horns because of this passage, thereby capturing in marble the power of the Ignorance Factor.

Many non-Jews, especially those who lived far from Jews, maintained as a matter of course that Jews had horns. It was not unusual for a Jew, venturing into an area where Jews had not been seen, to become an object of fascination to the populace, who would inquire about his horns. One verifying account comes from the author of a book on the Christian theology of the Jews as devils. Joshua Trachtenberg, author of *The Devil and the Jews* published in 1943, noted that he himself had encountered such an experience in America. "It was on a trip through Kansas that I once met a farmer who refused to believe that I was Jewish because there were no horns on my head. And I have since learned that this experience is not uncommon."

Probably the most intriguing belief about a Jewish physical trait was that Jews had a special body smell characteristic only of those who practiced the Jewish faith. This distinctive odor even had a scientific-sounding Latin name—*foetor Judaicus*.[2]

The amazing aspect about this aroma of the Jews, according to the medieval believer, was that if the Jew would convert, upon baptism the smell would immediately disappear. Such a belief is indeed surprising because not always did conversion change a Jew

---

[2] The belief in a distinct body smell is not confined to the Jewish-Christian sphere. Numerous cultures have believed the members of other cultures exuded characteristic odors. One notable example: a Japanese anthropologist reported that the Japanese originally found Europeans to have a pronounced smell, chiefly in the armpit area and unremovable by soap or water. Another example: French doctors during World War I swore they could detect even a single wounded German POW in a French military hospital by the German's "characteristic unpleasant odor." [*Gasette Medicale de Paris*, number 267, June 24, 1915]

in the eyes of his new coreligionists. Thus, it is intriguing to realize that the medieval world's distorted conception of the Jew was so extensive that the one element they saw conversion really changing was a distinct body smell that never did exist.[3]

Another misconception about the Jews involves the fabled "Jewish nose." This is a feature all anti-Semites know and love. An anti-Semitic cartoon would be lost without a Jew cavorting about with what could only be described as a Jimmy Durante nose (who, by the way, is not Jewish, but Italian). So prevalent a concept has this been that even Jews have believed the stereotype that says most Jews have large hooked noses. (Theodor Herzl, a handsome man who was able to gain a vast following in part because of his dramatic looks, writes in his diary about his "Jewish nose.") W. S. Gilbert of Gilbert and Sullivan, referred to this nose in the *Bab Ballads*, in which a Jew with one so large (he was referred to as a "bus-directing Jew") underwent a conversion to Christianity and—in an echo of the disappearance of the Jewish body smell—experienced the replacement of his Jewish proboscis:

> The organ which, in man,
> Between the eyebrows grows,
> Fell from his face, and in its place
> He found a Christian nose.

The reason for the "Jewish nose" has even been the subject of solemn scholarship. One research work concluded that the nose of the Jew was the hereditary outcome of a habitual expression of indignation. This concept was advanced by an expert physiognomist, Robert Bennett Bean, in an article in the *American Anthropologist* of 1913 (volume 15, pages 106–108) entitled, believe it or not, "The Nose of the Jew and the Quadratus Labii Superioris Muscle."

Bean also goes so far as to see a Darwinian principle involved in those Jewish features of nose and expression: "Having become a recognizable characteristic, it was used in sexual selection. Those who showed it most strongly would be selected in marriage by the

---

[3] Trachtenberg in *The Devil and the Jews* notes that some Christians did not think even baptism helped the peculiar odor, since in fifteenteeth-century Spain the charge was made that the converts smelled bad.

most orthodox, and would transmit a natural endowment to their offspring. Those who gave less evidence of it might marry outside of the race. In this way the feature became fixed, and it is as much an inheritance as any other characteristic."

I am sorry to deflate such scholarship or ruin the fun of anti-Semitic cartoonists, but the facts just do not support the existence of a predominantly dominant "Jewish nose."

Bergen Evans in *The Natural History of Nonsense* points out that "only a minority of Jews" have what could be considered a nose above average in size, and even this trait is shared "with the American Indians and with certain Asiatic, Mediterranean, and Alpine peoples."

An American scientist even went so far as to measure Jewish noses to see if the stereotype were true. This survey and results are reported on as part of what has been termed one of the most extensive research works on the question of the Jewish "race."

This is the 578-page *The Jews: A Study of Race and Environment* by Dr. Maurice Fishberg.[4]

On the subject of noses, Dr. Fishberg says he investigated "among the Jews in New York City and also in various countries of the East and West of Europe, in North Africa, and among Jewish immigrants from various countries of Asia." "The results," writes Dr. Fishberg, "do not bear out the popular opinion that the hook nose is to be considered the 'Jewish' nose because only a small minority of Jews have the privilege of possessing this kind of nose."

Dr. Fishberg's findings also come from what must have been a picturesque survey—he physically measured the noses of 2,836 adult male Jews and 1,284 Jewish females in New York City. The percentage of types of noses he found among the men were:

Straight or Greek	57.26 percent
Retroussé or snub	22.07 percent
Aquiline or hooked	14.25 percent
Flat or broad	6.42 percent

[4] Dr. Fishberg is listed in the book as a Fellow of the New York Academy of Sciences, and as a member of the American Ethnological Society, the American Association for the Advancement of Science, and the American Anthropological Association. His book on the Jews, published in 1911, was one of a science series edited by Havelock Ellis. It was the only major work of its kind for decades.

Among the females measured, "the percentage of straight noses was even larger" (59.42 percent), "and of aquiline and hooked noses even smaller" (12.70 percent).

Thus, concludes Dr. Fishberg, the predominant type of Jewish nose is actually straight: "It may consequently be surprising to some that observations among the Jews show that there is no valid reason for considering the arched or hooked nose as peculiarly Jewish. The reverse is rather true. If the most prevalent type of an organ is to be considered as typical of a race or people, then the Jewish nose is the straight, or Greek variety." [5]

Indeed, if only 14 percent of the Jews showed the "typical" nose, it may also be surprising to realize from Dr. Fishberg that the hook nose "is not infrequent among non-Jewish people"—with one study showing that aquiline and hook noses were found among 31 percent of Germans in Bavaria.[6]

But all this nose counting and measuring, while a noble enterprise to clear up a persistent stereotype of the Jewish people, is indicative of the mental wrestling that has been going on between those who would like to categorize Jews as somehow physically different and those who would show the Jews are physically no different from anyone else. What it all comes down to is the old questions of "Who is a Jew?" and "What is a Jew?"—is he the member of a race, religion, or nation?

The "Who is a Jew?" question has been answered by using definitions ranging from the simplest—that given by Jewish law (the child born of a Jewish mother)—to the simplest-minded—that given by the anti-Semite who declared, "I myself decide who is a Jew." This was the definition offered by Karl Lueger, the openly avowed anti-Semite who was elected five times in a row as Mayor

---

[5] According to Dr. Fishberg, the phrase "Greek nose" is derived from the common practice of ancient Greek sculptors to produce statues with faces having straight noses. But a perfectly straight nose does not seem to have been the rule in ancient Greece. Dr. Fishberg notes that only the good Greek gods had straight noses, but figures representing evil gods had other types of noses. And Socrates, for instance, is not shown with a "Greek" nose, but with a snub nose.

[6] Born in an Austrian town near the border with Bavaria was a non-Jew who seemed to be afraid that he had a "Jewish" nose—Adolf Hitler. One historian has speculated that Hitler, who feared his unknown grandfather may have been Jewish, grew his famed mustache primarily to reduce the look of his nose so that no one would say it looked "Jewish."

of Vienna during the days of Freud and a struggling young man by the name of Adolf Hitler.

In one respect, as pointed out by the anthropologist and historian Dr. Raphael Patai in *The Jewish Mind*, the Judaic definition is perhaps none at all—it is the same as defining a sheep as an animal born of a ram and a ewe. But in terms of providing a realistic, workable definition, it is remarkably pragmatic. Since except in the direst of circumstances it is the mother that stays with the child, the child can know its lineage more directly through the mother. Also, in recognition of the rapacity of the world in which Jewish communities lived in the Diaspora, a Jewish woman raped and impregnated by a Gentile could at least know that her child would be considered Jewish and part of the fold of her people.

But even more importantly—and this is something I have yet to see discussed—the Judaic law's definition of a Jew leaves open the possibility for the genes of non-Jews to enter more easily into the body of the people of Israel. The rabbis were not confining Judaism to the practice of a small band of people who could point to an unbroken descent from ancient Israel and the original Twelve Tribes. This was no closed society. The rabbis acknowledged that Judaism was not to be a race but was to be a religion by opening up the list of the Jewish people both to sincere male and female converts and, through the conception by a Jewish female, to the possible introduction of outside genes, although the liaison of a Jewish girl with an unconverted non-Jew was devoutly to be avoided. But, again, the acceptance of the child of a liaison between a Jewish female and a non-Jew showed that, in Jewish thinking, Nazi-like concepts of pure blood and special race lineage were never considered. Indeed, Jewish law is more liberal about who is a Jew than Nazi law was. The early Nuremberg laws of 1935 defined a full Jew as a person with three, or under certain circumstances two, Jewish grandparents, while according to Judaism a person could conceivably have only one Jewish grandparent (grandmother on the mother's side) and still be completely Jewish. In fact, the Nazi definition placed a person with just one Jewish grandparent as a "half Jew of second degree," and half Jews were not equated with full Jews. According to Nora Levin in *The Holocaust*, half Jews of the second degree "generally speaking were

[34]

not subjected to the destruction process." Many of them, however, *were* Jews in Jewish law. As we will see later, misconceptions about Jews as the Chosen People must be reexamined in the light of such a Jewish attitude to heritage.[7]

Thus, if Judaism could accept the progeny of those outside the faith or newly entered into it, then the Jews are far from a race. Jews are not a physical entity, but a spiritual entity. And as such, Judaism is open to all those who sincerely embrace it.

Because of this mingling of Jew and non-Jew, such a "non-Jewish characteristic" as blond hair can be found among Jews in a proportion reflecting the physical characteristics of the surrounding peoples. One research study showed that while 3 percent of Turkish Jews had blond hair, Ukrainian Jews had 15 percent, English Jews 26 percent, and German Jews 32 percent.

Although an anti-Semite may swear he can spot a Jew at twenty paces and may dismiss a blond-haired-blue-eyed Jew as the exception that proves the rule,[8] the evidence, as can be seen in Israel where Jewish immigrants from more than one hundred nations now live, is that the Jewish face, nose, eyes, hair—and horns—come in all sizes, shapes, and colors. There are black Jews and oriental Jews, blond Jews and bald Jews, husky Jews and frail Jews. But what there is not, when viewed on a world scale, is a possible physical stereotype of the Jew. In fact, history reveals some interesting statements by those who show how far apart is their own view of the Jew from what has become rooted today in the swarthy, Semitic stereotype. The German leader Bismarck, whose concepts of "iron and blood" set the stage for a later Hitler, could at one point tell his fellow Junkers, whom he thought overly stiff and inbred, to loosen up and acquire some élan by marrying Jews. The perfect marriage, according to Bismarck, "would bring

---

[7] Bergen Evans in his *The Natural History of Nonsense*, discusses how the anti-Semite could find fault even with Judaism's open attitude about who is a Jew: "One of the most 'insidious' things about the Jews is that one is never sure who is a Jew. One would think that this would knock the props out from under anti-Semitism, but, in actuality, it serves as an added grievance: they 'conceal' themselves cunningly, and 'polite' people have to feel out a strange company very gingerly before they may safely air their prejudices."

[8] The phrase "the exception that proves the rule" is another widely accepted misconception: "prove" is used here to mean "to test, to make trial of." The true meaning is not that an exception proves anything but that "the exception *tests* the rule." (See Eric Partridge's *Dictionary of Effective Speech*, page 254.)

together a Christian stallion of German breed with a Jewish mare." [9]

And then, too, there is the observation in an Arabian Nights tale: "Thou must know that we people of Persia are skilled in physiognomy; I saw the woman to be rosy-cheeked, blue eyed and tall statured ... and I knew she was a Jewess."

To see finally how the Jewish physical stereotype evaporates on scrutiny, let us look at the most recent major work since Fishberg's to study the Jew as a possible race.

Writing in the *The Myth of the Jewish Race*, published in 1975, Dr. Raphael Patai reports on findings about Jewish physical characteristics in such areas as height, hair and eye color, nose shape, cephalic index, hand clasping and arm folding, and finger print patterns. As far as the Jewish height, hair, eyes, and nose, he found:

> each shows such variability among the Jews and such correspondences between the Jewish and non-Jewish values in each locality that they constitute definite counterindications to the hypothesis of Jewish racial unity. . . . On the basis of these four features alone, one would have to conclude that the Jews are about as remote from constituting a single human race as would be a group composed of Russians, Germans, Italians, Spaniards. . . .

Dr. Patai goes into a United Nations listing, but you get the idea.

The fingerprint analysis, however, indicated the rest of the picture of the origin of the Jewish people. The fingerprints showed a relatedness among such different and separated groups as German, Turkish, Moroccan, and Yemenite Jews. "The pattern found in all these groups is suggestive of a Mediterranean origin. The picture which emerges is of a group of people who originated in the Mediterranean region and subsequently have diversified greatly in their genetic make-up."

---

[9] Of course, the children of such marriage, according to the laws of Judaism, would be Jewish. Bismarck's plan, without his realizing it, would have filled Germany with Jews.

Such a conclusion is borne out in further studies of morphological traits, blood group genes, and red blood cell and serum proteins. The notion is further supported by findings involving tests for glucose-6-phosphate dehydrogenase deficiency (mercifully referred to as G6PD deficiency), PTC test sensitivity (phenylthiocarbamide), color blindness ("the Jewish frequencies generally reflect the local non-Jewish frequencies"), and genetic distance between Jewish and non-Jewish groups.

The genetic distance computations, done with the aid of a computer, seem to sum up the results found over and over again in each of the other areas studied. These conclusions, writes Patai, were: "(1) that Jewish groups from different parts of the world are very different genetically; (2) that Jews of a certain area tend to resemble the surrounding non-Jews more than they resemble Jews from other parts of the world; and (3) that European Jews have a residue of non-European (Mediterranean) genes."

Thus, science bears out what history and common sense tell us: the Jewish people, who obviously began in the cradle of civilization, have over the course of thousands of years of migration and acceptance of converts expanded into a religion of near universal composition. But the Ignorance Factor and Goldberg's Law show that the common person is no respecter of common sense. Thus the myth of an alien Jewish race—the concept that Jews represent a separate and therefore different racial rather than religious grouping—has persisted with special vehemence among anti-Semites. *The Natural History of Nonsense* puts this in its stark paradoxical perspective: "That those who believe in racial differences have selected the Jews for particular attention is an ironical refutation of their whole theory, for it would be hard to find any groups on the face of the earth more thoroughly mixed, biologically, than they are."

Why are Jews so susceptible to so much ignorance?

Many of the reasons can be found in the special situation of the Jews. They are small in number. They have been scattered. They are not dominant anywhere, except now in the State of Israel, which exists in a precarious position even today. Viewed for so long as adversaries by Christianity and Islam, two dominant religions in different parts of the world, Jews and their religion have been subjected to the kind of gossip, tale-bearing, innuendo, distortions, misinformation, and outright lies that adversaries have always hurled at opponents. It is such an atmosphere that gives birth to Goldberg's Law and affects the Jew's ability to tell his true story.

But Jews as a minority group must also face a world influenced—as we saw at the beginning of this chapter—by the mistrust people often feel toward the member of any minority. The combination of ignorance and distrust is what makes it difficult for minority groups to find, if not acceptance, at least understanding.

In fact, the basic problem Jews and other minorities face in getting a fair hearing can be seen in—of all places—that famed Will Rogers quote about his never meeting a man he didn't like. We have been right to marvel that someone could mentally cut through the animosities and ignorances between people to arrive at such friendliness and love, for the surprising truth is that upon investigation I learned that Will Rogers did not have such heart-warming love for everybody and he did not say that statement in the way it has come to be accepted and embraced.

According to Homer Oroy, a close friend of Rogers during the last part of the humorist's life, the statement that was so close to America's heart "was mostly a happy accident" and "in reality there were many men he couldn't abide." In the biography *Our Will Rogers*, Oroy writes that the cowboy philosopher "had a hot and nasty temper" and "dodged" the people he didn't like—but still wound up in "two fist fights."

How then did Rogers come to be associated with a quotation of such brotherly love?

Oroy says that Rogers had a strange interest in constructing imaginary epitaphs for himself, always with a reference to the politicians he ribbed. Speaking in 1928 in Iowa City, Iowa, he had told an audience that he would like to see his tombstone read, "He joked about every prominent man of his time, but he never met one he disliked." Two years later, in a Boston church, when asked unexpectedly to say a few words following a sermon by the minister, he relied on telling one of his favorite epitaphs and then reworked the one he had given before to read now, "Here lies

Will Rogers. He joked about every prominent man in his time, but he never met a man he didn't like."

The *Boston Globe* recounted the story in its June 16, 1930, edition, on page 12, column 7, hardly highlighting it. But the Associated Press picked it up and, as Oroy relates, "it was the shot heard round the world." No one, it seems, was more astonished by the widespread interest in the statement than Will Rogers. "He had used it many times—or others almost like it—and it hadn't created a ripple."

What was overlooked in all the furor was that Rogers was not referring to all men, but to the prominent men of his day whom he had always needled. Oroy points out, "He had in mind only politicians and was limiting his statement to them."

Will Rogers, though, did not go out of his way to point out the error, Oroy writes. "He was enough of a showman to realize its value and to keep quiet about fine distinctions." But Will Rogers's friend and biographer makes no distinction about the famous quote: "It came to be applied in a way that he had not meant at all, for there were plenty of people he didn't like."

Not only that, but it seems the line caused Rogers discomfort. "Sometimes, however, it caused him inconvenience, for, now and then, he would meet a person he did not care for, but he had to pretend that he loved him as a brother."

The pervasiveness of the Ignorance Factor can be seen here. A slight mistake in communication, followed by repetition in the media, leads to widespread acceptance—so much so that the mistake creates a new reality to which even the originator of the statement must bend. In essence, a stereotyped vision of Will Rogers was established, and although in this case the result is a fostering of a love for Will Rogers and an endorsement for the inherent goodness in everyone, the truth is shaded by our misconception.

If an erroneous perception could happen to someone America admired, how easily could a distortion occur with someone a nation was uncertain about? Especially a minority group burdened by years of distortions?

And then, too, there is the further realization we must face: If lovable Will Rogers could engage in fist fights and know "plenty of people he didn't like," then we can begin to see how truly rare—if possibly nonexistent—is the person who could like everyone he would ever meet. We can begin to see why Jews and other minority groups are so susceptible to misunderstanding and prejudice, for the friction that appears to exist naturally between people is always ready to be inflamed by the Ignorance Factor.

But Jews have another problem just because they're Jewish. They not only have to contend with the Ignorance Factor. They also have to worry about Goldberg's Law.

GOLDBERG'S LAW

If anything can be misconstrued about the Jews, it will be . . . and has been.

Exhibit B: THE JEWISH "LOOK"

ONE OF THIS CENTURY'S LEADING ZIONISTS WAS MISTAKEN
FOR ONE OF THIS CENTURY'S LEADING ATHEISTS

Those who say that Jews have a certain "look" about them—and those anti-Semites who claim to be able to spot a Jew no matter what—have had some embarrassing moments.

Chaim Weizmann, second only to Theodor Herzl as a great leader of Zionism and the man who served as Israel's first president, had such a remarkable resemblance to Lenin, the leader of atheistic communism, that, according to John Gunther in *Inside Asia*, "when Weizmann happened to be at an international conference, the Russian delegates—this was in 1923 or thereabouts—kept staring at him as if he were a ghost, and the Swiss detectives set up a guard at his hotel door thinking that he *was* Lenin."

Some other examples are also revealing.

William Shirer reports in *The Berlin Diary*, the book which spans his years as a foreign correspondent covering Nazi Germany, how storm troopers one day mistook his good friend for a Jew and roughed him up: he was, however, "the purest of Scots." Jean-Paul Sartre, in *Anti-Semite and Jew*, tells how he had two French friends in Germany during the days he lived in Berlin at the start of the Third Reich. One was "a Catholic, the son and grandson of Catholics," but because he had black, slightly curly hair and was short and fat, the German children "threw stones at him and called him 'Jude.'" The other friend was a Jew who, because he was blond, the Germans thought a non-Jew. So taken in were they that this Jew "occasionally amused himself by going out with SS men, who did not suspect his race." In fact, one day one of the SS men told him: "I can tell a Jew a hundred yards off."

III
About That Religion Which Brought You The Ten Commandments

*Misconceptions about
the faith of the Jews*

FACT: The Romans believed that Jews secretly worshiped the pig.

FACT: An unusual remedy for drunkenness during the Middle Ages was based on a misconception about the Jewish prohibition against eating pork.

FACT: "Love thy neighbor as thyself," often thought to be Christian in origin, is first stated in the Hebrew Bible.

FACT: The Biblical statement calling for "an eye for an eye" was actually an advance over primitive forms of revenge.

FACT : Although the Bible endorses capital punishment, a Jewish court that invoked the death penalty once in seventy years was called "destructive."

> The Judaic law is the only one in the universe which ordained human sacrifices.
> —VOLTAIRE

THE ROMANS, those people who brought civilization such great advances as the codification of law and gladiator fights to the death, seem to have had some trouble understanding the Jewish faith. They especially could not fathom Judaism's prohibition against eating pork. Plutarch spent an entire treatise discussing how this could be. There are recorded cases of Romans jeering at Jews for not eating the flesh of the pig and, as a joke, forcing Jews to partake. In their search for a reason for this Jewish law, the Romans hit on an explanation and spread it amongst themselves in that most ancient, but pervasive, medium of communication—rumor and gossip. The Roman grapevine, which could transport quicker than an aqueduct, had it that the Jews did not eat the flesh of the pig because the Jewish people—aha!—secretly worshiped the pig.[1]

But the Romans did not stop there. The even sharper Roman mind undoubtedly asked itself why the Jews worshiped the pig. And so an explanation was devised for this, too. The Jews, declared the Romans, worshiped the pig because they were descended from the pig!

One should not be too hard on those empire builders for such logic. After all, they thought themselves the descendants of twins suckled by a wolf.

The Roman problem with the Jewish abstention from ham bones and pork chops is indicative of the larger ignorance with which the Jewish religion has been greeted throughout history. After all, no matter what the dietary observances of individual

---

[1] Tacitus, the Roman historian, thought otherwise. He said Jews worshiped the ass, because asses guided Moses and the people to a spring in the desert.

Jews, there has been at least one law of Judaism every non-Jew knew about: Jews do not eat the flesh of a pig. Yet, even such a well-known edict has been misrepresented. As the *Book of Jewish Knowledge* points out, "The baffling fact is that no Jewish religious observance aroused so much ridicule and resentment among the anti-Semites through history as the taboo against eating pork."

Before reviewing the ways in which some of the major aspects of the Jewish religion have been misunderstood or even perverted, let us look at how this one simple law—the prohibition against eating the flesh of the pig—has been misconstrued and ludicrously applied.

First, the true basis for the law.

In Leviticus 11:1-8, it is stated that only those animals which chew their cud and have cloven hoofs may be considered to be eaten as kosher food. The Bible then mentions that four animals which have only one of these signs also may not be eaten. They are the camel, the hare, and the badger, which chew their cud but do not have cloven hoofs, and the pig which does not chew its cud but has cloven hoofs.

As can be seen from the Biblical statements, no reason is given for abstaining from eating animals which lack the two requisite signs. The pig is simply one of four animals mentioned as still being prohibited even though possessing one of the two signs. Over the years, various explanations have been offered for this and the rest of the dietary laws. But one reason seemingly offered more than others is that the laws are hygienic in nature. Many of the nonkosher animals and fish are scavengers that can transmit disease. The pig, it has been pointed out, is a potential carrier of trichinosis, which only proper cooking can prevent.

The scientific rationale for the laws certainly speaks incredibly well of Judaic law which thousands of years ago could have seen what the Romans and the rest of the world then did not see, but the Bible does not give any reasons of hygiene for abstinence from pork, and Jewish religious thinkers down through the centuries are quick to note the absence of any given reason. Yet there are those who dismiss such a law as no longer valid because scientific advances have removed the medical and health problems of eating pork and other unkosher food. The trouble with this reasoning is that trichinosis is still a threat, as shown by a 1977 nationally syndicated newspaper article headlined, "Trichinosis remains a risk," by Dr. Jean Mayer.[2]

Forgotten in all the debate about the validity of the dietary laws is God's simple command to the Jews at the end of the presentation of these laws (Leviticus 11:44): "Sanctify yourselves . . . and be ye holy, for I am holy."

Here are some of the difficulties Jews have encountered with so simple and well-known a law as the one about the food of the swine:

- One Jewish war actually started over the pig. The Maccabee revolt in 168 B.C.E., which is celebrated in the Chanukah holiday, first started because of the order by the Sileucidan King Antiochus IV that Jews should sacrifice pigs on the temple altar.

- Beginning in the thirteenth century, anti-Semites delighted in showing Jews with pigs, as though that really denigrated the Jew. One of the oldest German caricatures of the Jew, which could be found in numerous books and broadsheets, was to depict a rabbi sitting backwards on a fat sow—it came to be called the Jewish Sow, or *Judenschwein*—and sucking on its tail, while other Jews suckled directly from the swine. Three-dimensional representations of this scene could be found in town halls and churches in Europe. The Cologne Cathedral had it represented in a wood relief on a chair from the fourteenth century. Several churches even made this the subject of sculpture that became a permanent part of the structure.

- As if it would really throw fear into a Jew even to touch the pig, a secular oath for Jews during the Middle Ages required the Jew to place his right hand up to the wrist on the Five Books of Moses and utter a long list of curses that would fall on him if he did not tell the truth. The scene had to take place, however, in a certain posture: "The Jew shall stand on a sow's skin."

---

[2] Unkosher shellfish also continue to pose health problems. A *New York* magazine cover story on fish on April 10, 1978, noted that, although the incidence is low, one can still get hepatitis from eating raw mollusks, primarily clams and oysters, and gastroenteritis which is "usually traced to inadequately cooked and/or refrigerated shellfish." The article also advised not to eat shellfish in places where outbreaks of hepatitis A, cholera, and typhoid have occurred because these are "the three most common illnesses sometimes associated with shellfish."

- The belief that Jewish abhorrence of the pig could be transmitted for other purposes figured in an unusual remedy for chronic drunkenness. As told about in the book *Alcohol: the Delightful Poison (A History)* by Alice Fleming, "A formula that was popular in Russia during the 12th century was to conceal a piece of pork in a Jew's bed for nine days. The pork was then mashed up and given to the drunkard, who would supposedly avoid alcohol as faithfully as Jews avoided pork."
- Since Jews were seen to be either in league with the devil or the devil himself, pork was latched onto as a good way to keep out of the house an evil spirit representing those wicked Jews. This continued into the nineteenth century in some sections of Germany where country folk believed a spirit called the *Jüdel* lived in their oven, leaving it to attack the children and other members of the household. How better to lock the *Jüdel* in the oven than to use the one thing a Jew—even a folk representation of the Jew—would obviously not cross? And so the Germans smeared the mouths of their ovens with pork.
- During the Inquisition, the populace was instructed to keep watch for one telltale sign above all others to see if any converted Jew was backsliding into the secret practice of Judaism. The sign: if these New Christians avoided eating pork. And then the Inquisition adopted a special name for these converts who did secretly practice their Judaism. The Spanish called these secret Jews "Marranos"—which is simply Spanish for "pigs." [3]
- And then there is the case of non-Jews who obviously thought eating pork would be a fate worse then death—and a Jew who erroneously believed the same. During the Civil War, upon discovery that one of the soldiers taken prisoner was Jewish, Gentile soldiers tried to break his will by offering him only pork to eat. The Jewish soldier steadfastly refused to eat it and eventually died of starvation—in itself an ignorant act, since to save a life a Jew is allowed to break the dietary laws.

Ironically, since the camel, the hare, and the badger are also prohibited, one can only wonder why the same mystique and misconceptions have not arisen in connection with these other ani-

---

[3] In another situation, Jewish converts to Christianity who were suspected of reverting to the secret practice of Judaism were called "Chuetas," which means "swine."

mals. But then only the pig is eaten in quantity by the non-Jew and so the Jewish religious prohibition may seem to stand as a rebuke to the non-Jew. One may ask why the Jews alone are considered anti-pig. The 500 million Moslems also do not eat pork, yet one rarely sees the Moslems attacked for their abstinence.

Jews, no matter what their individual practice, seem destined to continue to be known as the People Not of the Pig. As the TV character Archie Bunker said after learning that his fellow worker Stretch "Jerome" Cunningham was Jewish, "A Jewish name ain't supposed to have ham in it." [4]

How did Judaism—the religion that gave such monumental contributions to the world as ethical monotheism, the Bible, and the Ten Commandments—become so misunderstood?

Part of the explanation is that any religion to an outsider can seem labyrinthian in its thinking, the tenets and practices of a faith appearing odd, even incomprehensible. What one religion believes in with the deepest fervor may be the object of ridicule or puzzlement to another. The Ignorance Factor is rampant here, because most people are never schooled in other religions; they pick up those bits and pieces of information that, when put together without the guiding hand of a religion's leaders and thinkers, often create a bewildering maze of its own.

In this respect, Judaism is certainly not alone. As example, if one were to ask a non-Catholic what the doctrine of Immaculate Conception refers to, most people would say that it means that Jesus was born of a virgin, that Mary, his mother, conceived without the means of an earthly husband. But this is wrong, and the misunderstanding is so widespread that the *Dictionary of Misinformation* offers a discussion of this as one of the misinformations much of mankind has. The Immaculate Conception refers not to Jesus' birth, but to Mary's birth, that she was born without sin. The doctrine that Jesus was born of a virgin is given a different name—the Virgin Birth.

The widespread misconceptions about the basic tenets of Judaism, however, are ironic, for a historical development that should

---

[4] During the Spanish American War, when one of the Jewish soldiers serving with Teddy Roosevelt's Rough Riders would not eat unkosher meat, he was nicknamed "Porkchop."

have helped the world understand the religion that gave civilization so much has actually hindered that understanding. Out of the Jewish faith have come Christianity and Islam, but the historical fact that these three major world faiths are part of the same family, sharing much history and heritage, has led not so much to brotherhood as to a certain intensity of dispute that otherwise might have been absent. Not only do the trio fight over the same religious turf, as can be seen in Jerusalem, and argue about much the same religious principles, but the three religions squabble over who possesses the true faith, with the intensity and rivalry and friction that are usually seen only in bitter family feuds—which of course this is.

Take, for instance, the fact that in spite of being the religion that declared that what the Lord required of man was only "to do justly, and to love mercy and to walk humbly with thy God" (Micah 4:8), Judaism is often portrayed as harsh, authoritarian, the religion of "an eye for an eye" lacking in love and mercy, its leaders concerned primarily with the fine points of legalisms and the letter, rather than the spirit, of the law. It is certainly more than coincidental that Christianity claims to be the exact opposite—to being the faith full of love and forgiveness—for after breaking away from the religion from which it sprang and seeking its own following, Christianity had portrayed itself as virtually a mirror image of Judaism.

I am always reminded of a letter to the editor that appeared in the *Wall Street Journal* several years ago. The writer was trying to make the point that the absence of religion in our schools was promoting secular humanism and "its false basic premise that man is perfectible and only his environment is responsible for his faults and shortcomings." The letter writer went on to say that "the substitution of secular humanism for the Judeo-Christian ethic is resulting in a steady decline in the quality of human civilization."

So far, so good. But then the writer concludes by saying, "What is needed is a return to the authoritarianism of the Old Testament combined with the love and compassion of the New Testament."

Here we see the schism that has been made in the public's mind between Judaism and Christianity. Here we can begin to understand the job that has been done on Judaism.

The image of the Jewish religion as authoritarian and without compassion is often a result of that ever-constant companion of mankind—ignorance. "Do unto others as you would have others do unto you" is referred to as the Golden Rule, but it is invariably taken to be an exclusively Christian concept, based on such sentiments as "Love thy neighbor as thyself," which is usually thought to come from the New Testament. But the truth is that "Love thy neighbor as thyself" actually comes from the Hebrew Bible. It is mentioned in Lev. xix. 18, ". . . thou shalt love thy neighbor as thyself. . . ." There is such widespread ignorance about this that James Parkes, the English churchman, says in his book *Anti-Semitism*, "I have met ministers who believed that 'Love thy neighbor as thyself' was an entirely New Testament idea, and are unaware that Jesus is quoting and endorsing the teaching of the Mosaic Law (Lev. xix. 18), not giving original teaching himself in the passage."

Even a noted scholar on the Roman era—Michael Grant, who has been President and Vice-Chancellor of the Queen's University, Belfast—errs in his understanding of Judaism's origination of this concept. Writing in his book *Jesus: An Historian's Review of the Gospels*, he acknowledges that "as had been enjoined by Leviticus ... the Jewish Golden Rule was 'what you hate, do not do to anyone' " but that "Jesus converted this negative formulation into a positive: 'always treat others as you would like them to treat you.' " However, as we have just seen, this overlooks one fact: it was in Leviticus that the Golden Rule is stated in the unmistakably positive terms of the famed "Love thy neighbor as thyself." The reference to a negative in Judaism turned into a positive by Christianity is simply part of that old syndrome: the erroneous portrayal of the Jewish religion as supposedly lacking in the fullness of the positive love of Christianity.

Consider another way—subtle, but highly significant—in which the image of Judaism has been unfairly downgraded. Notice the label Christianity put on the Hebrew scriptures. These were now the "Old Testament" and the Christian scriptures were the "New." The covenant spoken about in the Bible between God and the Children of Israel was viewed as the "Old Covenant" that was now supposed to be supplanted and replaced by the newer relationship between God and the Church—which was termed the

"New Covenant." And finally the Christian religion was seen—by Christianity, itself—as the new chosen faith.

While there is a brief mention in Hebrew scripture of a possible new covenant (the reference is made by the prophet Jeremiah, but there is no indication that God means any changes in the existing covenant or intends any new revelation, only a strengthening of His relationship with Israel), the wholesale relabeling of the Jewish canon as the "old" Testament was, first and foremost, a masterful way to downgrade another religion's image. By the same token, the use of "new" when speaking of Christian scripture or the Christian Church was a stroke of public relations genius.[5] According to advertising theory (and all you need do is look at the ads), the strongest word in the advertiser's arsenal—the one word which can move minds and products better than any other—is the word "new." For "new" connotes fresh, modern, young, alive, vibrant, with-it-ness. "New" also means improved (which is why we so often see "new" and "improved" linked together on boxes of detergent).

Now, what word conjures up the very opposite of these attributes? Why, the very antithesis of new—which is "old." "Old" implies outmoded, stale, stodgy, archaic, arthritic, obsolete. Except for a mental association with words like "venerable" and "antique" (when applied to Model-T Fords and Louis XIV furniture), to label something, especially an idea or thought, as "old" is to denigrate it.

Which is what Christianity did when it began calling the Hebrew scriptures the Old Testament.

Wouldn't the image of the Jewish religion have been different if its scriptures had not been saddled with a name that compared it unfavorably to another faith's scriptures or if, at the very least, non-Jews had named the Jewish canon something less demeaning—such as the Original Testament? After all, "original" has more positive connotations than "old" and in reference to the

---

[5] The concept of a "new testament" begins with several such references in Christian scripture. Interestingly, the labeling of all the Gospels and other Christian writings as the New Testament and the Jewish scripture as the Old Testament did not come for more than a century. (For a discussion of the slow evolution of the term 'New Testament', see page 64 of volume I of *The Interpreter's Bible*, a twelve-volume work combining the thinking of numerous churchmen and termed "Christendom's Most Comprehensive Commentary.")

Hebrew Bible is certainly more accurate in describing when God's word—His Testament—was originally revealed to the world. Also, any work termed "original" indicates that the work possesses a continuing merit on its own terms and has established certain standards by which any later works in the same category must be measured. The Original Testament versus the New Testament has a different ring to it—indeed, the integrity of the Jewish religion is preserved in such a mental confrontation of words—than the Old Testament versus the New Testament.

We can now begin to see how even choices of words have helped distort the Jewish image. And the fact that Judaism and Christianity share so much in their origin and common history has only fed the muddling of the Jewish image. Growing out of the body of Judaism, Christianity, especially in its early development, had to feed on that body, as does the child with its mother; the result was a sapping of strength by one from the other. It is because of this that Jews today have a holy scripture which has been inherently downgraded by being referred to as the Old Testament—and Jewish teachings are not read and discussed on their own merits, but have to contend with the filtering thoughts of another religion, which presents itself as a new and improved version of the old.[6]

Voltaire's comment at the beginning of this chapter about Judaic law being "the only one in the universe which ordained human sacrifices" is really a result of this effort to depict the Jewish religion as primitive, punitive, part of an older, barbaric epoch in man's development. The truth, of course, as corroborated by archeology is that many ancient—and not so ancient—peoples sacrificed humans to their gods. Interestingly, Dr. Edward Westermarck, in *The Origin and Development of the Moral Ideas*, states, "We meet with human sacrifice in the past history of every

---

[6] Mohammed actually did to Christianity what Christianity did to Judaism. He claimed to offer the final revelation of God's word that he said Jesus and Moses before him had only partially delivered. He conceded that Moses and Jesus were true prophets and that Jews and Christians had once received authentic divine revelation, but taught that they had lost God's special favor by rejecting the final revelation contained in the Koran. Mohammed said that its contents completed and superseded Christian and Jewish scriptures. I have often thought that Christians would better understand what Christianity had done to Judaism if the Moslems called their scriptures not the Koran, but "The New, Improved Testament."

so-called Aryan race." Voltaire, the lover of India, should also be interested to know that "it occurred, at least occasionally, in ancient India, and several of the modern Hindu sects practiced it even in the last century."

Some of the other peoples said to have practiced human sacrifice included early Greeks, early Romans, Celts, Teutons, Slavs, ancient Semites, Egyptians, early Japanese, the Mayas, the Incas of Peru, and the Aztecs (who were said to have used it on such a scale that a minimum of twenty thousand such sacrifices a year were conducted throughout the empire).

The irony, in view of Voltaire's statement, is that the one people who did not practice human sacrifice were the Jews. In fact, so abhorrent was child sacrifice to the Jews that the Hebrew word for Hell is *Ghennah,* the name of the valley outside Jerusalem where the Molokites sacrificed children before the Israelites conquered the area and stopped the practice.[7]

At the root of this image of Jews and Judaism as stern, unyielding, repressive, even brutal, is the erroneous view of the Jew as the killer of Christ. Around this image of Christ killer can be seen swirling virtually all the stereotypes and misconceptions about the Jew and his religion. Not only has this charge caused much mistrust and misinformation, but the cry of "Christ killer" has propelled pogromists and crusaders into numberless Jewish communities to pillage, rob, rape, and—interestingly for those who espoused turning the other cheek and ending the supposed eye-for-an-eye vengeance—kill those said to be killers of Christ.

The labeling of Jews as Christ killers is an astonishing part of

---

[7] Such a fact did not stop Dr. Westermarck from quoting a Professor Kuenen in *Religion of Israel* who saw a connection between the Hebrew ban or *cherem* placed on an evil doer and the sacrificing of a human. Since the ban was really "dedication" to God and this "amounted to destruction or annihilation," according to Kuenen's reasoning "the persons who were 'dedicated,' generally by a solemn vow, to [God], were put to death, frequently by fire, whereby the resemblance to an ordinary burnt-offering was rendered still more apparent." This is a complete distortion of the Jewish practice of banning a person, from which the Christian practice of excommunication evolved. Those who doubt a scholar could distort religious history should note Dr. Westermarck's comment on this statement: "The sacrifice of offenders has, in fact, survived in the Christian world, since every execution performed for the purpose of appeasing an offended and angry god may be justly called a sacrifice." I think such comments may be more justly called scholarly sacrifice of common sense.

history for several reasons. First, on a purely practical level, crucifixion was not a Jewish form of punishment. The Jewish religion had specifically limited the imposition of the death penalty and the manner in which it could be carried out, and crucifixion was not one of the four methods that had been permitted by Jewish law. In fact, because of rabbinic restrictions placed on carrying out executions, by the time of Jesus capital punishment was rarely, if ever, invoked by the rabbis. And, as for crucifixion, there is no recorded case of a Jewish-conducted crucifixion. This was a Roman form of capital punishment, used by Romans to kill common criminals as well as enemies of the state. Many Jews were put to death in this way (during the siege of Jerusalem, the Romans crucified as many as five hundred Jews a day). Also, Jesus died on a Friday (thus the reference to Good Friday) during Passover (the Last Supper was a Passover seder) yet Jewish law specifically prohibited a court-ordered execution on Friday, the eve of the Sabbath, or during a holiday. So, without question, the Jews—physically at least—could not have killed Jesus or controlled his execution. Only the Romans could have decreed and carried out the crucifixion.

As for the supposed influence of the Pharisees on the Romans to carry out the crucifixion, the English churchman James Parkes in his book *Anti-Semitism* castigates the churches for such a belief: "With sublime indifference to the evidence of the Synoptic Gospels themselves (which contain no mention of the Pharisees in the events of the arrest, trial and death of Jesus) they [the churches] lay the blame for the crucifixion on Pharisaic shoulders."

Indeed, the early Gospels do not single out the Jews in general as at fault for the crucifixion, but the last in the series of Gospels to be written down, the Gospel according to John, does: it is the most anti-Jewish and pro-Roman of the Gospels. The reason given by many Bible scholars is that by the time this Gospel was written Christianity had turned away from its links to Judaism and was pursuing adherents in the Roman world. In this way, Roman ruler Pontius Pilate, known in all other histories for his ruthlessness, is in Christian scripture said to "wash his hands" of the execution of Jesus, deferring instead to the pressure of the Jews—a deference he failed to exhibit in his other dealings in Israel.

The implied involvement and collective guilt of all Jews as killers of Christ also does not quite hold up in the light of logic. Only a tiny number of the Jews in the world at the time were involved in the episodes that led to Jesus' death. The Diaspora had already begun nearly five hundred years before—in 586 B.C.E. when the Babylonians destroyed the first Temple and transported the Jews to Babylonia. Although the Jews were allowed to return when Cyrus of Persia later conquered Babylonia, many did not leave their new-found homes outside the Land of Israel and began a dispersal that was to become more permanent after the Roman destruction in 70 C.E. Indeed, at the time of the crucifixion, more Jews were living outside of Israel than inside, with more Jews residing in Alexandria, Egypt, than Jerusalem. And these Jews would have been totally unaware at the time of the scenes being played out in the Holy Land.

So the accusation that the Jews killed Christ must instantly be modified by asking: What Jews? The Jews in Jerusalem? The Jews living outside of Jerusalem but in the Land of Israel? The Jews living in another country like Egypt or Babylon? The question is more than rhetorical. Since Jesus' early followers were all Jews, they obviously could not be called killers. What, then, about the other Jews at the time who were totally uninvolved? And what about Jews yet unborn? [8]

Thus, Goldberg's Law may have its most outlandish example in a myth that sees all Jews as killers of Christ, even though non-Jews (the Romans) did the actual killing and used a totally non-Jewish method of execution, even though only a small number of Jews were said to have pressed for Jesus' death, even though the main followers Jesus did have during his life—the Apostles—were Jews, and even though virtually all Jews had the greatest of alibis ("I was somewhere else when the murder occurred, your honor").

The ridiculousness of all this has always been borne out for me by the story I once heard my mother tell. As a child growing up in America in the early 1900s, she had been subjected, as had many other Jewish youngsters, to the epithet from Christian children

---

[8] Harry Golden, author of *Only In America*, wrote that his "first brush with anti-Semitism" came when he once ventured into a Gentile neighborhood and wound up being chased by some young toughs yelling "Christ killer!" Golden was ten years old at the time.

[57]

that she was a Christ killer. Once she had even been slapped by an older girl. Finally, one day this eight-year-old child accused of a two-thousand-year-old murder turned on her tormentors and declared, "I didn't do it. My aunt did!"

The church finally put to rest much of this fiction with its statement on the Jews issued by the Second Vatican Ecumenical Council. According to *The Declaration on the Relationship of the Church to Non-Christian Religions* issued in 1965, what happened in the crucifixion of Jesus "cannot be charged against all the Jews, without distinction, then alive, nor against the Jews of today. Although the Church is the new people of God, the Jews should not be presented as rejected or accursed, as if this followed from the Holy Scriptures." A 1964 draft of the text had gone even further, using the word *deicide,* but this was replaced in the final version by a more ambiguous phrasing because of objections by some of the more conservative church leaders (and, interestingly enough, because of objections by Arab nations who feared such a statement would be the beginning of Vatican recognition of Israel).[9] The more cautiously worded 1965 document, however, was still a significant action by the Church. Although an emphatic rebuke of the deicide charge as Pope John XXIII envisioned would have been more helpful in laying to rest this cause of anti-Semitism, Vatican II broke the long-standing deadlock in Christian-Jewish relations over this issue. But it had taken the church nineteen hundred years to act.

If the charge of Christ killer has fostered an unpalatable image of the Jew and his religion, one passage in the Torah has been misinterpreted to such an extent that the entire Mosaic law has suffered because of it. This is the Biblical passage of "an eye for an eye."

---

[9] *Time* Magazine, in its issue of September 24, 1965, reported that one of the major reasons why the deicide clause had been replaced was "to satisfy anxious Middle Eastern Catholics, who mysteriously see in exoneration the first step toward Vatican recognition of Israel." *Time* also related that in the previous week at the urging of the Moslem mayor of Jerusalem, a number of Christian communities in Jordan "agreed to toll their church bells for ten minutes in protest over the council's expected endorsement of 'the Jewish declaration.'" That the ancient deicide issue could be inferred to affect current Mideast politics is yet another example of Goldberg's Law.

"An eye for an eye" has led to continuous and continued misinterpretations, serving throughout history and especially today as another supposed piece of evidence that Judaism is "vengeful" while only Christianity is "loving" and "forgiving." Ever since Israel was founded in 1948, an Israeli response to terrorism has invariably been labeled by the media as an act of "an eye for an eye" or, as one commentator once said, "two eyes for an eye." Not once can I remember such a phrase used to label an American retaliatory act during the Vietnam War or any other military response to an attack (were the allied revenge bombings of German cities called that?). Although the Bible's language has been freely adopted by the world, the "eye for an eye" reference has been clearly reserved for use in describing Jewish actions.[10]

Let us study the meaning of this passage more closely—especially as it has been viewed and interpreted by the rabbis. An investigation of "an eye for an eye" beyond its literal reading is rarely done, and yet the interpretation given by religious leaders and thinkers to a faith's scriptures is really a more valid way to understand that faith than the direct reading of its scriptures. The Bible is meant to be interpreted, analyzed, and debated so that its truths can be learned. The Bible has always had its commentaries. The works of Rashi, the great Jewish commentator, have themselves been the subject of over two hundred major commentaries.

Indeed, it has been the great religious thinkers of each religion who have helped by their analyses and interpretations to give contemporary meaning to their scriptures and direction to their faiths. Surely, no Christian wants his religion to be judged by any one simple, bare statement in his religious literature that comes unadorned of commentary and insight by Christian authorities, for it is really the direction given by these insights that the faithful are following anyway. Times change; the meanings of words shift. Without interpretation, everything on the printed page—from the Bible to the American Constitution—would be crippled in its own verbiage. For instance, Christian scripture quotes Jesus as saying (Matthew 10:34), "Think not that I am come to send peace on

---

[10] In 1972, less than a year before the Yom Kippur war, an Arab guerilla attack killed eleven Israeli youths. Israel's military response was discussed in *The New York Times* Week in Review section, in a lead article headlined, "The Planes' Message—An Eye for an Eye."

earth: I came not to send peace, but a sword." Are Christians to take this literally? If they are, then who would take Christianity seriously, especially since it presents itself as based on love and teaches that Jesus was the prince of peace. The Koran, too, is sprinkled with statements that on the surface can be taken as harsh and vindictive.

To understand truly the concept "an eye for an eye," we must see what Jewish thinkers through the centuries have said about it. And we must learn what was done when the rabbis were in a position of power to invoke "an eye for an eye." Did they carry out the literal reading of the passage or did they follow some other interpretation?

Let us first put the statement into the context of the ancient world. Civilizations ruled by law had wrestled with the problem of formulating laws of retaliation *(lex talionis)*, the compensation of one person for a loss suffered because of another. This was referred to as "measure for measure." The problem is that in an ancient civilization such as that ruled by the famed Code of Hammurabi, measure for measure was vengeful. If a man's ox gored and killed another man, the owner of the ox was to be killed. If the ox killed a son or daughter of another man, then the son or daughter of the owner of the ox was put to death. This was measure for measure as applied by the Code of Hammurabi.

Now let us take a look at the Biblical and rabbinic discussion of "an eye for an eye," remembering that what we will be seeing is the Jewish approach to the law of retaliation.

The "eye for eye" passage occurs first in Exodus 21,[11] a chapter devoted to "the ordinances which thou shalt set before them." Here are listed laws concerning the treatment of servants, murder, crimes against parents, kidnapping, and personal injuries. The actual presentation of "an eye for an eye" occurs from sentences 22 to 25:

> And if men strive together, and hurt a woman with child, so that her fruit depart, and yet no harm follow, he shall be surely fined, according as the woman's husband shall lay upon him;

[11] It is restated in slightly different form in Leviticus 24:19-21.

and he shall pay as the judges determine. But if any harm follow, then thou shalt give life for life, eye for eye, tooth for tooth, hand for hand, foot for foot, burning for burning, wound for wound, stripe for stripe.

Upon examination, then, we find that "eye for an eye" is introduced in the case of a pregnant woman who gives birth early because she comes into contact with men who are fighting. We also find that no premeditated murder or injury was intended. This is certainly an unusual example with which to teach "life for life, eye for eye." Since the Torah is sparing in its words, the mere stringing out of retaliatory statements is the first indication that we are not to read the passage literally. "Life for life" coupled with the personal injury of "eye for eye" would have been sufficient to convey any concept of strict retribution as the proper approach to punishment. But the Torah continues on and on ... tooth, hand, foot, burning, wound, stripe. Something is profoundly unusual about the Torah plunging into such normally unnecessary verbiage. Notice, for instance, that only one case—the pregnant woman—was given. Why, then, such a long listing of possibilities for punishment?

The answer is that "eye for eye" is the term for a remarkable concept—the law of monetary compensation. This is the conclusion given by the Talmud in the tractate Baba Kamma, which lists the extended debate of twenty-three sages who unanimously agree the Biblical phrase means compensation, not retaliation.

In the Torah, the only literal application of "an eye for eye" punishment is with a murderer: "Ye shall take no ransom for the life of a murderer that is guilty of death: but he shall surely be put to death" (Numbers 35:31). But in other instances, ruled the rabbis, monetary compensation rather than retaliation was called for. This can be seen in Leviticus 24:21: "He that killeth a beast shall make it good; and he that killeth a man shall be put to death." It is, therefore, all the more revealing of the meaning of the "life for life, eye for eye" declaration when this very last sentence is matched with Leviticus 24:18: "He that smiteth a beast mortally shall make it good: life for life." Since the Bible does not call for the death of a man who kills an animal, we can now see from the other reference in Leviticus that compensation of a different sort is intended. Wrote Dr. J. H. Hertz, Chief Rabbi of the British Empire, in his commentary on the "eye for eye" declaration: "physical injuries which are not fatal are a matter of *monetary compensation* for the injured party. Such monetary compensation, however, had to be equitable, and as far as possible *equivalent*. This is the significance of the *legal technical terms*, 'life for life, eye for eye, and tooth for tooth.'"

Indeed, ancient peoples practiced not an eye for an eye, but two eyes for an eye, a whole family for a single life. In our own times, we have seen such wild revenge in the actions of the Nazis—murdering ten hostages for each German soldier killed by partisans, destroying whole towns for the death of a German official. We can see such revenge in the historic warring of families, where the killing of one member of a family leads to the killing of several members of the other family.

The mere mention of "eye for eye" and its symbolic repetition in the references to such other areas of the body as tooth, hand, and foot emphasize that what is here being introduced to humanity is the substitution of legal punishment—the comparable, appropriate punishment—instead of the brutal revenge mankind had been used to employing for punishment.

We can see that this is the intended meaning of the passage by looking at what immediately follows in the Torah (Exodus 21:26–27):

> And if a man smite the eye of his bondman or the eye of his bondwoman and destroy it, he shall let him go free for his eye's sake. And if he smite out his bondman's tooth, or his bondwoman's tooth, he shall let him go free for his tooth's sake.

Thus, in the very examples that follow the original statement of "eye for eye and tooth for tooth," precisely where an eye and a tooth have been put out, the result is that an eye is *not* taken for an eye. The Torah calls not for the loss of the guilty one's eye or tooth in a savage act of revenge, but for equitable compensation—here, in the case of a slave, the most precious compensation of all: freedom.

Where is the revenge, the harshness ascribed to Jewish law because of the "eye for an eye"? The answer is that it evaporates upon an intelligent reading of the passage and a knowledge of its context in both the Bible and history. It is also interesting to note that the very example used to illustrate how "eye for eye" was to work was that of a man or woman slave abused by an owner. This was the second great humanitarian principle advocated here. For not only does "eye for eye" enjoin a fair relation between the crime and the punishment, it also maintains that all citizens are equal under the law and that the injuries of all should be valued according to the same standard. The poor man has the same rights as his rich assailant; the slave as his owner; the woman as the man.

The humanizing feature of this Jewish law—its introduction of kindness in place of vindictiveness—can further be seen in contrasting this law with another in the Code of Hammurabi, which said: "If a man has caused the tooth of a man who is his equal to fall out, one shall make his tooth fall out." This is repeated in no less than fourteen other similar examples in the Code. Notice, too, that the example expressly states "a man who is his equal"—a far cry from the Torah's example of slave abused by master. Furthermore, the Code of Hammurabi carries the principle to grotesque extremes. For example, if someone by his faulty work constructing a house causes the death of the owner, the builder is killed. But if he causes the death of the son or daughter of the owner, then not the builder but his son or daughter is killed!

Thus, the Jewish law of "eye for eye" was actually an advancement over the ancient practices of wild revenge and illogical methods of fitting punishments to crimes. "Eye for eye" established the basic principle of monetary or compensatory restitution as payment for injuries that could be repaid in no other form. And how do we know this for a fact? Because never does the Talmud or any other rabbinic literature endorse any other interpretation of the "eye for eye" passage. Indeed, the Hebrew scriptures show that God himself applies "life for life, eye for eye" in this way. As a result of the first crime between man and man—Cain's killing of Abel—God does not take "life for life, eye for eye," but punishes Cain in a different way. So, too, did Jewish courts of law refrain from invoking the death penalty. Although endorsed in the Bible ("he that killeth a man shall be put to death"), so many restrictions were placed on the presentation of evidence and witness testimony, and judges were so reluctant to impose capital punishment, that a famed rabbinic statement was that "a Sanhedrin which executes a person once in seventy years can be called 'destructive.' " [12]

As for lesser crimes, the Talmud even worked out a table of fines to be used in place of physical revenge (one punch equaled one shekel, a kick with the knee three selas, a kick with the foot five selas, etc). Based on the injury, compensation had also to be paid for pain, loss of income, and medical treatment.

Thus, consider the irony: a study of Jewish scripture and a knowledge of Jewish practice show no indication of a harsh, vengeful "eye for eye" culture. Yet, while Romans crucified criminals or broke their arms or legs, while the Koran called for cutting off the hands of thieves, while England had debtor's prisons that disrupted entire families, while France had Devil's Island and Russia had Siberia, the Jews have been labeled as the people of "eye for eye." [13]

"You are a people holy to the Lord your God, Who has chosen you from all the nations on the face of the earth to be His own possession."

This passage in Deuteronomy 14:2, one of numerous such statements made by God to the children of Israel, has led to the Jewish people being referred to as "the Chosen People." Indeed, the beginning of one of the holiday prayers of the Jews is *Attah Bechartanu*, "You have chosen us."

Needless to say, such a sentiment, seemingly so tied into specialness for the Jews, can be open to misinterpretations and, according to Goldberg's Law, it has been. One of Adolf Hitler's

---

[12] The Sanhedrin was the Supreme Court in Jerusalem. Its members are the ones the Gospels infer agitated for the killing of Jesus, and yet the Sanhedrin is on record as abhorring the death penalty.

[13] One fact of modern life shows how far from a vengeful people are the Jews. The State of Israel is one of the few countries to outlaw capital punishment. Not even Arab terrorists are put to death. The only person ever executed by Israel was Adolf Eichmann, architect of carrying out the Final Solution. The taking of one Nazi's life in punishment for his helping murder 6,000,000 Jews can be considered an example of "eye for eye" only by those who are blind to morality and mathematics.

first references to the Jewish people in *Mein Kampf* is a sneering reference to "the moral stains of this 'chosen people'" and in the very next page, "It was terrible, but not to be overlooked that precisely the Jew, in tremendous numbers, seemed chosen by Nature for this shameful calling [usury]. Is this why the Jews are called the 'chosen people'?"

Should the reference to the Jewish people as the Chosen People cause a Jew discomfort or an anti-Semite distaste? What is the meaning of the term 'Chosen People'? Isn't this in opposition to Judaism's own emphasis on the brotherhood of man?

First of all, the Bible seems to have made everybody forget that many other peoples have called or at least thought of themselves as chosen people. The German Kaiser William II, in a speech to his soldiers on August 4, 1914, declared: "The German people are the chosen of God."

Did not Hitler himself call the German nation the Master Race, chosen to lead all others? Isn't the whole Aryan myth simply a means by which the white European of the nineteenth century could feel himself superior to the non-European, nonwhite, and non-Christian? Didn't Germany's embrace of the Aryan race as their original forebearers signify their belief in being chosen by the force of history for a destiny different and better than other nations?

Wasn't the "white man's burden" in the nineteenth century a statement that the white race and its Christian religion were the chosen race and religion?

And which religion really considers itself the chosen religion—is it Judaism, which considers the righteous of all religions as worthy of the world to come, or Christianity, which states that only through belief in Jesus as the Messiah can one find grace and salvation?

Indeed, the original Calvinists convinced themselves that they were among "the chosen" even of other Christians.

So the Jews are not alone in having the concept of chosenness linked to them. But what is different about the Jews—and what makes others so uncomfortable—is that the Bible, the great religious authority in the western world, says that the Jews are chosen.

Thus, those who in a growingly secularist world would want to strike out at the notion of God must strike out at any notion of Jewish chosenness. Also, Christians must fit Jewish chosenness into their own view of a world in which Christians are said to supplant Jews in God's favor, so Jewish chosenness must therefore be replaced by—what else?—Christian chosenness. And this is what we find when we remember that the Church saw itself as chosen to be "the new Israel." In other words, the Bible could not be questioned, just updated. The chosenness of the Jews would do very nicely as a way to picture the specialness of Christianity in the world. The church fathers simply draped the chosen mantle on themselves, a bit of Gentile chutzpah which underlines one fact usually ignored: the Church does endorse the Jews as the Chosen People, but with a qualifier—the Church claims Jews stopped being chosen when they rejected Jesus as the Messiah.

In any case, the concept of the Jews as the Chosen People certainly makes everyone squirm. And it does so on its most basic level because no matter what people want to say about the Jews, certain chosen qualities still seem to exist: the Jews have lasted longer and with more vitality through more difficulties than any other ancient people; the Jews have influenced the world through their Bible, religious teachings, moral precepts, and Ten Commandments far out of proportion to their numbers.

The trouble with all this—the worry and discomfort of the anti-Semite, the pride but bewilderment of Jews schooled to believe in the value of everybody—is that, once again, few consider how Jewish religious thinkers view the subject. As with "an eye for an eye," we must look to see what the rabbis say about the meaning of Biblical statements referring to the Jews as the Chosen People.

The overwhelming majority of Jewish thought on these Biblical references is that for a people to be chosen by God conveyed not superiority of position, but responsibility for service. Although in the darkest days of the exile some Jewish thinkers found solace in the thought of a Jewry superior to their surrounding neighbors, even this superiorty was felt to be spiritual and not ethnic or physical. The essence of Jewish philosophy has been that the Jews were chosen by God not to dominate, but to teach—and to teach not by authoritarian methods, but by the example of their national life.

Indeed, Jewish chosenness has been interpreted by Jewish scholars to mean that Israel has been chosen to carry out a special mission of service to God and does not imply exclusive possession by Israel of divine love and favor. The Jewish people were to put the precepts of the Torah into daily practice and, by setting an example in their own righteous national existence, inspire all the other peoples of the earth to embrace God.

Thus, Israel was the servant of God, not the master of humanity. Indeed, the fact that the Jews were the Chosen People meant only that more was expected of them than of others, and furthermore that their actions would be judged by higher standards. In Amos 3:2, the Lord says, "You only have I known of all the families of the earth," but in what the Chief Rabbi of England, Joseph Hertz, termed the most famous *therefore* in history, the sentence continued, "Therefore I will visit upon you all your iniquities." The Almighty thus demands higher, not lower standards of goodness from Israel and will punish lapses more severely. Says one Biblical commentator, "The higher the privilege, the graver the responsibility. The greater the opportunity, the more inexcusable the failure to use it."

This is why Jewish scripture endorsed the inherent value of each person and the protection of the stranger. The Jews, whose origin as a nation was in slavery (no other people traces their origin back to the lowly state of slavery), were continuously reminded about the many aspects of mankind which show the brotherhood of man: "The voice of God at Mount Sinai sounded in all the seventy languages of mankind." "He who hates another human being hates God." "The Gentiles are my handiwork even as the Israelites are my handiwork. Shall I therefore destroy the Gentiles for the sake of the Israelites?"

This is why, the rabbis point out, the Torah begins not with the story of the Jewish people but with the creation of the world—to show that all mankind emerged from one man, Adam, and therefore historically and genetically everyone has the same roots. (Contrast this thought with the Aryan myth that advocated superior origin to one group of people.)

But most importantly of all, the Jewish religion has never excluded the non-Jew from the divine blessing. Whereas a number of other religions maintain that the Jew or other "nonbeliever" is doomed to Hell, Judaism states, "The righteous among the Gentiles will have a share in the World to Come."

Far from aiming to build itself up as a superior, an elite, or "master" race, the Jewish people, according to fundamental tradition, has been dedicated to bringing all the peoples of the earth into a common brotherhood, bestowing an equal worth upon each. Thus, Israel was elected for special service in the divine scheme to bring about the ideal of a united mankind.

To see that this is indeed how Jews are to view their being the Chosen People, let us look at how the rabbis present it to the Jews themselves. For in religion, as I have said, the interpretation and presentation of a faith's ideals are the truest guides to understanding that religion.

The following is an excerpt from one of the most widely used Orthodox prayerbooks in the United States today—*Prayer Book for Sabbath and Festivals*, published by the Hebrew Publishing Company of New York, with translation and annotations by Dr. Philip Birnbaum, an author of numerous books on Judaism. Here is his explanation to the worshipper of the meaning behind *Attah Bechartanu* ("You have chosen us"), the opening sentence in the holiday prayers that I cited at the beginning of this discussion:

> Israel's character as a chosen people does not involve the inferiority of other nations. It is the *noblesse oblige* of the God-appointed worker for the entire human race. Israel feels itself chosen not as a master but as a servant. It separates itself from others for the purpose of uniting them. The people of Israel affirm not that they are better than others, but that they ought to be better.

Why aren't these aspects of Judaism better known? Why has "an eye for an eye" been so misinterpreted? Why has the concept of the Jews as the Chosen People been misunderstood?

Part of the fault may lie within the Jews themselves, in not making emphatically clear to the world their own perceptions of their faith. But a larger part of the fault must lie with the adversaries of the Jews—be they the Romans or rulers of other ancient nations, be they the early leaders of Christianity and then Islam—who often had a vested interest in misrepresenting the faith of the Jews. And over the centuries, one misrepresentation fed another, all abetted by the Ignorance Factor, until the image of the faith of the Jews had been altered.

The irony is that those who would seek the truth about Judaism would find in this faith one of the most open and accessible religions of mankind. There are today no secret societies, no secret rites, no secret ceremonies in Judaism. There is nothing that would bar a Gentile from learning about Jewish practices. In the past, only a few of the temple services were barred to non-Jews. And yet this did not stop non-Jews from speculating the worst about Jewish activities, such as the High Priest's actions in the Holy of Holies on Yom Kippur to atone for the people's sins. Closed to the eyes of Jews as well as non-Jews, this sacred ceremony was misconstrued by some of Israel's ancient enemies who, in an obvious display of Goldberg's Law, thought the High Priest went in to worship a donkey.

But unlike the Druse who do have a secret ceremony and secret rituals only the faithful may know, unlike the Moslems who permit only their adherents to enter Mecca during the pilgrimage, unlike Catholicism with its confessional, unlike numerous fraternities and societies that have their secret rites, Judaism is open. In fact, because of the communal needs of the Jewish faith, the Jews have had to join together in communities, rather than retiring to monasteries or splitting into narrow groups hidden from view. Jewish prayer requires ten men to form a congregation. Jewish rites of circumcision, Bar Mitzvah, wedding, and funeral need a public of witnesses.

Even Jewish history is an open book—literally. The whole world can look into the Bible, the Jewish history book, and see what it says. The goings and comings of the Jewish people have been recorded in secular histories for centuries. Jewish practices are as old as much of recorded history. In fact, Passover has been cited as "mankind's oldest continually observed religious ceremony." So there are no surprises with the Jews and their religious faith.

The Jews have not lived apart from, but have very much lived with, virtually all the nations of the world.

And yet the ignorance about so much in Judaism persists.

The continued influence of the Ignorance Factor in the area of religion is especially regrettable because of the possibilities now for greater understanding between members of faiths so much in close proximity throughout history. James Parkes has noted in his book *Anti-Semitism* how much Christian clergy lack in knowledge and understanding of Judaism. Having first written about this seventeen years before in another book, *An Enemy of the People: Antisemitism,* Parkes repeats his statement that, with notable exceptions, the clergy's "ignorance is both dishonourable and disgusting":

> They maintain missions to convert the Jews, while at the same time they will not spend a penny of either time or effort to see that Judaism and the story of the Jewish people are fairly presented to their congregations . . . and nine-tenths of those references [that are made about the Jews] are ill-informed, often to the point of being definitely untrue. They don't mean to be prejudiced; they are not conscious of antisemitic feeling; but the share that they bear for providing a fertile breeding ground for every kind of antisemitic misrepresentation is an exceedingly heavy one. . . . They talk of 'the Law'; and they have not the slightest idea what 'Torah' (the Hebrew for Law) means to a Jew. They speak of 'the Jews' when they describe the less attractive activities of the early Israelites, with complete indifference to the fact that the congregation will relate their words to the conduct of a contemporary 20th-century Jewish community. This is particularly the case in their ignorant contrasts between the 'Jewish' and 'Christian' ideas of God.

Concludes Parkes, looking back at this statement, "There is unhappily nothing in the history of the past seventeen years which would make me modify this condemnation."

Judaism, however, has been able to make its contributions to the world in spite of centuries of such ignorance. As though in fulfillment of the Jewish role as Chosen People to spread the concept of God, Christianity and Islam have emerged out of the body of the Jewish faith; and important ingredients in the culture of the world today are such Jewish teachings as ethical monotheism, the Bible, and the Ten Commandments.

In fact, the influence of Judaism has so spread throughout the world that Judaic concepts once mocked by others are now widely imitated. The Jewish observance of the Sabbath, for instance, was ridiculed by the Greeks and the Romans, who hooted at the idea of a seventh day of rest, especially as the Jews advocated a rest not only for the master, but for slave, servant, stranger and even the animals one owned. Apion, a noted first-century Alexandrian, offered an explanation for the Jewish Sabbath: he claimed that the Jews, after having traveled six days in the wilderness, "had buboes in their groins; and on this account it was that they rested on the seventh day." Seneca, the Stoic philosopher, found the Jewish day of rest to be a ridiculous denial: "This most outrageous people ... by taking out every seventh day lose almost a seventh part of their life in inactivity...."

And yet, today not only do Christianity and Islam also celebrate a once-a-week special day of rest, but so do most working people in the world. The idea has so spread that much of mankind is up to a two-day-a-week rest, and there is now talk of a three-day-a-week cessation from work.

The Sabbath is but one of many contributions to the world by Judaism—the religion that brought you the Ten Commandments ... and the Original Testament.

GOLDBERG'S LAW

If anything can be misconstrued about the Jews, it will be . . . and has been.

Exhibit C: THE TEN COMMANDMENTS

THERE IS NOT ONE BUT MANY VERSIONS OF THE TEN COMMANDMENTS—AND THE BIBLE CALLS THEM BY A DIFFERENT NAME

Even the Jewish people's best-known religious contribution to the world has been misunderstood and altered.

The Jewish version of the Ten Commandments is not followed by Christians, who not only adopted a different listing but disagree among themselves about the correct format for the Ten Commandments. Although everyone has always agreed that there are ten edicts in number, the argument arose over the way in which the Biblical text was to be read to arrive at that total.

Jewish tradition begins the listing with the declaration "I am the Lord thy God." Christians, however, take what is the second commandment in the Jewish format as their first ("Thou shalt have no other gods before me"). Roman Catholics and Lutherans then divide up the rest of the statements covering the Ten Commandments in one way, while most other Protestants follow yet another method.

To add to all the general confusion, the Bible itself lists two slightly different versions (Exodus 20:2–17 and Deuteronomy 5:6–21, with the reference in Deuteronomy offering a different reason for the commandment to keep the Sabbath).

The greatest ignorance about the Ten Commandments, however, may be in the use of the name itself. For the Hebrew Bible *never* calls these ethical and spiritual guidelines the "Ten Commandments." The correct name for them—because it is the only one used by the Bible (Deuteronomy 4:13 and 10:4)—is the "Ten Words."

IV
Praise the Lord and Pass the Ammunition

A study of the most dangerous Jewish stereotype

FACT: More Jews died fighting for Germany in World War I than have died fighting for the State of Israel.

FACT: In one country during World War II, Jewish soldiers fought alongside Nazi soldiers and even reported to German officers—without any discrimination.

FACT: A Jew, referred to as "Two-Gun Cohen," helped build the Chinese army and was named a general in China's armed forces.

FACT: Three Jews are among nine individuals honored in the United States Military Academy at West Point as history's greatest warriors.

FACT: Fifteen Jewish officers fought in the Battle of Waterloo.

FACT: At one time, so many Jews were soldiers in the French Foreign Legion that a Passover seder was held for fifteen hundred Jewish legionnaires.

> Among other evils which being unarmed brings you, it causes you to be despised.
> —MACHIAVELLI

As THE FIRST fingers of light began shredding the Mideast morning sky, the Mirage jets swooped in from the Mediterranean, swung low across the Nile Valley, and, hugging the land in daringly shallow flying to avoid radar, roared across the Egyptian airfields. The Israeli pilots strafed and bombed the parked MIG planes and the air hangars with such accuracy and audacity that within hours of the start of what came to be called the Six Day War, Israel was able to destroy three hundred Egyptian planes and nineteen airbases. The same massive display was being repeated in other Arab countries so that by the end of twenty-four hours on June 5, 1967, the air forces of four Arab nations lay on the ground like charred birds of prey. The feats of those Jewish pilots that day, declares Anthony Sampson, the author of *The Arms Bazaar* writing ten years later, "altered the whole picture of modern warfare."

The Israeli military strategy was so daring, the resulting victory so complete and crushing, that at first many military analysts found it hard to believe. Britain and France had tried to do much the same thing against Egypt in 1956, with far less result. How could the Israeli Air Force do so much in just hours? How could the greatly outnumbered Jews so overwhelmingly defeat the Arabs?

And what about the accuracy of those Jewish fighter pilots? The photographs and films of the wreckage at the Egyptian airfields were studied worldwide. *Life* magazine ran large spreads of the reconnaissance photos, and television aired the film footage. What everyone saw was not only that the Egyptian plane carnage was complete—it was neat. Few holes on the runways or the airport aprons. Little evidence of wasted bombs or bullets. Not many near-misses. The remnants of countless Egyptian MIGs sat there as though shot by a rifle from the sky, with not much of the indiscriminate destruction usually left by fighter planes on strafing runs.

The eerie nature of this accomplishment led to wide speculation even by military specialists. Writes Howard Singer in *Bring Forth the Mighty Men*, "The gunnery was so accurate that for quite some time foreign military experts assumed the Israelis must have developed some secret weapon . . . a new weapon with some kind of homing device."

We now know that there was no secret weapon. Just highly skilled, intensively trained Israeli airmen and an audacious battle strategy. But the Jewish flyers did have a secret going for them that day—the Jewish ability, long ignored, for physical courage on a battlefield, an ability that the world had actually covered over in its creation of the stereotype Jew.

Indeed, the suddenly new image of the Jew as victor, rather than victim, the warrior and not the sufferer, had as much to do with the world's bewilderment over Israel's stunning military victory as the scope and rapidity of the victory itself. One could almost hear the world asking itself: How did the Jews get to be such good fighters? One could sense many Jews, too, asking the same question.[1]

Yet, so ingrained is this picture of the Jew as a poor fighter and reluctant soldier that even the stunning Israeli military victories in wars with the Arabs have not wiped out the stereotype in the minds of Israel's enemies. A pamphlet written by an Egyptian army colonel and distributed at an international military conference in Cairo several years ago, well after the Six Day War, claimed that "no country admits Jews into its armed forces." The weapons of Jews, who were said to care only about hoarding money, are "cheating, deceit and exploitation of other people's

---

[1] In fact, Jews had been asking themselves this ever since the new nation of Israel began beating the Arabs in warfare. Writing in *For 2¢ Plain* after the 1956 Sinai War, Harry Golden noted the emerging image of the fighting Jew, but quipped that it paralleled the tarnishing of the image of the Jew as an able businessman because of Israel's economic problems and unbalanced budget. Thus, for Golden, there could be a switch coming in the Jewish stereotype: people might now say, "Them Jews are great fighters, but they are certainly poor businessmen."

misfortunes." In a masterful muddling of several false stereotypes about the Jews, the Egyptian colonel noted that since "the image of the Jew is . . . that of usurer" it was apparent why Jews were not in the military: "a usurer cannot be a combatant."

The influence of the Ignorance Factor on the persistence of this stereotype can be seen in the case of Mark Twain. Exceedingly favorable to the Jews in most of his writing (he once declared that the Jew "has made a marvelous fight in this world, in all ages; and he has done it with his hands tied behind him") Twain nevertheless wrote an article in the September, 1899, issue of *Harper's Monthly* dismissing the Jew as a soldier. When some prominent Jews protested, Twain did an unusual thing: he went back and searched out the facts. Based on his findings, he later admitted, in a postscript to another article, "Concerning the Jews," that when he had written "The Jew as a Soldier"

> I was ignorant—like the rest of the Christian world—of the fact that the Jew had a record as a soldier. I have since seen the official statistics, and I find that he furnished soldiers and high officers to the Revolution, the War of 1812, and the Mexican War. In the Civil War he was represented in the armies and navies of both the North and the South by 10 per cent of his numerical strength—the same percentage that was furnished by the Christian populations of the two sections. This large fact means more than it seems to mean; for it means that the Jew's patriotism was not merely level with the Christian's, but overpassed it. When the Christian volunteer arrived in camp he got a welcome and applause, but as a rule the Jew got a snub. His company was not desired, and he was made to feel it. That he nevertheless conquered his wounded pride and sacrificed both that and his blood for his flag raises the average and quality of his patriotism above the Christian's. His record for capacity, for fidelity, and for gallant soldiership in the field is as good as any one's.

Twain then went on to discuss the "common reproach that the Jew is willing to feed upon a country but not to fight for it." Concluded Twain:

That slur upon the Jew cannot hold up its head in presence of the figures of the War Department. It has done its work, and done it long and faithfully, and with high approval: it ought to be pensioned off now, and retired from active service.

But the slur never has quite been pensioned off. No matter what Jews do, they do not seem able to convince the rabid anti-Semite of their willingness to fight—and fight well—for the country in which they live. Soviet dictator and widely acknowledged hater of Jews Josef Stalin once cracked that "the Jews are rotten soldiers"— a distinctly irrational statement to come from the leader of a nation in which during World War I five hundred thousand Jews served in the Russian army, with several thousand winning awards for bravery, and in which during World War II:

• Among the Soviet Union's 150 nationality groups, the Jews had the highest percentage of those serving in the military and winning the largest number of honors—all according to the Soviet Union's own data.

• Jews ranked fourth among the 150 nationality groups in number of "Heroes of the Red Army."

• One hundred twenty-four thousand Jewish officers and enlisted men were decorated for bravery *in battle*.

• The Soviet army had at least one hundred Jewish generals.

• The commander-in-chief of the Soviet Air Force at the beginning of the war was General Jacob Smushkevich.

Thus, for Stalin to have been right in his assessment of Jewish fighting ability, Russia would have to have been in the habit of enlisting, training, and decorating a great many rotten soldiers.

Of course, all of these facts, even if shouted repeatedly into Stalin's left ear, probably would not have altered the dictator's mental image of the Jewish soldier. In addition to being a long-held belief, the stereotype of the Jew as a nonfighter has been a most damaging, dangerous one, warping the Jew in the minds of both non-Jew and Jew. For this picture—of the Jew as weak and passive, as cerebral and not physical—undoubtedly enabled many a pogrom to occur. If nature abhors a vacuum, human nature abhors a power vacuum. Once Jewish communities in the Diaspora, already small and isolated, were thought to be defenseless and unlikely to fight back in the face of attack, they became even more tempting and vulnerable targets to the pogromists. And a world which had witnessed centuries of such attacks would be fertile ground for the most massive pogrom of all—the Holocaust, in which even today the seeming lack of Jewish physical response is debated. For this reason, this stereotype may be directly responsible for more Jewish deaths than any other false image of the Jew.

Indeed, so deep did this image of the Jew become that even many Jews misunderstand what appears to be Jewish cowardice in the face of centuries of pogroms and persecution. Except for the exploits of the Israeli army today, people in general do not know the Jewish history of physical courage that makes this stereotype crumble.

The image of the Jew as a nonfighter seems to have emerged only after the Romans drove the Jews out of the Land of Israel. The Romans themselves could not have stereotyped the Jews in this way, for the Israelites held off the mighty Roman legions for four years in the battle for Jerusalem. "Only the numerical superiority of the Romans and the strength of their equipment had overcome the Jewish resistance," wrote a Christian historian in *Jerusalem—A History*. Then the Zealots resisted Roman might for three more years at Masada, and just sixty years later, the Romans had to put down yet another Jewish rebellion—this one led by Bar Kochba.

But in the exile that followed, discrimination, verbal and physical abuse, expulsions, ghettos, crusades, and pogroms all conspired to make, then keep the Jew downtrodden as a rejected or reluctantly accepted minority. Such a situation, fostered and reinforced over two thousand years, creates its own realities, altering the image of a people—often in their own minds as well as in the minds of their adversaries. The inevitable wheel of prejudice—in which a country browbeats a minority and then heaps scorn on it for acting browbeaten—rolled back and forth over the body of Jewry throughout Europe and Asia, in century after century. But in the area of military affairs, the cycle of prejudice had one further impetus the modern world seems to forget: the non-Jew may have never seen the Jew as a fighter or soldier because after the fall of the Roman empire, few European countries permitted their Jews to enter the army or rise to officer status.

Serving in the military was considered a right of citizenship—and Jews were not often considered citizens. The first nation to welcome the Jews into the military on any appreciable scale was the United States, but that came as late as the eighteenth century. Thus, another case of Goldberg's Law: the Jew could hardly be viewed as a soldier if he was not permitted to step onto a battlefield.

The exclusion of Jews from many of the armies of the world for so long is in itself an intriguing commentary on the psyche of man. One would think that anti-Jewish discrimination, which automatically places less value on Jewish life, would have fostered an atmosphere in which the armies of non-Jewish nations would have at least sought to use Jewish manpower for the proverbial cannon fodder. But mankind appears to have a special mystique about its armies and the people who lead them.

Armies have invariably been exclusionary. In many countries, it is the military that provides the power structure for the nation, as can be seen openly in South America and Africa today. In ancient times, the leader of the war-making apparatus was the king or emperor himself. From Alexander the Great through Julius Caesar through Charlemagne through Napoleon up through Mao Tse-tung, the strong leaders of nations have been active leaders of the armies. So inbred does this seem to be that, even in modern times, those heads of state who wish to gain the tightest control of their people not only take over the mantle of chief of the armed forces, but even dress in military clothes. Stalin, Mao Tse-Tung, Hitler, Mussolini, Castro, Idi Amin—few are the times when they could be seen in anything but an army-type uniform. Czar Nicholas II, made a general at twelve, dressed in military clothes throughout his life.

Even the United States has not been too far removed from the mystique of the military. The father of America, George Washington, the first to become president, was originally Commander-in-Chief of the Continental Army, the country's revolutionary forces. Among other war heroes raised by Americans to the

Presidency have been Andrew Jackson (a major general in the War of 1812, he became a national hero when he defeated the British at New Orleans), William Henry Harrison (he was given command of the Army in the Northwest in the War of 1812 following his involvement in the Battle of Tippecanoe, for which he became famous), Zachary Taylor (a career soldier), Ulysses S. Grant (General-in-Chief of the Union Army at the end of the Civil War), James Garfield (he was first elected to Congress at thirty-one while a brigadier general), Theodore Roosevelt (hero of the Spanish-American War), and Dwight David Eisenhower (commanding general of the victorious forces in Europe in World War II)—not to mention those who were able to highlight their military record for political advantage, such as John F. Kennedy (PT-boat commander) and Jimmy Carter (Naval Academy graduate). At least one out of every five presidents of the world's leading democracy gained his position either directly or indirectly through his military exploits.

Thus, with the power structure of so many countries tied into the armed forces, with the military supplying even today many of the more schooled elements of a country—especially in the backward nations—the army has been seen as the center of leadership and control of a people. The Jew, viewed as the alien, was not welcome in this structure. And the atmosphere for any Jew who might wish to enter was strongly assimilationist—which in turn made Jews shy away from the military. Even when needed to fight, the Jew was kept in a downtrodden capacity—he was not usually allowed by law to become an officer.

In Europe, only with the advent of emancipation during the nineteenth century were Jews able to enter the military to any large degree (some nations, such as Poland, Germany, and Sweden, had intermittently allowed Jews to serve, but then would later withdraw the privilege). When finally accepted, Jews were often subjected to insults, and Jews who wanted to make a career of the military were especially victimized by prejudice. One such case: In the United States Navy in the 1800s, Uriah Phillips Levy, who eventually rose to become a Commodore and is credited with bringing an end to flogging as a punishment in the American navy, was court martialled six times during his career (the court martials often arose over his fighting back in anti-Semitic incidents, but he was vindicated each time). Another case in point: In the czarist army during the entire nineteenth century, only one Jew—Zvi Herz Zam—was able to become an officer. He eventually was promoted to captain but only just before his retirement after forty-one years in the military.[2] And then, of course, there is the famous episode involving Alfred Dreyfus, a captain in the French army, charged by his government with providing military secrets to the Germans. Later cleared of what proved to be an anti-Semitic inspired campaign, complete with forgeries and false testimony, Dreyfus was such a devoted military career man that, even after years of brutal imprisonment on Devil's Island and several trials, this French Jew went back into the army and fought for France in World War I. Although in his fifties then, he commanded a fortress in Paris. After the war, he retired as a lieutenant colonel in the French army.

The Ignorance Factor has helped reinforce the Jewish passivity stereotype by wiping out in the world's mind the connection between the ancient and the modern Jew. To comprehend the true Jew, one must begin by looking at the earliest days of the Jewish people.

What seems to be overlooked, if not totally forgotten, is that the Israelites may have been promised the Promised Land, but they weren't given it—they had to fight to win it and, later, to preserve it. And they had to win wars against some of the ancient world's strongest armies.

Ironically, those battles for the Promised Land have been immortalized by history, and so have the leaders of those victorious Jewish armies. Joshua, remember, is the one who "fit (fought) the battle of Jericho." David defeated the tough army of the Philistines (a name now associated with the antiintellectual and anticultural), and, in slaying Goliath, became literally a giant killer. Judah Maccabee turned back the assault of the mighty

---

[2] When Zam was first promoted to vice-captain, he was ordered by the war minister, surprised that a faithful Jew was an officer, to command the worst company in his regiment. But one year later, Zam had so shaped up the soldiers under him that they were judged the best company. Zam still had to wait years to be made a full captain.

Greek nation and restored the Temple worship to become the hero of Chanukah (a holiday that celebrates a military, as well as a spiritual, victory).[3] And the military prowess of these Jews has not been forgotten by the professionals today. In the Military Academy at West Point, the Academic Board Room contains base-reliefs of nine famed warriors from history, each one carved into the massive stone mantel over the fireplace. There, alongside Hector, Alexander the Great, Caesar, King Arthur, Charlemagne, and Godfrey de Bouillon, are Joshua, David, and Judah Maccabee.

The heroic exploits of Judah Maccabee have also been celebrated in another unlikely way—by George Frederick Handel, the famed composer of the Christian oratorio, "Messiah." In fact, Handel's creation of the oratorio *"Judas Maccabaeus"* saved his career. Handel (1685-1759) had fallen into difficult financial straits until on April 1, 1747, he launched the oratorio retelling the story in the First Book of Maccabees about the Maccabee-led Israelite victory over Antiochus. The work became a popular success, mainly for two reasons that say something about the Jewish stereotype we have been discussing. Sir Newman Flowers, one of the most important biographers of Handel, has written that "a Jew on stage as a hero, rather than a reviled figure, was a thing practically unknown in London." As a result, "Handel found himself possessed of a new public." A large part of that "new public" became the Jews of London, who flocked to see an artistic work acclaiming a Jewish national hero. The theatre attendance swelled by Jewish ranks enabled Handel to present the oratorio forty times before his death. "A grateful Handel," writes Will Durant in the *Age of Voltaire*, "took most of his oratorio subjects from then on from Jewish legend or history: *Alexander Balus, Joshua, Susanna, Solomon, Jephtha.*" But in further indication of how the story of the true Jew has often been covered over, the Nazis changed the title of Handel's oratorio to *Hero of a People* to wipe out its Jewish reference.

Handel's *Judas Maccabaeus*, however, touches on a theme that indicates another reason for the absence of Jews from the ranks of

---

[3] One history book notes that during this war, latkes, a Jewish food of pancakes made out of potatoes, were hardened and then used as ammunition—they were hurled at enemy soldiers.

soldierdom for so long. For while the Jewish people admired the military leadership of such figures as Joshua, David and Bar Kochba (who led the last revolt against the Romans), their victories were viewed not so much as military as spiritual. They were, after all, instruments of God, seeking to preserve religious values. This is why King David, the warrior, is not as celebrated in the Jewish mind as much as King David, the psalmist. Handel seems to have understood this—and it is possibly why he touched the sensitivities of his Jewish audience who could respect the fighter and his act of heroism but who felt that his success emanated from a God who admires peace more than power. As Judah sings at one point: "How vain is man who boasts in fight, the valour of gigantic might!"

What Judaism fosters is a religion not of weakness and passivity, but abhorrence to violence and fighting for its own sake. The Jewish religion is not a faith of pacifism. The Hebrew scriptures tell of numerous battles for national survival. The Bible even sets the age for military service at twenty (Numbers 1:3). The Israelite kings had standing armies, with draftees called to duty for wartime. King Solomon, for instance, had an army of approximately twelve thousand calvary, fourteen hundred chariots and forty thousand chariot horses (1 Kings 10:26).

But the Jewish nation engaged in warfare imbued with religious values. The Ark containing the Ten Commandments was said to be brought onto the battlefield, and the army of the Israelites was always accompanied by a priest who would give spiritual counsel and inspiration to the soldiers before battle. Sometimes the High Priest accompanied the Ark onto the battlefield. Indeed, even the Maccabee name, according to one version, originated from a religious message contained in the Hebrew letters Judah carried on his flag: M.K.B.Y.E., which is the abbreviation for the Hebrew original of "Who is like thee, O Lord, among gods?"

Thus, Judaism did not glorify war. According to the Bible, an altar made of stone could not be touched by iron, because this metal signified bloodshed and weapons of war. And Jews can well be proud that theirs is the religion that spoke of the vision, in Isaiah's words, of a world in which nations "shall beat their swords into ploughshares and their spears into pruning-hooks." [4]

Although Jewish armies ceased to exist with the Roman destruction of the Second Temple and the expulsion of the Jews in the year 70 C.E., Jews were permitted according to Jewish law to serve in the armies of the nations in which they settled. Extensive rabbinical literature was written voicing no objection, counseling Jews to try to maintain the Torah laws of Sabbath and diet during peacetime but absolving adherents during times of war. Maimonides, the great Jewish philosopher, in his *Hilchoth Melachim*, stated that in the case of war, the Jewish soldier was to act as he would when faced under any other conditions with saving a life: such a situation took precedence over the maintenance of Sabbath or dietary laws. As H. L. Mencken recognized when he reprinted the Hebrew proverb in his *New Dictionary of Quotations* (page 613), "the law of the land is the law for the Jew."

During the long years of Jewish exile, then, the glaring absence of Jews from many of the armies of the world was not a reflection of Judaic law, lack of Jewish capabilities, disloyalty to a nation, or desire on the part of Jews to avoid military duty. Indeed, where the Jew was allowed to serve, the story of Jewish heroism and national commitment is replete with surprising facts and incredible individuals.

In *The Jewish Connection*, I created the imaginary Goldbergian Institute, where the amazing but unknown accomplishments of Jews could be on display in exhibits and pictures. The military involvement of the Jews is such an important yet overlooked part of the Jewish experience that to tell adequately this aspect of the Jewish condition—indeed, to rid the world of its Ignorance Factor in this case—an entire floor of the Goldbergian Institute would have to be devoted to showing the unusual, yet true story about Jews in the military.

Here then is the military exhibit I envision. It begins with a mural depicting the first group of Jewish settlers in America in

---

[4] So prevalent has this Jewish-sponsored concept become that just one of its words was needed to be used in a *New Yorker* cartoon to make its point. A suddenly indignant wife looks over at her husband, decked out in his general's uniform, and says, "I bet you don't even believe in ploughshares."

[86]

1655 petitioning Peter Stuyvesant, the governor-general of New Amsterdam, for permission to stand guard at the stockade and to participate in the defense of the colony like other men. Stuyvesant had excluded the Jews from bearing arms—he, after all, was just following what was the practice in Holland and throughout much of the rest of Europe in those days. In place of military duty, Stuyvesant wanted the Jews to pay a tax—another common idea (they were not going to let the Jews off that easily). But the Jews, with men by the name of Asser Levy and Jacob Barsimson leading the way, protested to Stuyvesant. He rejected their request. The Jews then protested to the Dutch West India Company controlling New Amsterdam. Levy, however, hit on what must be considered a Jewish solution: he decided to stand guard without authorization and showed up so many times to keep watch that the tax was eventually dropped and the Dutch allowed Levy and others to become part of the guard. A small victory for the Jews, but a most meaningful one in many ways: this debate over the right of Jews to serve in the military force literally began the march of freedoms Jews won in the developing New World. It also marked the beginning of wide-scale Jewish participation in the armed forces of this new land—and thereby set into motion the eventual acceptance of Jews into the armed forces of a growing number of nations.[5]

The scope of this Jewish participation in America can be seen on a statement affixed to the front wall of the exhibit. Here is revealed that more than 2 million Jews have served in all the conflicts in which the United States has ever been engaged, from the American Revolution through the Vietnam War. And on the wall, underneath that statistic, is another interesting fact: the Jewish War Veterans, founded in 1896 by Jews who had served in the Civil War, is the oldest active veterans organization in America. (The American Legion was not founded until 1919; the Veterans of Foreign Wars, 1913; Disabled American Veterans, 1923; and Catholic War Veterans, 1935.)

A special display in the Goldbergian Institute has to be set up to

[5] The first Jew to serve in an armed force on North American soil actually goes back to the sixteenth century when a Marrano, Hernando Alonso, fought in Mexico with Cortes. When Alonso was discovered to be a secret Jew, he was burned at the stake as a heretic.

show the many ways in which Jews participated in the Civil War because this conflict marked the first one in which Jews became immersed to an unusual degree. With two hundred thousand Jews in all of America, over six thousand fought in the Union Army and thirteen hundred in the Confederate Army.

On the Union side, for instance, it has been said that as many as nine generals were Jewish. But the seven we are certain about, each of whom rose to the rank of Major General or Brigadier General during the war, are prominently on display: Edward Solomon (whose bravery at Gettysburg attracted wide attention); Frederick Knefler (who served under top Union Generals Grant and Sherman); Max Einstein (who fought in the Battle of Bull Run); Philip J. Joachimsen (who before the war earned the thanks of President Franklin Pierce for becoming, as Assistant Attorney of the United States District Court in New York, the first to prosecute slave dealers vigorously); Leopold Blumenberg (who as a major commanded Maryland's 5th Regiment, which he had assisted in organizing, in the Battle of Antietam); Abraham Hart (who was involved in the defense of Washington, D. C., and in the second Battle of Bull Run); and Leopold C. Newman (who, while dying in a Washington hospital from a cannonball wound, was visited by President Lincoln to be commissioned as a Brigadier General).

Statistics show some of the rest of the range of Jewish involvement. On the Union side, for instance, Jews numbered 21 colonels, 9 lieutenant colonels, 40 majors, 205 captains, 325 lieutenants, 48 adjutants, and 25 surgeons.

But it was among the foot soldiers that Jews distinguished themselves. So involved in the fighting were Jewish soldiers in the Confederate Army that John Seddon, Confederate Secretary of War, refused High Holy Day furloughs for the Jewish soldiers because "it would disintegrate certain commands if the request was granted." One of those Southern soldiers has a special niche in this display. He is Max Frauenthal, whose heroism in battle became so legendary that his name, corrupted into the easier-to-pronounce Fronthal, actually became used by Confederate soldiers as a synonym for courage.

As for the Union, two generals are on record citing the performance of Jewish soldiers. Said Major-General O. O. Howard, who had a Jewish aide-de-camp in the first Battle of Bull Run and another assistant who was killed at the Battle of Chancellorsville, "Intrinsically, there are no more patriotic men to be found in the country than those who claim to be of Hebrew descent and who served with me in parallel commands or more directly under my instructions." [6] Said a General Stahel: "There were many Hebrews under me ... I always found the soldiers of Jewish faith as firm in their devotion to the cause of the country they were serving as any others, and ever ready to perform any duty to which they might be assigned."

Such talk was not mere flattery. During the Civil War, seven Jews won the Congressional Medal of Honor.

There is much to see on this floor of the Goldbergian Institute, so the visitor, to see it all, must glance only quickly at the next series of display cases—ones showing the military exploits of individual Jews in a wide range of unusual situations. Here, in a mini gallery of military heroes, is:

• Joseph Trumpeldor (1880-1920), who was one of the first Jews to hold commissioned rank in the Russian Army. He served with the Siberian regiment in the Russo-Japanese War (1904), where he volunteered for dangerous missions. Badly wounded, he had to have his left arm amputated, but upon recovery he insisted on being sent back to the front. His act received special mention, and he was later awarded the Order of St. George, Russia's highest decoration, and made a captain. After the war, he lived in Palestine and became involved in early efforts by Jewish settlers to found a military force as a prelude to establishment of a Jewish state. He served as deputy commander of the Zion Mule Corps and later worked with Vladimir Jabotinsky, the fervent Zionist leader, to form a fighting unit in the British Army that became the Jewish Legion with 10,000 volunteers. When he died during an Arab attack in Palestine, his last words were, "Never mind; it is

---

[6] Mark Twain cited this quote in his retraction on the Jew as a soldier. He also cited the fact that during the Civil War, fourteen Jewish Confederate and Union families contributed a total of fifty-one soldiers. One family had a father and three sons serving; another, a father and four sons.

good to die for our country." Songs, poems and stories have been written about his exploits.

• The lieutenant from Brooklyn, New York, Louis Cohen, who, following World War I, was awarded the French Croix de Guerre with palm, the Cross of St. Stanislaus, the Order of the Bey of Tunis, and a medal from the French Minister of the Interior.

• Major General Maurice Rose, the son of a synagogue sexton in Denver, Colorado, who commanded the United States 3rd Armored Division in World War II and accomplished three firsts—he was the first army commander since Napoleon to invade Germany from the West, he headed the first army division to breach the Siegfried Line, and he led the first American unit to capture a German town.

• Sam Dreben, a soldier of fortune known as "the fighting Jew," who was born in Russia in 1878, relocated to Texas, and fought for the United States in World War I (winning the Distinguished Service Cross for attacking a machine-gun nest and killing thirty-two German soldiers, winning the Croix de Guerre and other citations)—all after he had participated in the Spanish-American War, wound up in China during the Boxer Rebellion, engaged in fighting in Nicaragua, and served in Mexico with General Pershing. He died far from a battlefield as a proud Jew, making an especially large donation of money to the American Jewish Joint Distribution Committee.

• The man who became a general in the Chinese Army, Morris Abraham Cohen (1887-1970), known as "Two-gun Cohen" for his skillful marksmanship, also called "Cohen Moisha" by the Chinese. Cohen, born in London but growing up in Canada, became friendly in 1908 with the Chinese nationalist leader Sun Yat-sen, then living in exile and planning the revolution he was later to lead. In 1922, following service in World War I with a Canadian regiment on the western front, Cohen became aide-de-camp of Sun Yat-sen in China and later also advisor to Sun's successor, Chiang Kai-shek. In these capacities, Cohen helped organize the Kuomintang Army. He was commissioned a general of the Chinese Army and was attached to the Chinese Ministry of War from 1926-28, operating virtually as the Chinese Nationalist war minister. Admitted to the highest officialdom of Chinese politics, he became an important power in both political and military circles in China. He was involved in military operations against Communist rebels and the Japanese, who considered him a dangerous foe and once stopped a British liner suspecting he was on board. He was finally captured by the Japanese in 1941, but was exchanged two years later and returned to Canada. He tried several times following the Communist takeover to heal the rift among the Chinese factions.

• And the Liuzzis—son Giorgio, who was chief of staff of the Italian Army from 1956 to 1958, and father Guido, who as director of Italy's military academy after World War I built up one of Europe's most outstanding army schools.

A special display in this section is reserved for Berek Yoselovich, a Polish Jew who helped open up the ranks of European armies to the Jews. It was he who in 1794 asked Polish General Tadeusz Kosciusko, who had participated in the American Revolution and was flushed with ideas for organizing a similar revolt among the Poles against the Russian Czar and the King of Prussia, that Jews be allowed to participate. Except for France, where the Revolution of 1789 had opened up equal rights and therefore the army for Jews, European countries at the time did not allow Jews to be soldiers. Poland had intermittently allowed Jews to take part in wars, but pressure by the Catholic authorities in the eighteenth century had put an end to it in Poland. Now, however, Kosciusko decided to respond favorably to Yoselovich's petition and permitted the Jews to form a regiment of volunteers for a light calvary unit. Yoselovich was made commander, and he set about to collect money from Warsaw Jews to buy arms. On October 1, 1794, a call for volunteers went out in Yiddish.

Five hundred Jews volunteered. They eventually formed a unit that battled Russian forces in an attempt to defend Warsaw, with most of the Jews perishing in the brutal fighting.

Berek Yoselovich survived and later fought in the Napoleonic War, where he died in battle at Kotzk on May 5, 1809. Several patriotic Polish folksongs still celebrate his actions in behalf of Poland.

His son, Yossel, followed his footsteps. In 1830, he organized a Jewish regiment of 850 youths. This group was incorporated into the national guard in Warsaw and although they were scrupulously religious (they ate only kosher food, rested on the Sabbath, and wore beards, for which they were called "the Beardlings"), they proved remarkably brave soldiers, moving the Polish Commander in Chief to state, "The spectacle of the Jewish militiamen and their sacrifices for Poland must have convinced everyone how much we have sinned against the Jews."

Berek Yoselovich's actions, along with the spirit of emancipation beginning to influence the governments of Europe, had started to open up the military to Jewish participation, as is shown by a display depicting the Battle of Waterloo. Napoleon formed an all-Jewish unit in his army in 1805 and a number of Jews took part on both sides in the Battle of Waterloo in 1815. In fact, 235 Jewish soldiers were killed at Waterloo and, according to an article in an issue of the *London Times* in August, 1833, the Duke of Wellington reported that a number of the officers on the battlefield at Waterloo were Jewish. Said Wellington: "No less than 15 officers of the Jewish faith took part in the Battle of Waterloo; I, myself, made the acquaintance of many excellent and distinguished officers of that religion." [7]

The visitor to this floor of the Goldbergian Institute is now led by a short corridor to the next section of the exhibit. This display is entitled, "Jews in the World Wars." Here is fresh evidence, right in our century, that dispels the ever-lingering stereotype of the Jew as unsoldierly.

The official United Nations statistics for World War I are shown. They reveal that a total of 1,172,000 Jews served in the armies of nine nations. This included 250 thousand Jews in the United States armed services, a figure that represents 5 percent of the Jewish population in the United States—an interesting statistic since only 3 percent of the rest of the American populace served in World War I.[8]

---

[7] Another unlikely military spot in which to find Jews is surely the French Foreign Legion, and yet numerous soldiers of the Jewish faith have served in that exotic, yet harsh, army. In fact, according to one source cited in a book on the subject *(Jews and the French Foreign Legion)*, "the Jewish communities of Algeria in April, 1940, prepared a Passover for 1,500 Jewish legionnaires."

[8] Among other pieces of evidence of the Jewish role in the American war effort: over fifteen thousand Jews were killed or wounded, six Jews won the Congressional Medal of Honor, and among the ten thousand Jewish officers were three who rose to general.

Austria-Hungary, a hotbed of anti-Semitism (Karl Lueger, the Mayor of Vienna from 1897-1910, had dismissed Jewish officials and introduced segregation in his city's schools), had the second highest participation of Jewish soldiers—275 thousand. But the most ironic involvement came in Germany, where 90,000 Jews served the Kaiser, 11,500 were awarded the Iron Cross, one of the German war aces was a Jew, and 12,000 Jews died fighting for the Fatherland. The dramatic aspect to this statistic is that in modern Israel's wars with the Arabs, less than ten thousand Jews have died on the battlefield.

The death of twelve thousand Jews and the participation of ninety thousand in the German army—one of whom, Hugo Guttmann, served as Lance Corporal Adolf Hitler's regimental adjutant—did not stop the ugly charges in Germany following the war based on that Jewish stereotype: Jews, some claimed, had either not enlisted in sufficient numbers or had avoided combat. The German War Ministry even ordered a survey to find out, but some of the findings aroused heated debate. According to the *Encyclopaedia Judaica*, "the percentage of Jews was almost equal to that of Christians" and would have been higher but for a diminishing German Jewish birthrate that started in 1880. Jewish deaths in battle, where upwards of eighty thousand Jews served in frontline trenches, were actually proportionately higher than non-Jewish deaths. Ben Hecht is quoted in *Before the Deluge* as saying, "More Jews were killed in battle than Germans. The Jewish population of Germany was only one half of one percent. The Jewish deaths in the war were three percent."

Ironically, a Jew did have much to do with stopping Germany on the battlefield. From June, 1918, until the war's end, Lieutenant General Sir John Monash (1865-1931), son of a Polish immigrant Jew, commanded the Australian army in France. He led the Allied assault on the Hindenburg Line, breaking it with five Australian, two English, and two American divisions. According to the *Encyclopaedia Judaica*, normally reserved in its comments on individuals, Monash "was responsible for the breach of the German lines . . . which led to the collapse of German resistance. He was considered the outstanding army commander of World War I."

So the Germans do not have to worry that they lost the war, as

Hitler claimed, because the "Jews stabbed them in the back." The Jews, thanks to Monash, stabbed them in the front.

World War II, the subject of the next exhibit, tells much, if not more, of the same story—widespread Jewish participation in the armies of the world, but an involvement which much of the world has ignored. Again, the United Nations figures are presented: this time they show that 1,397,000 Jews served in the world's armed forces. The United States had 550 thousand, Russia had 500 thousand, with the rest of the Jewish total spread between Poland (140 thousand), Great Britain (62 thousand), France (46 thousand), Canada (16 thousand), South Africa (10 thousand), Czechoslovakia (8 thousand), Belgium (7 thousand), Holland (7 thousand), Australia and New Zealand (3 thousand), and Palestinian units in the British Army (35 thousand).

This last figure (the number of Palestinian Jews who fought in World War II) is indicative of the Jew's problems with the Ignorance Factor, as can be seen in a story recounted by a Jewish chaplain who served in Palestine during much of the war and wrote about his experiences in a book entitled *Soldiers From Judea*. Major Lewis Rabinowitz, appointed in 1941 Senior Jewish Chaplain in Britain's Middle East Forces, recalls:

> Shortly after my arrival in the Middle East (May, 1941), I received a communication from an official military source in London: "Statements have appeared in the Jewish Press here that there are 9,701 Palestinian Jewish soldiers in the Middle East. *This number must be exaggerated.* Will you please find out the facts?" There was no exaggeration at all, as I hastened to inform the enquirer after the necessary verification had been made. Two and a half years later I returned to England. The number of Palestinian Jews with the Forces had grown to 25,000; the Royal Navy, the A.T.S. (Auxiliary Territorial Service) and the WAAF (Women's Auxiliary Air Force) had opened their ranks to them; Jewish units were in Sicily and Italy; but the same ignorance prevailed.

The figure eventually reached thirty-five thousand. But no wonder the British were startled. As Major Rabinowitz points out, those 35,000 Jewish volunteers "represent as large a percentage of the Palestinian Jewish population of under 600,000 as eight million volunteers would constitute in relation to the population of the United States."

Jewish participation in World War II had some fascinating—and ironic—overtones, as the exhibit shows. In the United States, sixteen Jews became either admirals or generals, ten thousand were decorated for heroic action, fifty thousand were killed or wounded, Jewish women served in the WACS and WAVES, and two Jews were awarded posthumously the Congressional Medal of Honor (one of whom, Isador Jachman, attended the Talmudical Academy of Baltimore). But American Jewry also has another distinction. The shortest man to serve in the United States Army in the Second World War was Nissum Attas, from New York's East Side. Attas stood 4 feet 5 inches tall.

Included in the World War II exhibit is the story of one of the most ironic events of that war, in which a set of circumstances led to a strange sight—Jewish soldiers fighting alongside Nazi soldiers.

This happened on the Finnish-Russian front. During the Finnish-Russian war of 1939-40, the able-bodied Jewish citizens of Finland served in the army. When Finland joined with Germany during the Second World War to attack Russia in order to recapture lands lost in that earlier war, Jewish soldiers continued their service to their country. Finland refused to enforce any anti-Jewish legislation, and the commander of Finland's armed forces in both wars, Field Marshal Mannerheim, would not yield to strong Nazi pressure to de-Judaize the Finnish army. In fact, no Finnish Jews were ever turned over to the Germans. Rabbi Frederick E. Werbell, who wrote about this in the April 24, 1977, issue of *The Jewish Week-American Examiner*, reported that on a visit to Finland he "met several Finnish Jewish soldiers who actually reported to German officers, without being discriminated against!"

The visitor now enters the last exhibit area on this floor of the Goldbergian Institute. Here are shown some of the exploits and achievements of the Israeli Defense Forces, the first Jewish army since the Romans defeated the Jews in ancient Israel.

In photos taken during Israel's wars with the Arabs and in 3-

dimensional mockups of such daring military exploits as the Entebbe rescue, the fighting skills of Jews can be seen.

Especially noteworthy in this exhibit is the material on the Yom Kippur War. Israel's success in her confrontations with the Arabs is well known, especially in the Six Day War, but the results of the 1973 Yom Kippur War seem to be less clear in the public mind, possibly because of Israel's early losses due to the surprise Arab attack, and because of the diplomatic halt to the fighting before a logical end came on the battlefield. But the surprising truth, as the exhibit points out, is that in many ways the Israeli achievements in the Yom Kippur War even surpassed those in the 1967 Six Day War.[9]

One military correspondent, for instance, termed Israel's performance in air-to-air combat during the Yom Kippur War as incredible. The Israelis were able to shoot down 334 Arab planes; the Arabs, in the air, were able to down only 3 Israeli planes. In all, Israel lost 115 aircraft, mainly to the sophisticated Russian-supplied surface-to-air missiles, but Israel was able to demolish a total of 387 Arab planes, which means that she destroyed enemy planes at a greater ratio than the Arab nations' 2.5 to 1 ratio superiority in aircraft.

Also, hard as it may seem to believe in light of what the world thought during and right after the war because of the initial successes of the missile system thrown up against them, the Israeli Air Force's performance was actually superior in the Yom Kippur War to that in the Six Day War. As the highly respected American magazine *Aviation Week and Space Technology* pointed out in an article following the war, the loss rate per sortie (the flight of an aircraft from its base to attack a target to its return to base) is the real guide to performance. In this regard, *Aviation Week* noted that Israel's loss rate was one aircraft per hundred sorties—considerably less than her four per hundred sorties of the 1967 War.

The Yom Kippur War also saw history's biggest tank battle, when Israeli and Egyptian tanks dueled in the Sinai desert. The results of all the tank activity on all of Israel's fronts was that 420

---

[9] Because of the cost to Israel, the Yom Kippur War could also be called the $6 Billion War (Israel had to expend more than $250 million a day for twenty-one days, versus the $100 million daily in the Six Day War).

of Israel's tanks were knocked out, with approximately 200 totally destroyed. The Arabs, on the other hand, suffered knockout damage to 2300 tanks, with 1270 demolished. Thus, the Arab tank loss ratio to Israel was an incredible eleven to one.

Finally, the Yom Kippur War saw Israel's navy totally rout Arab naval units. In ten engagements, the Israeli Navy won ten times.

Following that war, the Commanding General of the United States Army Materiel Command, General Henry A. Miley, Jr., led a team of military men to Israel to assess the American resupply effort and Israel's utilization of the war materials. It was under General Miley's command that the massive American airlift of tanks, as well as other army weaponry, had been carried out. He later reported on the results of his factfinding mission in a speech before the National Security Industrial Association in Washington, D. C.

Among some of his findings:

• The Israelis would fire gun tubes on both tanks and artillery until the guns wore out ... and then would replace them in a procedure they had developed for changing the tubes right on the firing lines. The Israelis would swap 175mm gun tubes for 8-inch tubes in three hours. "My artillery friends and ordnance experts," General Miley said, "tell me that it is quite a feat even under ideal conditions."

• "The Israeli forces properly anticipated a high washout rate of engines because of the severe sand and dust conditions in the Sinai desert. They beat this one by stockpiling tuned-up engines at the front."

• When replacement tanks got scarce at one point, repair teams came forward and swapped the components of two or more damaged tanks to come up with one workable tank—"all this within a stone's throw of the still-raging battle."

Concluded General Miley after citing numerous such incidents, "All in all, we brought back reports that would be hard to believe except that there were photographs and eyewitness accounts to substantiate those reports. . . . What the Israelis did borders on the miraculous."

The visitor completes his tour of the Goldbergian Institute's special one-floor exhibit on Jews in the military by coming into contact with one last display—a wall panel that depicts a special irony of history. Here is shown a painting of that crucial Roman battle for Jerusalem two thousand years ago. A printed message on a card alongside the picture reads:

> We hope this entire exhibit has convinced you that the Jewish ability in military affairs is strong, no matter what history or the generally accepted stereotype of the Jew implies, and that Jewish courage down through the ages is something of which each Jew can be proud. In fact, Jewish achievements in this area are so pervasive that when the Roman army, as depicted in this painting, eventually conquered Jerusalem, the Romans actually did so with the help of a Jewish military mind. Generally overlooked by history is that the Chief of Staff and main advisor to the Roman General Titus during the siege of Jerusalem—indeed, the highest-ranking officer in Titus's army in Judea—was a Jew: Tiberius Alexander, nephew of the great Jewish philosopher Philo. Just think what might have been if the Roman army, like so many other armies, had not accepted Jews.

GOLDBERG'S LAW

If anything can be misconstrued about the Jews, it will be ... and has been.

Exhibit D: THE TWELVE-YEAR-OLD JEWISH SOLDIER

CZARIST RUSSIA, WHICH ORIGINALLY EXCLUDED JEWS FROM ITS ARMY, AT ONE TIME DRAFTED TWELVE-YEAR-OLD JEWISH YOUTHS FOR MILITARY SERVICE LASTING TWENTY-FIVE YEARS

Czarist Russia, which expelled the Jews twice during the eighteenth century, tried numerous methods to convert Jews during the nineteenth century. One of the six hundred restrictive orders and regulations issued about the Jews by Czar Nicholas I during his reign (1825–1855) was his infamous decree creating the "cantonists"—twelve-year-olds who had to be supplied by Jewish communities for military service of twenty-five years. The purpose was not to involve Jews in the army—only one Jew was allowed to rise as high as captain—but to use the military as a way to forcibly assimilate Jewish youngsters.

Once in the service, Jewish youths were subjected to consistent attempts to break their spirit and make them become Christians. Many did convert, but many others refused. Because of the conversions and deaths that resulted, Jewish parents often went to extremes to protect their children from being drafted, even taking drastic action to make them unfit for military service (such as severing a thumb so a rifle could not be fired). As a result of such acts and the difficulty in finding enough twelve-year-olds to fill a community's quotas, it was not unusual to see Jews as young as eight or nine years old being drafted into the Russian army for twenty-five years.

Needless to say, Russian Jews developed a hatred for Nicholas I and his army, but this still did not stop Jews from serving later in the Russian Armed Forces during World War I. At that time, under a different Czar, Jews were drafted for tours of duty like everyone else—and did not have to serve until well after their Bar Mitzvah.

V
"A Jew, I Presume?"

*A gallery of Jews
who shatter the stereotypes*

FACT: In the 1920s, the son of a Jewish blacksmith was recognized as one of the world's two strongest men.

FACT: The "father of ballet" was a fifteenth-century Italian Jew who wrote the first known work on the dance. His writings are preserved today in the national museums of France and England.

FACT: At one time, there were 100 thousand Jewish farmers in the United States—with Jews involved in every branch of farming and Jewish farmers located in every state.

FACT: The codesigner of the MIG jet fighter plane was a Jew whose name is part of the word "MIG."

FACT: Superman, the most popular comic book hero of all time, was created by two Jewish high school students— and the "S" on Superman's uniform represents their last names.

"Work Shall Make You Free"
—Sign over entrance to Auschwitz

DO YOU REMEMBER this story from history?

The famed nineteenth-century explorer Henry Morton Stanley has been cutting his way through the jungle underbrush of Africa for months now. With him is a veritable army of natives assembled for this special expedition. Back in Europe an entire continent has been eagerly reading his dispatches and waiting for word of the outcome of his mission. Finally, one night, in a lakeside clearing in the lush forests of this fabled dark continent, Stanley sees the man for whom he has been searching so long and diligently—a white man who, although trained in Europe as a doctor, is now serving in the heart of Africa. Wasting no time, Stanley strides over to him, raises his cap, offers his outstretched hand in greeting, and says:

"Dr. Schnitzer, I presume?"

What? That is *not* the famous remark you remember? Wasn't Stanley looking for a stranded medical missionary and explorer named Dr. David Livingstone? Weren't Stanley's first words of welcome a clipped understatement that became world renowned: "Dr. Livingstone, I presume?"

You're right—partially.

Stanley is said to have uttered such a remark when he found Livingstone in Africa.[1] But what has been generally forgotten—

---

[1] Although there is no actual record of Stanley's first words to Dr. Schnitzer, Stanley's historic first words to Dr. Livingstone were brought into question several years ago. In a 1972 interview, Stanley's grandson was quoted as saying he had been told that Stanley had not used the greeting, which really was a takeoff on the line in an old English play, "Mr. Stanley, I presume?" But a biographer of Livingstone, Tim Jeal, researched the matter and concluded that Stanley did greet Dr. Livingstone with those now immortal words—probably. Finally, a myth preserved—maybe. (Stanley's real name, though, was not Stanley; he was born John Rowland.)

[104]

although not by those history books which still tell the story—is that in 1888, seventeen years after his famous exploit with Livingstone, Stanley followed with another equally daring expedition in search of another European doctor and explorer in dire straits in Africa. And this other rescue mission, which generated the widespread concern and support of the German and British people, was as closely followed at the time as the Stanley-Livingstone story had been.

Who was the object of all this interest?

His real name was Eduard Schnitzer, and he was a German Jewish physician in his forties.[2] Born in 1840 in the Prussian province of Silesia, he studied medicine at Konigsberg, Germany. After a brief period in private practice, he decided to give in to a long desire for travel. He journeyed through southern Europe, then to Turkey, set up another private practice in Khartoum, closed that down and eventually wound up on April 17, 1876, in Lado, capital of the Equatoria Province of Egypt, where General Gordon, the Governor of Equatoria, appointed him provincial medical officer. Two years later, when Gordon left to become Governor General of the Sudan, Schnitzer, who had previously changed his name to Emin Effendi, was appointed Governor of Equatoria Province. He changed his name to Emin Pasha and for the next ten years ruled this vast area that measured 100 thousand square miles—twice the size of present-day Czechoslovakia.

But Emin did more than rule. He broke up the slave trade, explored sources of the Nile, and—in his favorite pastime—journeyed into unexplored jungles to secure collections of plants and

---

[2] Here is another of those discrepancies in historical sources. Everyone agrees that Schnitzer was born a Jew. He is profiled, with his own entry, in *The Jewish Encyclopedia*, *The Encyclopaedia Judaica*, *The Encyclopedia of Jewish Knowledge*, and *They Are All Jews*. But at some point in his life he appears to have converted, although what he converted to and when is in dispute. *The Lunatic Express*, a book about nineteenth-century Africa, says this "German-born Jewish physician" converted to Islam after reaching Africa, but a biography—*Emin Pasha: His Life and Work*—states that at the age of six, after his father had died, he was converted to Protestantism and makes no mention of any later conversion to Islam. Despite conversion, according to Jewish law (and according to such other quaint definitions as the Nazi's Nuremberg Law), Eduard Schnitzer was a full Jew. In fact, Stanley, writing in his book *In Darkest Africa*, which is about his finding not Livingstone but Emin Pasha, mentions Schnitzer's "Jewish parents" but makes no reference to any conversion. (As another indication of how error creeps into historical sources, throughout his book Stanley mistakenly refers to Schnitzer as Schnitzler.)

birds. He constructed forts, roads, and clinics, and began numerous agricultural irrigation and livestock breeding programs.

A brilliant chess player, pianist, and master of many languages (some said he knew a dozen, others that he could speak more than twenty), Emin presented an unusual figure. Photographs and drawings show him to be a small fastidious man with rimless glasses, neatly cropped mustache and beard, and a fez atop his head that made him look as if he were wearing a yarmulkah. One famed drawing of the day shows him—fez, eyeglasses, and all—leading a charge of soldiers on horseback.

And serving him as his trusted assistant was a Turkish Jew, Vita Hassan, who accompanied Emin on his explorations and journeys in Africa. Hassan, mentioned frequently by Stanley in the book *In Darkest Africa*, wrote a two-volume work on his life in Africa with Emin Pasha.

An uprising eventually isolated him and his troops from the outside world in April 1885. When Europe learned of his situation, a German Emin Pasha Relief Committee was formed to fund a rescue effort. The British, too, became involved, and a rival private expedition under Stanley was established.

By April 1888, Stanley, at the head of what has been termed "a formidable expedition, one of the most aggressively outfitted that had ever entered Africa," met up with Emin Pasha in a scene that historians have noted for its similarities with Stanley's meeting with Livingstone. Stanley then led Emin Pasha to the coast, and all of civilized Europe breathed a sigh of relief. But by 1890, Emin, who now longed for his adopted country, was back inside Africa, undertaking an exploration of the Victoria Nyanza. Because of his continued opposition to the slave trade, during the course of this expedition he was assassinated by Arab slave dealers.

The story of Dr. Schnitzer, alias Emin Pasha, leaves us with intriguing questions: how could all this happen and we know so little about it today? And how could a Jewish-born physician—interested in botany, zoology, language, chess, and piano—wind up as a governor and an explorer in "darkest Africa"?

The image of the Jew as rooted to the narrow streets and the supposedly narrow-minded world of the European ghetto has so warped our ideas of Jewish vocations and avocations that we cannot conceive of a Jew of ages ago in any other setting than the stereotypical European one, a heavily bearded, long black-coated figure engaged only in intellectual pursuits. And even the modern descendant of the Jew is seen as part of an essentially typical milieu—involved in only such professions as accountancy, law, medicine, the rabbinate, science, teaching, or business (retail, but especially wholesale). While those with such a mental image of the Jew are able occasionally to make an exception to the rule, they are still willing to bet that if they wanted to find a Jew between 9 A.M. and 5 P.M. during the work week, they could find him either buying and selling (preferably suits and dresses), keeping the books for those who do, protecting before courts of law those who do not do it well, attending to the medical needs of those who overdo it, and always avoiding at all cost anything that must be done with the hand—pheh!—rather than the brain.

Minority members have a way of being confined to a few job categories by the majority. Many Chinese living in the United States were engaged in the hand laundry trade at its height, but at that very same time China itself was far from dotted with an endless string of laundries nor were the rivers of China choked with starch. Greek immigrants did open and operate numerous restaurants in America, but the Parthenon might have been nothing more than a magnificent eatery if all the Greeks in history bore out the stereotype placed on the Greek-American in this century.

Interestingly, statistics might very well bear out some of these stereotypes, but the basic interests of a people do not. For the truth is that when it comes to occupations, discrimination and a unique set of pressures are invariably the cause of a minority people's movement—usually transitory—into a certain line of work. This is why the stereotypes of ethnic groups in America bear little relation to these groups' occupations in their home countries. This is also why Jewish occupational stereotypes seem to linger. Only the Jew, for so long without a homeland in existence, was forced to endure the occupational stereotypes placed on him without the compensating effects of his own people active in their own country untainted by economic oppression. To earn a living freely, one must be able to live freely.

As for those many Jews who do gravitate to the professions and the use of their minds rather than their hands, it is probably more than pressure and coincidence that they do so. A people trained to treasure the Book of Books, to study, analyze, and follow an awesome library filled not only with major texts but commentaries and discussions on those texts, is ripe for producing generations of scholars or those interested in scholarship. As for the belief that Jews are more likely to work with their minds than their hands, one should remember that the whole thrust of civilization has been for man to lift himself out of the caves not by exercising his brute, animal strength but by sharpening his mind. The brain has long been recognized as a sturdier tool than the back. An Adolf Hitler could try to sully the Jewish image with that timeworn aspersion about Jewish absence from the ranks of the common laborer, as he did in *Mein Kampf:* "How far the inner Judaization of our people has progressed can be seen from the small respect, if not contempt, that is accorded manual labor." Only Goldberg's Law could explain how the Jews could be attacked for doing what the thrust of civilization has been to make all men do—use their brains.

Ignored by many is the fact that the rabbis of the Talmud, who made it a matter of principle not to derive their livelihood from the Torah but from a secular vocation, espoused the value of labor, even if manual. Talmudic sages are recorded as being sandal-makers, masons, carpenters. Hillel the Elder, one of the most renowed of rabbis, was a woodcutter.

Also usually overlooked or unknown is that the rabbis had long noted that in the Biblical injunction to "remember the Sabbath day to keep it holy" was also the declaration, "Six days shalt thou labor and do all thy work." This was interpreted to mean that work during the week was as important as the Sabbath rest on the seventh day. Not only was idleness regarded as the road to evil, but as the late Joseph H. Hertz, Chief Rabbi of the British Empire, writes in his commentary on the prayer book, "The Jewish Sages are tireless in their insistence that work ennobles and sanctifies."

While Jewish industriousness may not seem to need defending—after all, the rabbinic endorsement of labor set up a Jewish work ethic far before the Protestant work ethic—we need only remember that the Nazis sought to propagate even this misbelief about the Jews. For arched across the entrance to Auschwitz was a diabolical sign that was meant in part to mask the evil nature of the concentration camp, but was also intended to reinforce yet another damaging stereotype of the supposedly parasitic Jew living off other people's physical labor. Above the gates of the Auschwitz hell was a five-word message to those who were entering but would never leave: "Work Shall Make You Free."

From the sixteenth century until the French Revolution, the ghetto existence was the lot of most of European Jewry, and it allowed few of the freedoms necessary for the full flowering of occupational talents. Only mentally could the Jew leap the walls of the ghetto and the restrictions of the Gentile society. The discrimination against the Jew was so pervasive, arbitrary, and capricious that it encumbered the Jew's ability not only to live but to make a living.

What Jews could or could not do to earn a livelihood came under constant and conflicting restrictions. Some countries prevented Jews from being shopkeepers, others from being craftsmen. One country ruled that Jews could deal in wood and leather, while another country ruled they could not. The Jews would be encouraged to start a factory in one land, yet be prevented from doing so in another. One region of a country would decree that Jews were allowed to sell alcohol; a neighboring region would make it against the law. In the middle of the eighteenth century in Prussia, for instance, Jews found that the government permitted them to do business in raw calf and sheepskin, but not in raw cowhide or horsehides; a Jew could be involved with manufactured woolen and cotton items, but could not be involved with raw wool or woolen threads.

Indeed, the Ignorance Factor has caused most people to overlook how discrimination and persecution have resulted in Jews, even today, concentrating in certain occupational fields and being absent from others. During so much of the history of Christian Europe, the denial to Jews of the right to participate in any but a narrow range of usually unsavory occupations was a way both to denigrate the Jew and to keep him from competing.

Moneylending, for instance, was a role foisted on the Jews for several centuries during the Middle Ages because of the Church's position that Biblical law prevented Christians from lending money at interest. As we will see in a later chapter, Christians also engaged in moneylending when the Church finally differentiated between interest and a fair profit, which it permitted, and "usury," which was still prohibited. Yet the early restriction of the Jews to this field led the general populace to associate Jews with moneylending and other matters of business and commerce. The centuries of Jewish involvement with moneylending left its mark, for Jews eventually moved into fields allied with moneylending: pawnbroking, dealing in secondhand clothes, even sewing (clothing, put up as collateral, had to be repaired for resale).

The picture of the Jew working as a peddler is but a result of the few occupations open and practical for him in a world in which he was not even a second-class citizen (the Jew was often not considered a citizen at all) and could be expelled at any time. One can see how tenuous was the Jew's situation and how little was he really the all-powerful, wealthy moneylender when we realize how equally strong is the image of the Jewish peddler. (For an explanation of how the Jew could have the simultaneous image of powerful moneylender and parasitic peddler, see Goldberg's Law.)

While discrimination was forcing Jews into certain fields and preventing them from entering others (Christians also closed their guilds and crafts to Jews), Jewish religious needs were also shaping occupational pursuits. This is why, for example, Jews became so involved with tailoring and the garment industry.

The Jewish involvement with tailoring emanated from the Biblical prohibition against wearing clothing containing a mixture of linen and wool *(shatnes)*. To make certain the law of shatnes was carried out, the Jewish community needed tailors skilled in making garments free of such a combination and able to check other clothing. From this began family traditions in such trades. Eventually, Jews began performing tailoring services for the general community. In fact, although European governments denied Jews the right to serve in their armies, these same governments often looked to Jews to supply those same armies with the material and tailoring skills for military uniforms.

In this way, the garment industry began to become heavily Jewish. Once there were Jews in such a line of work, other Jews tended to follow for a very natural reason: owners and fellow workers in the garment trade would be Jewish and therefore more receptive to hiring Jews. In such a way was this industry built up in the United States largely by Jews: newly arriving Jewish immigrants in America found jobs more easily among their coreligionists, who were already in the clothing trade because of the presence of fellow Jews before them.

The needs of the Jewish community led to a thriving activity of skilled Jewish workers even in that traditional trio of manual occupations—the butcher, the baker, and the candlestick maker. The Jewish butcher was needed to provide kosher meat prepared in keeping with the laws of ritual slaughter. Bakers were needed to ensure that the dietary laws were followed in the preparation of baked goods (no lard could be used). And the Jewish interest in beautifying the rituals of the religion led to Jewish goldsmiths and silversmiths skilled in fashioning works for the synagogue service and accessories for the Jewish home, such as the ever-present Sabbath candlesticks.

But while the presence of Jews in certain occupations is a product of Jewish interests—intellectual, cultural, and religious—the truth is that even today Jewish presence or absence in many fields of endeavor is often a continuing result of the pressures and denials of centuries. Certain occupational restrictions, although eventually removed, were enforced for so long by so many countries that even when Jews were permitted to return to that vocation they tended not to come back in the numbers expected. This has fed the stereotypes. Thanks to the Ignorance Factor, the large-scale absence of Jews from a certain field led to the unfounded belief that Jews did not have an aptitude for that kind of work and that something must be wrong or different with the Jewish character. A case in point that warrants closer study is the Jewish experience with farming.

Since the late Middle Ages, the Jew has not had the image of farmer. This has been a problem for Jews because the land, as does the military, has a certain mystique. Even in early America, a great debate of the infant democracy was whether to reserve the vote only to landowners. The owning and the working of land implies attachment, loyalty, and love for a nation. It also signifies solid, tangible wealth. Until relatively recently in man's history, most people lived on farms or in rural areas. The city, a later development in man's progress, was often considered suspect, with urban dwellers seen to have different values and attitudes. The Jew, living for the most part in urban areas (ghettos were sections of cities), were often the objects of distrust and hostility for the sole reason that so many Jews could be seen living in the city and so few working the land.

But ignored or unknown by most people is that Jews were denied access to farming and owning land in many European countries after about the eighth century. Christian emperors in the fourth century began restricting Jewish ownership of slaves because the Jewish law granting eventual freedom to a Jewish slave was encouraging too many slaves to convert. This denied Jewish farmers and land owners an important source of farm labor then used by Christians. The next step was to exclude Jews from owning land altogether, and eventually official Church policy made it illegal to sell land to a Jew. As late as 1893, the Catholic Diet of Cracow, Poland, declared: "The Jews are our enemies; who sells a peice of land to a Jew or leases it to him is undermining the welfare of our nation." Adding to the Jew's problems was the fact that since in many countries he was not considered a citizen, he could not have permanent residence. Up until 1869, for instance, Switzerland, Bavaria, and Prussia refused to grant Jews such rights.

Jews had been able to farm in isolated instances. In what is now Iraq and Iran, Jews were farmers from 600 B.C.E. until 1000 C.E. Some four thousand Jews in India continue to raise jute as they have done since 600 C.E. Jews were also involved in farming in Italy, France, and Spain until the fourteenth century, mainly in grape production (the great Torah commentator Rashi supported himself by cultivating a vineyard in his native France).

The Jewish people's exclusion from farming is especially ironic because the Israelites were farmers, as can be seen in the fact that three major Jewish holidays—Succoth (or Tabernacles), Pesach

(Passover) and Shevouth (Pentecost)—are basically harvest festivals.

Indeed, the Bible and the Talmud are filled with laws about and references to this most basic of man's occupations. The first order of the Talmud is called *Zeraim*, meaning seeds, and deals with the agricultural laws. It was, in fact, Judaism that advocated the farming technique of rejuvenating the soil by letting it rest periodically ("The seventh year you shall let your land rest and lie fallow, that the poor of your people may eat," Exodus 23: 11). The word "jubilee" is really Hebrew and emanates from the Hebraic word denoting the major cessation from farming every fiftieth year—the year culminating seven of the seventh-year rest periods.

The modern Zionist movement from its beginning realized not only that farming was essential in any reestablished Jewish state, but that there was great symbolism in Jews returning to farming as a livelihood. Said Theodor Herzl in his address to the first Zionist Congress in 1897, "On the day the plow is again in the strengthened hands of the Jewish farmer, the Jewish question will be solved." The inherent meaning of farming for the future of the Jewish people was best summed up by the Yiddish poet Eliakim Zunser: "In the plow lies our bliss."

To help Jews return to the land, in 1891 the philanthropist Baron Maurice de Hirsch donated $36 million to what was called the Jewish Colonization Association to help settle about five thousand Jewish families in farming colonies in Argentina and Brazil. This immigration was the foundation for the large Jewish community in Argentina today.

Baron de Hirsch had first tried to better the condition of Jews in Russia by offering the Russian government 50 million francs for the purpose of establishing an educational system for Jews, which would include agricultural schools. His offer was never accepted.

The Baron also supported Jewish agricultural colonies in America. A 5300-acre tract of land was purchased in Woodbine, New Jersey, in 1891 for a series of 30-acre farms, a townsite of 275 acres, and the erection of factories: the idea was to combine agriculture and industry. In 1894, the Baron de Hirsch fund established in Woodbine the first secondary Jewish agricultural school in America. The school operated until 1917.

Twenty-five colonies of Jewish farming families were eventually set up in the early days of the Jewish farm movement in America, in such states as Louisiana, Arkansas, Kansas, Colorado, New Jersey, and South Dakota, as well as in Canada. Not all were successful. The historic estrangement of the Jew from the land was not easy to overcome, especially for Jews used to living in tight-knit urban communities. And yet, from a total of two hundred to three hundred Jewish farm families in America in 1900 with a population of about a thousand, the number of families by 1925 reached ten thousand, with a total population of fifty thousand.

The peak of the Jewish farm movement—as indeed the peak of American farming in general—was reached at the end of World War II in the 1945 to 1954 period. By then, there were an estimated twenty thousand families with one hundred thousand Jewish farmers in the United States. Jewish farmers were active in every branch of farming and could be found in every state of the union.

Because of the lower requirements for capital and land, the majority of Jewish farmers were engaged in poultry and eggs. Some distinguished themselves as egg farmers. In fact, during the 1950s, the New Jersey Jewish farmers were the top egg producers in the United States (an important Jewish farming center was in Vineland). In recent years, a Jewish farmer in California developed an operation so vast it had a half-million chickens. Jews also contributed innovative ideas to farming—such as the Jewish farmer who came up with the idea for an east-west coop house that enables hens to be exposed to the heat and light of both the morning and afternoon sun. An eminently sensible idea, the innovation received nationwide interest.[3]

---

[3] Not to be overlooked, of course, are the scientific advances of Jewish researchers that have helped agricultural productivity. Dr. Arthur Goldhaft, for instance, a veterinarian who grew up as the son of a pioneering Jewish farm family in New Jersey, developed successful fowl pox vaccines and other poultry medicines in the early 1920s. Aaron Aaronson, an agronomist who organized the Agriculture Experimental Station in Palestine, discovered "wild wheat," which has been used in the United States and elsewhere to strengthen cultivated wheat. David Lubin founded the International Agricultural Institute, an international clearing-house for agricultural data and information. His ideas influenced the King of Italy to convene a conference of forty governments in Rome in 1905 to listen to Lubin's approach to increasing agricultural productivity.

The number of Jews engaged in farming in the United States has declined in recent decades, paralleling the reduction in the number of American farmers in general. Also, the concentration of Jews in egg and poultry farming has made the Jewish farmer especially vulnerable to the steep drops in these segments of the industry. The number of farms in America has dwindled from a 1935 peak of 6,800,000 to approximately 3,000,000 by the beginning of the 1970s, with only 2 million farms considered truly commercial. The statistics on the Jewish farmer indicate that by the early 1970s his number had declined to seven thousand farm families, with four thousand in the northeast of the country and three thousand in California, the Midwest, and various other states. However, figuring an average gross production per farm of $75 thousand, the gross annual product generated by Jewish farmers represented a still potent figure of a half-billion dollars.

The modern State of Israel continues to put the lie to the myth that Jews have no interest in farming or doing hard physical work. The Jewish colonization of Palestine actually began with farming operations. The first agricultural school was operating at Mikveh Israel as early as the 1870s. The Bilu enthusiasts of Russian Jewish students, in the late nineteenth century, advocated use of Jewish laborers on farms and went to Palestine to work on the land. Aharon David Gordon (1856–1922) moved to Palestine in 1904, working as a manual laborer in vineyards and orange groves and becoming an outspoken advocate of physical labor and farming. His pronouncements had great effect on the founding of the kibbutz. The first kibbutz started in 1909, with the kibbutz movement seen as a way for Jews to plunge into farming on a wide scale and begin restoring the arid, agriculturally ravaged country to its historic condition of a land flowing with milk and honey. From the kibbutz idea eventually emerged the moshavim, a cooperative farming situation which is also operating today in Israel.

In recent years, as in the case of the United States, machinery and improved farming methods have reduced the need for manpower on the farms in Israel. Presently, about 8 percent of Israelis work the farms, a statistic that compares favorably with America's 6 percent.

And Israel has brought about many notable achievements in agriculture. New ways of irrigation have been developed to add to the productivity of the land. For instance, a method of bending down apple tree branches from early growth and using trickle irrigation (water combined with soluble fertilizers) has resulted in apple trees being ready for harvest in three years instead of the normally required six, and peak yields are possible at two hundred to two hundred and eighty tons per acre as against seventy in ordinary orchards. Such aggressive ideas have enabled Israel literally to make deserts bloom, and statistics tell the tale. One example: Israel has become the world's second largest grower of grapefruits (after the United States) with twenty-eight thousand tons squeezed and canned annually. Another Israeli achievement: Israeli cows have the highest milk production of any in the world—with 7300 kgs. per year (this time the United States is second, with 6400 kgs. annually). Other countries wishing to boost milk production have a special need for Israel's pregnant cows—as indeed did Iran, to which Israel once shipped four hundred cows on a specially chartered plane.

Thus, Israelis are on their way to restoring Israel agriculturally to a land flowing, if not with honey (although Israel exports honey, too), then certainly with milk. And other countries are realizing the Jewish way with farming. After all, Israel is the land that not only sells wine to France, but ships tulips to the country famed for its own tulips—Holland.[4]

The truth, then, is that only the Ignorance Factor enables people to persist in stereotyping the occupational pursuits of the present day Jew finally freed from the barriers of the past. Here is just a brief sampling of Jewish activity in modern times in roles still rarely associated with Jews.

At the very time the German Jew Einstein was earning renown as the greatest mind of the day (he was awarded the Nobel Prize in 1921), another Jew was earning his living as one of the two strongest men of his time. Sigmund Breitbart, born in a small

---

[4] Israel's growing season differs from Holland's. In an arrangement that has been going on for a number of years, Israel grows the tulips for Holland and ships these and other flowers by special El Al flight to Amsterdam, where they are resold.

Polish village as the youngest son of a Jewish blacksmith, had shown great strength even as a youngster. As an adult, he toured Europe and the United States to display his physical prowess, performing before large theatre audiences in such European capitals as Vienna and London, appearing at the Palace Theatre in New York, and traveling the famed Keith Circuit in America. Part of his performance is listed in the *Book of Lists* in its enumeration of twenty-four feats of physical strength: "With his teeth, Breitbart bit all the way through a 5-mm-thick steel bar and bit 1½ mm into an 11-mm-thick steel bar. Breitbart also broke chains by expanding his chest, and drove large nails through iron with his bare fist."

When Breitbart died unexpectedly in 1925 at the age of forty-two, just days after another strong man had also passed away prematurely, it moved *The New York Times* to comment on the two. On October 16, 1925, in an editorial entitled "Strength and Longevity," *The Times* termed them "the world's two strongest men" and noted among Breitbart's feats that he "played with drayhorses and bit iron chains apart."

Breitbart had been so concerned about the image of the Jew as physically weak that he used his performances to eradicate it. While he lay on the stage floor and lifted several horses standing on a platform, he had the orchestra play the haunting melody of *Kol Nidre*, the opening prayer of Yom Kippur. The music gave him an emotional push for the great physical exertion needed. It also enabled him to make the event a Jewish-oriented one: "I perform this feat of strength for the honor of the Jewish people," he would announce.[5]

Around the time Sigmund Breitbart was breaking chains with his bare hands and uncapped teeth, another Jew—the son of a rabbi—was earning his living by using strength and skill of a different sort to break out of chains, handcuffs, even strait jackets. While engaged in this "un-Jewish" occupation, he became so immensely popular doing these feats as well as other magical acts

---

[5] Interestingly, serving in the English language as a synonym for great strength is a Jewish name—Samson, who battled the Philistines and literally pulled the house down on Israel's enemies (see *Webster's New World Dictionary*, which defines Samson first as "an Israelite distinguished for his great strength" and then as "any very strong man").

that his name has entered our language as a synonym for magician. He called himself Houdini.

Born in Hungary in 1874 as Erich Weiss, he was the son and grandson of Orthodox rabbis. He grew up in Appleton, Wisconsin, where his father was a Hebrew teacher. (The future Houdini helped his father teach the Aleph Beis—the Hebrew alphabet—to beginners.) [6] The family eventually moved to New York, where Erich became Bar Mitzvah. The Weisses were so poor that his father at one point had to sell some of his collection of fine Hebrew books.

As a youngster of nine, Erich had become intrigued with the circuses that passed through Appleton, and decided to become a magician. After the move to New York, he took the name of Houdini from the great French magician Robert-Houdin and at the age of seventeen became a full-time professional. He soon began developing his own special act. This involved not only doing magic tricks in a spectacular style—such as making an elephant disappear on stage—but also performing as an escape artist, invariably in unusual settings: head down in a tank of water, suspended over a busy street, locked in a trunk immersed in a lake.

His mysterious ability to escape from locked places and free himself from handcuffs and strait jackets so impressed people that among those who were amazed by his abilities were officials of Scotland Yard and the Moscow Police Department (for whom he broke out of an "escape proof" Russian-made prison van).

Houdini, who died in 1926 (on Halloween), never publicly revealed his escape secrets, although he freely acknowledged they had nothing to do with mystical powers and actively campaigned against mediums and supernaturalists. "The secret will go with me to my grave," he said in an interview. "If it were anything in the nature of a contribution to science, anything that might help humanity, I would assuredly disclose it, but it is not."

But then, he alluded to what might have been the answer, and again another piece of the false Jewish stereotype is chipped away,

---

[6] Houdini showed much interest in Jewish philanthropies. In one of his projects, he assisted in the organization of the Rabbis's Sons Theatrical Benevolent Association, which had among its members Al Jolson and Irving Berlin.

for Houdini mentions his body's unique prowess. "The secret is peculiar to myself, and it is improbable that there will be another individual in several generations so oddly constituted. For one thing, I was born with an inordinate physical strength."

The Jew is supposed to be intellectual, right? Yes, but in the far from intellectual world of comic books, Jews have taken a leading role. The *Encyclopaedia Judaica* points out that Jews represent 80 percent of the pioneers and leaders of America's comic book industry. And while Jews comprise less than 3 percent of the United States' population, a survey in the 1960s found that Jews accounted for 10 percent of the creators of the country's comic strips. One of the more notable Jewish names behind the comics: Al Capp (née Caplin), creator of Li'l Abner and his decidedly "un-Jewish" hillbilly world. Another, Rube Goldberg, became so famous for his comically contrived cartoon inventions that his name is used to describe a complicated apparatus (as in "That's a Rube Goldberg invention"). Goldberg also won a Pulitzer Prize for editorial cartooning.

Even the most popular comic book hero of all time is the creation of Jews. Superman, published first in 1938 and since then translated into thirty-five languages, was the brainchild of two Jewish youngsters from Cleveland: Jerry Siegel and Joe Shuster. In a time of deep depression in the United States and spreading talk in Europe of fascism and an Aryan super race, the seventeen-year-old high school students came up with the idea for a super man who would do good in the world. According to Jerry Siegel, the hero they envisioned would be "a champion for good with the strength of Atlas, as invulnerable as a perfect Achilles, plus the morals of Galahad." They were also fascinated with Douglas Fairbanks, Sr., who was then dazzling audiences with his own stunts in movies like Robin Hood. After six years of rejections by various comic strip syndicates, a comic book company agreed to purchase the first Superman story for $130 and print it in the June, 1938, issue of a new publication called *Action Comics*. It was an immediate success [7] and the two were employed at $5 each per comic book page to turn out Superman stories on a regular basis.

---

[7] A copy of that issue is worth $3000 today.

Unwittingly, the two gave up rights to the Superman character when they signed that first agreement for $130. Although they continued to be paid to produce the comic strip for the next ten years, Siegel and Shuster never shared in the millions of dollars the Superman character generated in licensing rights for its use in toys, radio programs, television shows, books, costumes, movies, and a Broadway play. Prolonged court cases resulted in total recognition that Siegel and Shuster were the creators of Superman, but that they had signed over all rights to Superman in 1938 for $130.

The two Jewish cartoonists had, however, retained one aspect of their identity with Superman. Everyone thinks that the "S" on the hero's uniform stands for Superman's name. But it does not. According to an Associated Press story in December, 1975, on the plight of the two creators (because they were not receiving any royalties from the Superman character, they were both, then sixty-one years old, living in near-poverty), the "S" emblazoned on Superman's chest stands for their own names—Siegel and Shuster.

Another unlikely place to find a hidden Jewish reference is in the chic world of high-fashion cosmetics, which also can hardly be seen as a "Jewish" industry. Yet, not only is a Jewish name serving as that of a whole line of cosmetics (Helena Rubinstein), but the Hebrew word for rabbi is actually a secret part of the name of the world's largest cosmetic company. Revlon was started by the Revsons, a Jewish family whose name Revson means "son of a rabbi." When the Revsons founded their company, they brought in as a partner Charles Lachman. To show the merger the "s" letter of Revson was dropped and replaced by the "l" of Lachman. The word Revlon, however, retains the "Rev," which is Hebrew for "rabbi."

And what about the world of dance? Hardly Jewish, you say? Not only is one of the world's great male ballet dancers today Jewish—Yuri Panov, the Russian Jew whose two-year effort to emigrate to Israel earned the support of the world's artists—but the fifteenth-century dancer who has been termed "the father of ballet" was Jewish.

He was Guglielmo Ebreo de Pesaro, which means "William the Hebrew of Pesaro." Born in approximately 1440, he was the son of parents who were probably Marranos who had fled Spain and located in Italy. At a young age, Guglielmo showed a decided interest and ability in dance. He soon left Pesaro, a small town on the eastern coast of Italy, and went northward to the town of Piacenza to become the pupil of a man named Domenechino, who had become well-known as a dancing teacher. Guglielmo served his apprenticeship, a strenuous undertaking in that era because it involved sacrifices and menial work. But he must have excelled as a pupil because it was not long after he finished his training that he paid his teacher the highest compliment—he became even more renowned than his master. It was said that he "excelled all men in the dance" and poets of the day even wrote glowingly of his abilities not only as a dancer, but as a musician. He turned to writing and became one of the first to write on the dance, his work being used as a text by many dance masters then. His fifteenth-century manuscripts are preserved today in the Bibliothèque Nationale in Paris and in the libraries of Siena and Florence.

The story of Guglielmo Ebreo underlines the fact that Jews at the beginning of the Renaissance were so numerous as dancing masters and professional musicians that one historian of dance, Walter Sorell, has called them "professions as characteristically Jewish as those of pawnbroking and medicine." The Renaissance had brought to Jewish families an interest in dance and music, and the teaching of the two became a part of the education of many Jewish children, particularly in Italy where even Hebrew teachers were expected to be versed in music and dancing.

In fact, Jews became so dominant in these professions that Christian competitors complained. Writes Sorell: "In 1443, for instance, the authorities in Venice ordered schools of music, singing and dancing run by Jews to be closed, and 'they should be stopped from teaching these subjects under pain of imprisonment and fine.'"

Jewish dance masters teaching Christian pupils were not out of the ordinary. In 1313, a rabbi taught Christians a choral dance around the altar in a Spanish church. In 1443 in Venice many women nobles took dance lessons from Jewish women in the city of Parma (until the Jews were expelled from the city). In 1775, the Pope permitted a rabbi to teach dancing and singing.

According to Sorell, there were other Jewish dance instructors, but the social pressures for dancing artists undoubtedly caused conversions. This is another reason why we tend to be ignorant of the wide participation of Jews in so many areas. As Sorell writes, "And we may be sure that many more of the Italian and Spanish dance teachers than the records show were Jewish. For not everyone could withstand the outside pressure and face the danger of persecution as well as the envy of his baptized competitors. It is understandable that only those among them who achieved incontestable mastership added proudly to their name: *Ebreo.*" [8]

What about Jews in police work? Police are supposed to be Irish, you say? There are approximately one thousand Jewish police officers in the New York City Police Department, far from representative of New York's Jewish population, but still one thousand more than you probably thought there were. And with close to three thousand active and retired Jewish officers belonging, New York's Jewish police have the largest—but not the only— chapter in a national religious fraternal organization for Jewish police, the Shomrim Society, founded in 1924. Also, some notable chiefs of police have been of Jewish descent. Moses Judah Hays served as head of police for Montreal for sixteen years. The police commissioner of Berlin during part of the period of Nazi agitation for power was a Jew, Dr. Bernhard Weiss. Hitler's propaganda expert Josef Goebbels liked to picture him as an evil, corrupt police official out to persecute the Nazis—a portrait Goebbels laughed about in private. And for nearly a half century, from 1802 to 1849, Jacob Hays (1772-1850) led one of the world's largest police forces—the New York City Police Department. He also

---

[8] The Chassidic sect of Judaism, founded in the eighteenth century, has made dance an adjunct of prayer, and their vigorous dancing has proved a surprise to those who know only the stereotypes. In the book *The Making of a Musical* about the Broadway hit play *Fiddler on the Roof*, Sheldon Harnick, its lyricist, is quoted as saying he remembered how a reviewer of the show voiced his surprise at the dancing because he didn't associate Jewish dancing with such violence. Many Jews, too, are just as unknowledgeable about Jewish dance. Jerry Bock, who wrote the music for *Fiddler*, commented on his research into Chassidic dancing: "It was an interesting discovery to find out how physical and aggressive these people were."

earned an international reputation as a solver of mysteries.[9]

Aviation has proven to be one area of endeavor that has captivated the fancy—and a lot of the fantasy—of people. One of the great American folk heroes is Charles Lindbergh, the aviator. The symbol of courage and independence early in this century was the flyers: the World War I aces with their aerial dog fights, the pilots who flew the mail in rickety planes to launch air service. Today, the astronauts and cosmonauts have captured our imagination.

It may come as a surprise to find that the first person in history to make controlled glider flights was a German Jew, Otto Lilienthal, who flew more than two thousand such flights. His work and writings about his findings influenced the Wright Brothers, who openly acknowledged their debt to him.

And when the Wright brothers opened their first flying school to train future pilots (the Wright Brothers Flying School at Montgomery, Alabama), a Jew was in that first class of five. But not only was Arthur Welsh (his real name was Laibel Willcher) one of the Wright Brothers' first pupils, he showed such flying ability that Wilbur Wright later termed him "the peer of any man in the world as a pilot." Welsh also holds the distinction of being:

• The first pilot to fly a plane with a passenger more than two hours;

• The winner of a prize for flying a continuous flight of three hours and five minutes;

• The flying instructor of Henry A. "Hap" Arnold, who later became the first chief of the United States Army Air Corps and head of the United States Air Force during World War II.

Welsh, who was devoted to promoting flying, died in a crash testing a new military biplane.

When air mail service was instituted in the United States, the

---

[9] Although he converted to Christianity, Jacob Hays came from an illustrious Jewish family. The first Hays, Michael, came over to America in the early 1700s. Three grandsons became Jewish farmers and subsequently fought in the American Revolution. Later descendants served in virtually all of America's wars. In addition, another descendant—Isaac Hays—was one of the founders of the American Medical Association. During World War II, the chief of the Manhattan Project to build the atomic bomb was a Hays descendant—J. Robert Oppenheimer.

pilot of the first plane to carry mail was Captain Benjamin Lipsner, who was also America's first superintendent of air mail.

Following within days of Lindbergh's famous trans-Atlantic flight, the first person to fly over the Atlantic as a passenger was Charles Levine. He traveled 3,903 miles (New York to Eiselben, Germany), a world record at the time. In fact, on the Sunday that Lindbergh was returning to America from Europe, Levine's picture and story were featured on the front page of *The New York Times*. The *Times* called it a "daring flight" and even Lindbergh, as he traveled back to America on the cruiser *Memphis*, sent a message of good wishes to Levine and the pilot, Clarence Chamberlin.

When people were trying to become the first to fly over the continent of Australia, the winner—in 1910—was the great magician Harry Houdini, who had been intrigued with airplanes. Oddly enough, he had once said that while people might forget his feats of escape, they would remember his pioneering efforts as an aviator.

A Jew has even been a spaceman. One of the Russian cosmonauts who traveled into space was Jewish—Lieutenant-Colonel Boris Volynov. He was commander of Soyuz-5, the Russian spaceship that achieved the first link-up in space and transfer of people from one spaceship to another.

Jewish involvement in aviation has been so extensive that two of the world's greatest jet planes were developed by Jews—and one of the planes retains in its name part of the name of its Jewish inventor.

The French fighter planes the Mystère and the Mirage were developed by Marcel Dassault, who was the son of a Jewish doctor, Adolph Bloch. In 1909, inspired by the Wright brothers' flights, the seventeen-year-old enrolled in the College of Aeronautics, and during World War I established his own company to build planes. Although the company collapsed following the war, he was soon back as an aircraft designer for the French air ministry, which needed a bomber to respond to Hitler's buildup of his army. The French prime minister flew to Munich in 1938 in a Dassault plane.

During World War II, Dassault was captured by the Germans,

but refused to work for them as an aircraft designer. He was sent to Buchenwald, where he was saved from a death sentence only by the Allied liberation of the concentration camp.

Following the war, and after conversion to Christianity in 1947,[10] Dassault worked in earnest to rebuild the shattered French aircraft industry. He set up his own company, built and trained his own team of designers, and within a decade and a half of the war developed a series of jet planes, including the Mirage III that could fly at twice the speed of sound. "In a period of French humiliations in Algeria and at Suez, the Mirage was not only an aeronautical achievement but a glamourous symbol of French power," writes Anthony Sampson in *The Arms Bazaar*. Not only was the Mirage used by the French air force as a strike aircraft, but it was found to be effective for intercepting, ground attack, and reconnaissance as well. The Mirage also soon became unexpectedly "one of the most phenomenal of all French exports."

Dassault's plane provided France with one other very important side benefit. Says Sampson, "More important, it was regarded as a diplomatic as well as a military weapon, and in the following decade the Mirage became a major counter in French foreign policy." Indeed, Charles de Gaulle presented Dassault with a copy of his memoirs containing this inscription: "To Marcel Dassault, in memory of our struggle and of the part he has played in giving stature to France."

Another Jew even more prominently involved in the "un-Jewish" profession of aircraft weapons design was Mikhail Gurevich, a Russian Jew who was cocreator of the Soviet MIG fighter plane. The irony is that although Russia used this plane to help defeat Nazi Germany, it was the plane the Arabs used to try to defeat Israel.

Gurevich, who died in Moscow in 1976 at the age of 84, began specializing in aircraft design several years after the October Revolution. By 1929, he had become deputy chief of a leading Moscow aircraft factory and, working with another designer,

---

[10] Dassault's brother, who did not convert, was a French Army officer who, when France was liberated in 1944, was given the second highest rank in the French army and appointed governor of Paris.

created his first fighter plane. The man he collaborated with was Artem Mikoyan, the younger brother of the Soviet political leader Anastas Mikoyan. In recognition of their work, the plane was named for the two of them—"MI" for "Mikoyan" and "G" for "Gurevich." Which is how the name "MIG" was born.

During the Second World War and afterward, Gurevich, as deputy chief designer at the Soviet Ministry of Aircraft Production, continued to work on improving the MIG airplane. He designed the MIG-3, a potent match for the Nazi Messerschmidt fighter. Then, in 1949, he created the Soviet Union's first jet fighter plane, the MIG-15, followed soon by the MIG-17. By 1955, about the time Dassault was developing the supersonic jet fighter for France, Gurevich designed the first Soviet supersonic fighter, the MIG-19.

In recognition of his work, Gurevich was promoted in 1957 to chief designer of all of the Soviet Union's military aircraft production. He held this position until 1964.

The Jewish ability with aircraft design is shown today in Israel, another indication of how the presence or absence of a homeland can enhance or alter a people's image. Israel has developed her own jet fighter plane, the Kfir ("young lion"), and designed new and superior types of missiles, such as the Gabriel and the Jericho, which are bought by other countries. But Israel is also involved in promoting commerical aviation, manufacturing and selling a two-engine passenger plane called the Arava. As a result of such efforts in the field of aviation, today the Israeli Aircrafts Industries, which produces Israel's own planes as well as overhauls, repairs, and makes parts for aircraft, is one of Israel's largest companies, employing close to 20,000 skilled workers.

As this brief survey indicates, even in unlikely fields of endeavor there have been Jews who distinguished themselves as key innovators or leaders. This ironically reinforces another Jewish stereotype. Since accomplishment in this world is invariably an intellectual result—even the most successful farmer is soon seen as the shrewdest rather than the sweatiest—Jewish success means Jewish association with mental rather than manual labor.

[126]

The difficulty the Jew faces in escaping his stereotypes is manifested in even how he earns his daily bread. Myths and images die hard. Jews may have to wait quite some time before the world will instinctively respond to a picture of a farmer or explorer, a policeman or airplane pilot, by saying, "A Jew, I presume?"

GOLDBERG'S LAW

If anything can be misconstrued about the Jews, it will be ... and has been.

Exhibit E: JEWISH LANDOWNERSHIP

THE NEED FOR JEWS TO SUBDIVIDE SCARCE PROPERTY COULD RESULT IN SOMEONE OWNING 1/700TH OF A HOUSE

The falsity of the image of vast Jewish wealth and valuables can best be seen in how narrow the world was for most Jews in Europe. For instance, the restrictions on Jewish ownership of land—which hampered Jewish involvement in agriculture in so much of Europe for so long—can be seen in how houses often had to be passed from parents to children. Here the confinement of Jews to ghettos added to the lack of maneuverability.

Two examples on record from Germany:

In Cologne in 1322, a Jewish family sold a one-eighth and one-ninety-sixth portion of "a large house" in which two other Jewish families owned another quarter and one-sixteenth part. Thirteen years later another Jewish couple bought a share of one-third and one-sixtieth minus one-seven hundredth of a house from a Christian neighbor.

This type of situation did not occur too frequently, however. The reason is painfully simple. Jews were seldom allowed to stay long enough in a land to need to create such subdivisions for so many generations.

VI
Praise the Lord and Pass the Baseballs, Footballs, and Basketballs, Too

*More Jews where you'd
least expect them*

FACT: The first non-Latin to win fame as a matador was a Brooklyn-born Jew who was praised by Ernest Hemingway as among the best bullfighters in history.

FACT: For three years, a Jew was the highest paid baseball player in America.

FACT: More than twenty Jews have been world champions in boxing—and one was the first prize fighter ever to hold two world titles simultaneously.

FACT: The first professional baseball player was a Jew.

FACT: At one time, the record in basketball for most points scored in a career was held by a Jew—who had also until then played the greatest number of consecutive games in basketball history.

FACT: The first world championship in weightlifting was won by an English Jew.

FACT: A Jew holds the record for most gold medals (nine) ever won by one person in the Olympics.

> There never was a prominent Jewish athlete in history.
> —Brig. Gen. Charles H. Sherrill,
>   American representative to the
>   International Olympic Committee in 1936

Seville. 1929.

The matador stood poised in the center of the bull ring, his gold tights glistening in the sun, his outstretched hands calmly holding the crimson cape. Staring into the eyes of the massive ebony bull that snorted and swayed just yards in front of him, he calmly flicked the cape. The bull reared up its head, snorted again and charged, eyes bulging white. Skillfully, the matador brought the cape across his body and swished it close to his side, leading the rushing bull to brush so near that its gnarled horns flashed by only inches from his groin. The crowd roared in excitement. Again and again, the thin, dark-haired matador coolly led the bull through the full paces of the bullfighter's repertoire. And when finally his performance ended with a flourish, the fans rushed from the stands and carried him through the arena's Prince's Gate, reserved for royalty, an honor only four other matadors had experienced in that ring's 175 years.

As the bullfight aficionados showed that afternoon, this was no ordinary matador. But there were other reasons why he was different. First of all, he was American, not Spanish. Second, he was Brooklyn-born. Third, he was a Jew.

His name was Sidney Franklin, and he was a rarity. Born in 1903 as Sidney Frumkin, he left home at the age of seventeen after one of many arguments with his father. Franklin boarded a ship headed for Mexico and wound up in Mexico City working as a commercial artist. After several months, and just before he was planning to return home for a visit, he went to see his first bullfight. Mesmerized by the spectacle, he decided, in a process of thought he always said "puzzled" him, to become a professional matador. Beginning his career in the late 1920s, he performed for the next several decades in the top bullrings in Spain, fighting several thousand bulls before retiring in 1959. Although one other American had become a bullfighter briefly, Franklin was the first American to perform as a bullfighter in Spain and the first non-Latin to win fame as a matador.

And he was good. So good, in fact, that Ernest Hemingway, the self-styled authority on bullfighting and admirer of physical courage in and out of the bullring, praised Franklin in *Death in the Afternoon*, Hemingway's ode to bullfighting. Actually, Hemingway not only praised Franklin, but published two pictures of him in action and devoted a separate section in the book to an assessment of his ability as a matador.

"Franklin is brave with a cold, serene and intelligent valor but instead of being awkward and ignorant he is one of the most skillful, graceful, and slow manipulators of a cape fighting today," Hemingway wrote. He termed Franklin's cape repertoire "enormous" and his veronicas "classical, very emotional, and beautifully timed and executed."

"You will find no Spaniard who ever saw him fight who will deny his artistry and excellence with the cape."

Hemingway, who had seen many of the great matadors perform, even rated Franklin with the best: "He is better, more scientific, more intelligent, and more finished matador than all but about six of the full matadors in Spain today and the bullfighters know it and have the utmost respect for him."

The only fault Hemingway could find was that Franklin did not do his bull killing with enough emotion: "He does not give the importance to killing that it merits, since it is easy for him and because he ignores the danger." The novelist also criticized Franklin for trying to be his own business manager: "he does all his own business and is very proud of his business judgment, which is terrible...."

But Hemingway concluded his estimate of Franklin by noting that "he is a great and fine artist and no history of bull-fighting that is ever written can be complete unless it gives him the space he is entitled to."

One item was noticeably lacking in Hemingway's account, however. The great Nobel Prize winner, who had pictured a Jew named Cohn as ineffectual in his novel, *The Sun Also Rises,* never mentions what was well-known to him; that the American matador he called "brave with a cold, serene and intelligent valor" was Jewish.[1]

The stereotype of the Jew as a thinker instead of a doer, as intellectually rather than physically oriented—so much a part of the false Jewish image fostered by occupational and military discrimination—may be closer to the truth in the area of athletics, but while Jewish avoidance of sports was once true, it no longer is. Not many Jews can be found participating in organized and professional sporting events from the days of the Greeks to Jewish emancipation in the early nineteenth century, but since the abolishment of ghettos in the 1800s Jews have responded with a varied, and in many ways unusually successful, involvement in modern era sports. Not only have there been Jewish bullfighters, but Jews have now been elected to the official halls of fame of baseball, basketball, boating, bowling, boxing, football, handball, horse racing, lacrosse, rowing, speed skating, and volleyball.

The long Jewish avoidance of sports did not evolve directly out of Judaic teaching—indeed, there is nothing in Judaism opposed to physical education, and certain laws definitely support it. Parents are required to teach their children how to swim since their ability to swim could save their lives. Also, because the body is the Almighty's creation and the vessel of the soul, and because good health and the preservation of life are of first importance, the maintenance of physical fitness was devoutly encouraged. However, Judaism, which in all things teaches the golden mean, saw a consuming concentration on sport as a frivolous use of time—precious time that could be better spent in keeping mentally and spiritually fit through study.

Until the emancipation of the Jews and their release from the ghettos of Europe, all Jews were religious in their modes of

---

[1] Franklin is not the only Jew to become a bullfighter. Another was Randy Sasson of Colombia. He went by the name of *El Andaluz.*

behavior, if not of thought. The few rebels were either ostracized or themselves fled the ghetto by means of conversion. Today, whether individual Jews are religious or not has little bearing on the fundamental profile, attitude, and philosophy of the group, which bears its own special message.

As with any people whose mind is on the eternal, for Jews the expenditure of time is not taken lightly. Few if any are the religions that make a special case in behalf of a total commitment to athletics. Rather, in the ancient world it was the cultures that glorified the body—like Greece and Rome—and not the religions that glorified the soul—like Judaism and Christianity—that fostered athletics.

As such, Judaism quite logically urged spiritually oriented religious activities and studies rather than the self-adoration of athletics. Sigmund Freud noted the great psychological effect this has had on the Jewish personality. Writing in *Moses and Monotheism*, he said, "The preference which through two thousand years the Jews have given to spiritual endeavor has had its effect; it has helped to build a dike against brutality and the inclination to violence which are usually found where athletic development becomes the ideal of the people."

What also motivated the Jews in their attitude toward sports, however, was a bitter national experience with the very ancient cultures that glorified the athlete.

The early attempts to Hellenize the Jewish people were centered around athletics. In 174 B.C.E when the Land of Israel was under Greek control, the Greek influence could be seen in the construction of a gymnasium right outside the Temple in Jerusalem. The attraction for many Jewish youths proved too enticing, diverting them from their prayers and study. Even priests "were no longer intent upon their service at the altar, but disdaining their ancestral honors they hastened to the wrestling arena" (2 Maccabees 4:14–15). In Jerusalem, as in Greece, sporting events were conducted in the nude, and the homosexuality it encouraged was shocking to Jewish religious sensibilities. Also, since the Olympics in Athens were originally connected with idolatry (competing teams brought gifts to the Greek gods), Jewry resisted the Greek concentration on sports as the antithesis of Jewish ideals.

Later, when the Land of Israel fell under Roman control, the gymnasium outside the Temple was replaced by a circus where Jews engaged in gladiatorial contests, often to the death. This Roman emphasis on brutal gladiator contests and gory circuses soured the Jewish religious and intellectual mind even further against sports. Reinforced by an alternative Jewish emphasis on education and scholarship, this attitude toward the frivolousness and assimilationist pressures of sports was to last until modern times.[2]

Of course, such an attitude could be easily misconstrued by others and, as you know from Goldberg's Law, it was. The Jewish reverence for learning and its concomitant disinterest in sports was seen as simply further evidence that the Jew was not capable of being much of an athlete and was not willing to engage in physical activity. The Zionists realized the need both to counter this image of the Jew and to prepare Jews for the more physical life available to them in a hoped-for land of their own.

In 1898, at the Second Zionist Congress, Max Nordau, a physician and leading Zionist, declared that the Jewish people should adopt a program of physical fitness, especially for the youth, and renew their involvement in sports: "... gymnastics and physical training are exceedingly important for us Jews, whose greatest defect has been and is, lack of discipline ... nature has endowed us with the spiritual qualities required for athletic achievements of an extraordinary quality. All we lack is muscle, and that can be developed with the aid of physical exercise." And then he touched on what the cycle of prejudice and false images could do to people: "The more Jews achieve in the various branches of sport, the greater will be their self-confidence and self-respect."

In response, a Maccabi movement of athletic clubs for Jewish youth sprang up in Europe, Palestine, and elsewhere in the Diaspora. By World War I, more than a hundred such clubs were active in Europe alone. One of the largest and most successful of these clubs, from Vienna, fielded an all-Jewish soccer team which

---

[2] Also to be remembered is that a sports event is really a social event. This is why blacks were excluded from professional baseball in the United States until the 1940s. Similar social disabilities, which as we have seen often prevented Jews from serving in the military or owning land, also kept the Jew from freely participating in sports in Europe.

proved outstanding and virtually unbeatable in competition throughout the 1920s. The name they gave themselves—and a name used by many other clubs—says something about the hurt many Jews felt because of the stereotype of the Jew as unathletic and nonphysical, as well as the need many Jews saw to improve the Jewish physique affected by centuries of ghetto life. The club called itself Hakoah, which is Hebrew for "Strength."

By the eve of World War II, the World Maccabi Union, as it had been called since 1921, had a membership of two hundred thousand with branches in most European countries and in Palestine, Turkey, Egypt, China, Australia, South America, South Africa, and the United States. Following the war, World Maccabi leaders began to reviving the movement that had been devastated in Europe and dormant elsewhere. Holocaust survivors were aided in getting to Palestine, and clubs were reopened. One country which would not allow Jews to engage in sporting activities as Jews was the Soviet Union, and clubs in countries that came under Soviet domination after the war were not permitted to restart. But the movement picked up members and clubs with the formation of the State of Israel. Headquartered now in Israel, the Maccabi World Union reported at the beginning of the 1970s that it had clubs in thirty-eight countries with an estimated two hundred thousand members.

An outgrowth of this movement is the Maccabiah international games now held every four years in Israel. Open to Jewish athletes in all countries, the Jewish Olympics was first held in 1932 in Tel Aviv. Thereafter, it was held in 1935, 1950, and 1953, with the games going on at regular four year intervals since then. Competition is held in track and field, gymnastics, swimming, water polo, boxing, wrestling, fencing, tennis, table tennis, soccer, basketball, and volleyball. And all the athletic contests in these Jewish Olympics are recognized and approved by the International Olympic Committee.

With modern-era sports freed from religious and idolatrous overtones, with the acceptance of Jews into the mainstream of society this past century and a half, Jews have engaged freely in sports, although the reluctance to seek it as a professional occupation still marks the general Jewish attitude.³

But one unusual aspect marks the Jewish involvement in sports. Again, as in other areas of endeavor, Jewish achievement, while not one of quantity, has been marked by unusual quality.

Indeed, in my search for the incredible, ironic, and bizarre in the Jewish experience, I have encountered numerous examples of Jewish surprises in the world of sports. In fact, there are so many of them that I could see these surprises comprising a Jewish Athletes Hall of Fame in the Goldbergian Institute, which, as you know, is my imaginary museum for housing and displaying unusual achievements of Jews. Here would be revealed the untold story of the Jewish role in sports, a story which in its particulars destroys yet another part of that lingering stereotype of the ghetto Jew.

Such an excursion into the successes of athletes who are Jewish may strike some as simply chauvinistic, with little significance outside a seeming coincidence of religion. This, in fact, was the first reaction of the great Jewish prize fighter Barney Ross to a book on such a topic, *The Jew in American Sports*, by Harold Ribalow. Ross states in the book's preface how he first wondered why anyone should write such a book, feeling along with some friends he consulted that singling out any particular group—social, racial, religious or even fraternal—and writing about its ability in some particular field "seemed more of a chauvinistic indulgence than a contribution to either literature or history."

But the more he thought about it, says Ross, the more he realized that the book presented the story of athletes "who had an even harder struggle than usual in their climb to the top simply because they *were* Jews." And to those who would tell him that it did not matter if these athletes were Jewish, he responded that it did matter:

> I know from my own experiences that every Jew who enters a competitive sport (indeed, any field of endeavor) carries with

---

³ For the observant Jew, professional athletics can present problems. The constant travel and the holding of sporting events on Saturday play havoc with the maintenance of the dietary laws and Sabbath. This is another reason why fewer Jews proportionately can be found in professional sports.

him more than the burden of acquitting himself well as a human being and a specialist in his field ... he carries, too, the burden of being a Jew. It is a burden he carries in common with other minorities. ...

As I envision it, the Jewish Athletes Hall of Fame would begin with a look at boxing, a sport calling for brute physical strength and hardly the type of athletic competition that fits the Jewish image. And yet, Jewish involvement in boxing has been so extensive that more than twenty Jews have held world championships in prize fighting. Another Jew, Daniel Mendoza, who was proud of his Jewishness and possessed a Hebrew school education, is considered the father of scientific boxing for his transformation of the sport from vulgar fisticuffs to a pugilistic art. He was champion of England from 1792-95 and was one of the first to be selected for the Boxing Hall of Fame in 1954. Seven medals were struck in his honor in England and twenty-five portraits painted of him and his fights. Another English fighter, Samuel ("Dutch Sam") Elias, a contender in numerous important bouts between 1801 and 1814, is widely reputed to be the inventor of the wicked uppercut punch.

Among the Jews who have been world champions were such individuals as: Robert Cohen, of France, world bantamweight champion 1954-56, who was a religious Jew who had studied to be a cantor; Barney Ross (his real name was Barnet David Rasovsky), who was the first person ever to hold two major boxing titles at one time (he was world lightweight champion 1933-35 and welterweight champ 1934-38) [4]; Maxie Rosenbloom, who was history's busiest fighter while holding a title, defending his world lightheavyweight championship eight times and fighting another ninety-eight times during his 4½ year reign from 1930-34, an average of one fight every fifteen days; and then there was Benny Leonard, another observant Jew who never fought on Jewish holidays and who lost only 2 out of 210 bouts in a ring

---

[4] Ross, who came from a religious family, served in the marines in World War II, where he was badly wounded on Guadalcanal. Given drugs for his wounds, he became addicted. He struggled years to overcome his addiction and then worked to help other addicts. A movie was made of his life.

career that saw him retire at one point as the undefeated lightweight champion after holding the title eight years.[5]

Countless other Jews have also been professional fighters. Although the Jewish pugilist is once more a rarity, in the first half of this century the boxing profession held a special allure for the Jewish sons of poor immigrant parents, a reminder that social and economic conditions can determine professional sports activity as much as ability or interest. One Jew, however, may hold a special niche in boxing history that will never be dislodged. Actually, he achieved a record that in and of itself destroys the stereotype of the Jew as physically weak, lacking in courage, deficient in stamina. For the boxer who engaged in more professional bouts than any other fighter in boxing history was Abe, "the Newsboy," Hollandersky. Between 1905 to 1920, he fought in—and survived—1,309 fights. (He also wrestled in 387 matches.) [6]

Basketball, like boxing, is another sport that lends itself to poor boys in urban areas trying to make good. Not much equipment is needed, not many players are necessary, and little space is required. This is why Jews could be found in profusion in basketball until just recently, including players, coaches, referees, owners, and even commissioners (the first commissioner of the National Basketball Association was Maurice Podoloff, who served from 1946 until 1963).

The first Jewish professional basketball player—Paul "Twister" Steinberg—appeared as early as 1900 (the game was invented in 1891). Subsequently, Jews have produced many outstanding college players, more than sixty All-American selections, and at least two College Players of the Year (Len Rosenbluth of North Carolina in 1957 and Arthur Heyman of Duke in 1963).

---

[5] Leonard was named the outstanding lightweight of all time by *Ring* magazine. In 1977, Jim Bishop, the journalist who has covered numerous championship fights, wrote in a column about Muhammad Ali that "the only boxer I ever saw who could match his automatic grace in the ring was Benny Leonard." Active in many Jewish causes, Leonard served in 1935 as chairman of the Maccabi National Sports Board, which chose the American team for the World Maccabiah Games in Palestine.

[6] One boxer, usually thought of as Jewish, may not have been. The heavyweight champion Max Baer, who displayed a Star of David on his trunks, led people to believe his father was Jewish, but this has not been proven.

Most of the Jewish players who made All-American in college went on to play professionally. One of those, Adolph (Dolph) Schayes, had set the following records when he retired in 1963: until then, he had scored more points than any other player (19,115),[7] most free throws (8,216), played in most league games (1,035) and as of 1964 had played the greatest number of consecutive games (765 over a nearly nine-year span). In 1966, he coached the Philadelphia 76ers—and was voted Coach of the Year.

Among the many Jews who have served as basketball coaches, one stands out with the accomplishment of another record in basketball history—most coaching wins. This is Arnold Jacob "Red" Auerbach, one of the Jews in Basketball's Hall of Fame. In 1950, he took over the last place Boston Celtics and by 1957 had guided them to their first league title. From 1958-59 to 1965-66, his team won consecutive NBA championships—the longest string of championship victories in America's three major sports of basketball, football, and baseball. His trademark of lighting up a cigar every time his team won may have also earned him a place in the smoker's hall of fame: his teams won 1,037 times, the most victories by any coach.

Jews have also left their mark in basketball as referees. Among them have been Mendy Rudolph, who became head of NBA officials in 1969; Norman Drucker, who has officiated for twenty-seven years in nearly nineteen hundred games (and in an interview figured that he had run an estimated 10,800 miles officiating those games), and David Tobey, a referee for nearly thirty years, another member of basketball's Hall of Fame, and the author in 1943 of the first book on basketball officiating. Jews have also coached to gold medals the Olympic basketball teams of Canada (1936) and the Soviet Union (1964, 1968).

A Jewish Athletes Hall of Fame would not be complete in its basketball section without noting that among the Jewish owners of basketball teams, one owner surely stands out because he not only owns but founded and coached the world's best known basketball

---

[7] With this record, Schayes replaced George Mikan as the then highest scorer in basketball history. In 1950, sports writers had voted Mikan as the greatest basketball player of the first half century. Mikan, however, scored only 11,764 points.

team. That's Abe Saperstein. His team: the Harlem Globetrotters.

The look at Jewish participation in basketball must, of course, take note of the slack off in Jewish participation in this area these days, as black athletes come to the fore and the poor, crowded, urban conditions of an earlier America are replaced for Jewish youngsters by suburbia and more professional opportunities. One Jew who realized early that his success in basketball would not prepare him for earning a living later in life was Harry Boykoff, an All-American in college (1943, 1946). Towering 6 feet 9½ inches, he played professional ball for six years following his successful college career. Although paid the then princely salary of $10,000 for his first season in the pros, he was quoted as saying that "I don't want to be an athletic bum." He pointed out that since he would have to support a family after his playing days, "I'll only be able to do it if I can make something of myself." So Harry Boykoff, while playing professional basketball, became an accountant.

Football is one of those sports people rarely associate with Jews because of its bruising violence. And yet the Goldbergian Institute's Jewish Athletes Hall of Fame is able to puncture the myth that Jews have been absent from this endeavor. Literally hundreds of Jews have played college football, beginning with Moses Henry Epstein, who played in the third college football game ever—Columbia University against Rutgers in 1871 (the sport had started in American colleges the year before). Since then, nearly forty Jewish college football players have been named All-Americans and a half dozen have been enshrined in the College Football Hall of Fame.

In professional football, among the Jews who have stood out in spectacular fashion are Benny Friedman, Marshall Goldberg, and Sid Luckman. Friedman, who had been a unanimous first team All-American selection and member of the College Football Hall of Fame for quarterbacking the University of Michigan team to titles, started his professional career in 1927. During the next seven years he helped the fledgling professional sport by using the forward pass more expertly than any previous player, thereby opening up the game. He concluded his seven-year career by serving as both player and coach of the Brooklyn Dodgers football team (1932–33).

Marshall Goldberg, an All-American with the University of Pittsburgh, was a running back for the St. Louis Cardinals and achieved one of the longest touchdown runs in history—95 yards from the line of scrimmage. At the first awards dinner of the National Football Foundation in 1958, Goldberg, who was already in the College Football Hall of Fame, was selected for the Professional Football Hall of Fame.

After an outstanding college football career at Columbia University (he was named to the College Football Hall of Fame), Sid Luckman, who had been born in Brooklyn in 1916, began playing professionally with the Chicago Bears in 1939. He soon became recognized as the first great T-formation quarterback in professional football. This style of play was widely imitated after Luckman led the Bears to the world championship in 1940 against the Washington Redskins in the most one-sided game in the history of championship games—73-0. He quarterbacked the Bears to four championships and became the first to throw six touchdown passes in one game. In 1943, Luckman, who was also a good punter and defensive player, was chosen as the Most Valuable Player in professional football.[8] He was later named to the Professional Football Hall of Fame.

Baseball, which has reigned as the national pastime of America for more than a century (the first games were played in the 1840s), has been marked by that special aspect of Jewish participation—not quantity, but quality. In the early days of baseball, many of the players came not out of the major cities where most Jews lived but out of small town America, where land and climate were just right for the wide-open spaces and warm outdoors needed for this sport. Also, as the first of the three major sports to go professional, it attracted a rougher and more closed society of athletes, many of whom had not graduated from high school, let alone

---

[8] Overlooked usually is the fact that many of Luckman's passes were caught by another Jew—Johnny Siegal—who played with Luckman at Columbia and on the Bears.

attended college. It was, after all, basketball and football that had the tradition of college competition as a prelude to professional play. In baseball, an elaborate farm system trained players immediately from high school, bypassing the one place where most Jewish youth were interested in going—college.

But only the Ignorance Factor has kept most people from knowing the full and unusual story of Jews in baseball. For this story starts at the very beginning of professional baseball. A Jew by the name of Lipman E. (Lip) Pike actually holds the distinction of being baseball's first professional player. In 1866, when teams were composed of amateurs, he started drawing a salary for playing third base for the Philadelphia Athletics. His pay: Twenty dollars a week. This began a trend that saw teams composed of amateurs and paid players as a prelude to all-pro teams. Pike, though, was not only the first paid player, but one of the best of the early era. He once hit six home runs in one game.[9]

Several other Jews also played pro baseball before 1900. The first Jew to play in the major leagues in the modern era (from 1900 onward) was Johnny Kling, who in 1901 became a member of the Chicago Cubs team that featured the famous Tinkers-to-Evers-to-Chance doubleplay combination. The noted sports writer Grantland Rice termed Kling, whose real name was Kline, the smartest catcher in baseball. The number of Jews in pro baseball then began to increase. George Stone, an outfielder, led the American League in batting in 1906. Erskine Mayer had twenty-one wins as a pitcher for the Philadelphia Phillies in 1914 and 1915. (Mayer's grandmother on his mother's side, who could trace her ancestry back to the Mayflower, was a convert to Judaism.) And there were others in those early days, though not as successful.

Often overlooked is that in the 1920s some teams actually wanted Jewish baseball players as a way to attract greater crowds. With Babe Ruth packing them in at New York's Yankee Stadium, for instance, John McGraw, manager of the New York Giants, dreamed of an equal gate attraction—a Jewish home run hitter who could rival Ruth. In 1923, McGraw thought he had found his

---

[9] Pike was also one of the fastest runners of his day. He once raced against a famous trotting horse over the 100-yard distance and won—in less than ten seconds, setting an unofficial amateur record then.

answer in a Jewish player by the name of Moses Solomon. In response to Babe Ruth's moniker of "Sultan of Swat," Solomon was actually named "Rabbi of Swat." But the experiment did not work. Solomon could not field up to major league standards and by the end of the season he was back in the minors.

Since then, however, Jews have come forward to achieve virtually every honor in baseball. Jewish pitchers have thrown six no-hitters, Jewish batters have won batting titles, Jewish sluggers have held home run titles, and Jewish players have been selected for the highly prized Most Valuable Player awards. For instance, Al Rosen, third baseman for the Cleveland Indians, was the home run leader of his league in 1950 and 1953, as well as MVP in 1953. Another Jew—Arthur Shamsky, playing for the Cincinnati Reds—equaled the major league record of hitting four home runs in four consecutive times at bat (1966), a feat even Babe Ruth never accomplished.

But of the two Jews who stand out with the all-time greats in the history of baseball, one is a batter and one a pitcher—as though to spread the small Jewish quantity into the maximum quality possible.

The batter was Hank Greenberg. Born in the Bronx on January 1, 1911, to Orthodox parents from Rumania, Greenberg began playing professional baseball in 1930. Powerfully built and standing 6 feet 4 inches, he was voted the American League's Most Valuable Player by 1935 for his home run hitting for the Detroit Tigers, whom he helped lead to a pennant that year for the second year in a row.[10] By 1938, Greenberg had achieved one of the rarest feats. He hit fifty-eight home runs in one season, only two behind Babe Ruth's famed sixty homers. This achievement tied him with Jimmy Foxx for most home runs in a year by a right-hander. Although left-hander Roger Maris later hit sixty-one, no other right-hander in forty years has come close to hitting fifty-eight.

By 1940, Hank Greenberg was being paid the highest salary of any player in professional baseball. He responded by leading the

---

[10] In 1935, the year Greenberg won the MVP award, the batting champion of the American League was another Jew—Charles Solomon "Buddy" Myer, who batted .349 and came in second in total hits with 215. Playing for the Washington and Boston teams for seventeen years and in two world series, Myer compiled a .303 lifetime batting average.

Tigers to another pennant and Greenberg was named to another MVP award. In 1941, Greenberg was again the highest paid player in baseball. But then World War II came, and he volunteered at the height of his career for service in the United States Army Air Corps. Upon his return to baseball at the end of the 1945 season nearly four years later, Greenberg again helped the Tigers win the pennant, this time with a story book grand slam home run in the last inning that won the game and the league title. In 1946, Greenberg, again the highest paid player, captured his third American League home run crown.

When he ended his career two years later, Greenberg had compiled an incredible record, especially in view of his war-shortened career: a total of 331 home runs, which in terms of home runs per the present 162-game schedule placed him fifth as of 1975 on the all-time list of baseball athletes, with 38.49 homers a season (this surpassed such other power hitters as Jimmy Foxx, Ted Williams, Mickey Mantle, Willie Mays, and Joe DiMaggio and was just behind Henry Aaron's 38.60) [11]; a lifetime batting average of .313; and runs batted in of 1,276 (he had led his league in RBIs four times, driven in more than 100 runs a year every full year he played after his first with the Tigers, and achieved a one-year high of 183 RBIs which at the time was only one behind the record). In 1956, Greenberg became the first Jew elected to the Baseball Hall of Fame.

One of the greatest pitchers of all time, who threw more no-hitters (four) than any other pitcher in history, is another Jew— Sanford (Sandy) Koufax, who was born in 1935 and started his professional playing career at the age of nineteen. Also elected to the Hall of Fame, Koufax was named Baseball Athlete of the Decade for the 1960s.

Koufax's story is not just one of statistics, but of courage. Koufax suffered from traumatic arthritis in his pitching arm for several years. The only way he could pitch was to plunge the elbow into ice water for an hour a day. Even after his condition had been diagnosed, he pitched two of his four no-hitters. The

---

[11] This listing of home run hitters by average per season rather than by career totals, which is a revealing way to show the annual effectiveness of hitters, can be found in *The Sports Book* edited by Min S. Yee and published by Holt, Rinehart and Winston (page 24).

painful elbow finally forced him to retire from professional sports in 1966 at the age of only thirty—and yet, in that last year, he won twenty-seven games for the second year in a row and led both leagues in winning percentage, earned-run-average, and strikeouts.

Ironically, Koufax had an erratic beginning as a major league pitcher. He had a dazzling fastball he found hard to control. By the end of his sixth season in 1960, he had a lackluster record of thirty-six wins and forty losses. But the Brooklyn-born and reared pitcher had been constantly working to conquer his control and in the 1961 season his adjustments in his pitching finally started to have effect. He began to make a historic mark on the game of baseball by striking out 269 batters that season, breaking Christy Mathewson's long-standing National League record. And then began his string of no-hitters. He pitched his first no-hitter on Memorial Day in 1962, his second a year later, his third a year after that, and his fourth the following year—which was not only a no-hitter, but a perfect game in which no opposing batter reached base and Koufax struck out fourteen of the twenty-seven he faced, including all three batters in the last inning. Four no-hitters, four years in a row—an all-time pitching record.[12] The next year was 1966, his last before being forced to quit at the height of his powers (he said he didn't want to "wind up with an arm I won't be able to use for the rest of my life").

The Sports Book, using an elaborate set of statistics, lists Koufax as third in its cataloguing of All-Time Greatest Pitchers and cites him as "the greatest left-hander who ever lived." He is the only pitcher to average more than one strikeout an inning during his pitching lifetime (2,396 strikeouts in 2,325 innings) and is the first pitcher ever awarded the Cy Young award for best pitcher in his league three times (1963, 1965, 1966). He was also the youngest man elected to baseball's Hall of Fame.

Koufax has one other distinction. He would not play on Rosh Hashanah and Yom Kippur. This led Koufax's manager, Walter

---

[12] Only three pitchers in major league history have three no-hitters apiece—and only one, Bob Feller, had them all in the modern era since 1900. Another Jewish pitcher, Ken Holtzman, has two no-hitters (1969 and 1972 for the Chicago Cubs).

Alston, to check the Hebrew calendar to prevent any conflict in his scheduling of Koufax's pitching appearances.[13]

While basketball, football, and baseball reflect the participation of Jews in sports in America, what has been the situation worldwide?

One indicator may be seen in the range of some unusual firsts earned by Jewish athletes. Such as:

The first world championship in weightlifting ever staged was won by an English Jew—Edward Laurence Levy in 1891. Levy, who stood only 5 feet 3 inches tall and weighed 155 pounds, had been assistant master in a Hebrew school before starting his own. He once said that "a person who does not engage in sport is not worth educating."

The first men's world singles and doubles champion in table tennis was a Hungarian Jew—Dr. Roland Jacobi in 1927.[14]

The first walking champion of the United States at one and three miles was a Jew—Daniel Stern (1849–1923).

But the best indicator of the diversity and significance of Jewish athletic ability worldwide is the record compiled in the Olympics, and the Goldbergian Institute's Jewish Athletes Hall of Fame has a special exhibit for this.

The irony of course is that the original Olympics, as indicated earlier, had idolatrous overtones which repelled the Jews. But the modern Olympics, revived in 1896, have been far removed from religious or racial overtones (except for the 1936 Olympics hosted by Hitler's Germany).[15] With the emancipation of the Jews wide-

---

[13] Hank Greenberg's decision decades before Koufax not to play on Yom Kippur during a hot pennant race attracted national headlines. His team lost the game. Another great baseball player who decided not to play on Yom Kippur was not even Jewish. He was Rod Carew, the many-time American League batting champion. A black, Carew married a Jew and made plans to convert to Judaism, which strongly interested him. Featured on the cover of *Time* magazine, he wore a necklace with the Hebrew word Chai ("Life") clearly visible.

[14] One of the world's greatest male table tennis players may have been another Hungarian Jew, Viktor Barna. He won twenty-two world titles, including five singles championships. Barna became interested in the sport when his friend was given a table tennis set as a Bar Mitzvah present.

[15] Surprising as it seems, the Nazis let German Jews participate on Germany's Olympic team in 1936, but this was only in response to outside pressures and was largely a subterfuge. Helene Mayer responded by winning a silver medal in fencing. (Over the years, German Jews have been awarded seven medals in Olympic competition.)

spread by the time the Olympics were restored, Jewish athletes participated in modern day Olympics from the start. Thus, between 1896 and 1968, records tell a startling story: 131 Jews from seventeen nations on four continents won 236 medals. This included 101 gold, 68 silver, and 67 bronze.[16] Since 1968, the record of Jewish success in the Olympics has soared. In 1972, at Munich Mark Spitz won seven gold medals in swimming, the most gold medals awarded to an individual in any single Olympics. Coupled with the two he had earned in the Mexico City Olympics in 1968, Spitz's total of nine gold medals was another historic achievement—it meant that a Jew now held the record for most gold medals ever won by one person in Olympic competition.

(That Munich Olympiade was also marked by the Arab terrorist murder of Jewish athletes. Is it just coincidence that the terrorists struck at a sporting event in which Jews were once again putting to rest the myth of the weak ghetto Jew? Why were the terrorists intent on humiliating as well as killing some of Israel's finest young athletes? In addition to the international publicity they hoped to achieve, were the foes of a Jewish homeland disturbed by this different Jewish image?)

Oddly, Mark Spitz's Olympian achievements in swimming (he also won a silver and a bronze medal in 1968) were nothing new for Jews. At the first modern Olympics held in Athens in 1896, Jews completely dominated the swimming events. Jewish swimmers swept all three open events and won a total of four gold medals.

Significantly, Jewish achievement in the Olympics spans the range of athletics, from the fury of judo to the grace of fencing, from boxing to yachting. And the large number of countries from which Jews have participated, as well as the spectrum of sports activities represented, demonstrates again that the myth of the nonathletic Jew has been debunked across the world of Jewish communities and not in just one country or by one type of Jew.

[16] Leave it to the Jews to win Olympic medals not only for sports competition, but also for nonathletic endeavors. The Olympic Committee has awarded medals for special service in behalf of the Olympics. Thus, in addition to the medals listed above, a Jew won an Olympic gold medal for literature in 1928 (he was the official historian of the Olympic Games and wrote books and articles about it) and another Jew earned a silver medal in 1924 for architecture.

Jewish participation, let alone success, in the high-powered international competition is telling the tale that the individual accomplishments of Jewish athletes do represent a broader picture, not so much a new Jew as a newly perceived Jew. Indeed, when America's Olympic Committee representative General Charles H. Sherrill, as quoted at the beginning of this chapter, made his statement on the eve of the 1936 Olympics about the absence of prominent Jewish athletes, Jews had already won fifty-three gold medals in the ten modern Olympics.

All this is not to say that the modern Jew has become a super athlete, secretly ready and able to slay all indoor and outdoor sporting event records at the drop of an anti-Semitic insult. The State of Israel has yet to win an Olympic medal (although countries bigger than her have not, either). The Maccabiah Games do not always threaten to topple world marks. The number of professional Jewish athletes in baseball, football, and basketball has been on the decline in recent years.

But the point is that most people are ignorant of the Jewish people's diverse and substantial—let alone successful—involvement in sports for the past century. And that Ignorance Factor has hampered, and in many ways continues to hamper, what could be a positive impact on the Jewish image, for the human being thinks in symbols and the symbols offered in the world of sports spill over into the real world. Why else did Italians cheer so enthusiastically for Joe DiMaggio? Why do blacks embrace a Muhammad Ali? Why did whites mount a "great white hope" to defeat the first black boxing champion, Jack Johnson?

Why, in fact, are sports teams given the name of cities (such as the New York Yankees)? Why do citizens of these metropolises root for their "home team" as though the success or failure of paid athletes—invariably born and raised in other locales—reflects on the prowess and ability of the sedentary citizen and his city?

The answer is that we need symbols of our courage and strength. We need surrogates to carry out our flights of fancy. We must have our self images fulfilled, if not by ourselves, then vicariously by others. Those who sneer at an ethnic group's pride at the accomplishments of other members of that group fail to understand the most basic drive of the human being for identity with others and for pride in self. Sports and athletics, especially team athletics, are so successful in our times because they carry out that function of creating identity and instilling pride. And it is why when a team fails, the frustration and the boos begin because the self becomes frustrated at the failure of its symbolic representation.

Thus, the boxing match between a black champion like Jack Johnson and a white challenger was seen as a battle between the black man and the white man. The boxing matches between Joe Louis and the German Max Schmeling in the 1930s became a struggle between democratic America and Nazi Germany. This is why the Olympics became to Hitler in his day—and has become to the Soviet Union today—not just a sporting event but a nationalistic event, a way to vindicate through the actions of individual athletes the prowess and progress of a nation. Sport is all that—and, in the case of the Jew, it is more.

In the case of the Jew, his historic absence from athletics simply reinforced a host of other stereotypes. Since sport is social, the nonsporting Jew was seen as nonsocial; since athletics is physical, the nonathletic Jew was again seen as weak. Thus, the Jewish absence from sports set up a social vacuum in which the Jew had to struggle anew for acceptance and tolerance.

We can see what the absence or presence of Jews in sports can mean in the public psyche when we view what happened in the days of Daniel Mendoza, the proud Jew who became the English heavyweight boxing champion. In a manuscript preserved in the British museum library, the distinguished Gentile, Francis Place, who lived during the time Mendoza became famous, wrote how before Mendoza became known the Jews of London suffered from mounting prejudice because of the passage of the Naturalization Law of 1753:

> I then saw the Jews being chased, whistled at, beaten, their beards plucked and spat at in the public street without any passerby or officer of the law coming to their aid. . . . Dogs were not treated so shabbily as some Jews were.

But all of this suddenly changed. Why? Because a Jew entered sports. As Francis Place recorded it:

> One circumstance above all others brought the mistreatment of Jews to an end. In the year 1787 the Jew, Daniel Mendoza, became a famous boxer. He opened a school where he taught the art of boxing as a science. This sport spread rapidly among young Jews.... It was no longer wholesome to molest a Jew if he did not happen to be an old man....

Image. It is all image. Not every Jew was now a Mendoza. Not every Jew was now being schooled in the art of boxing. But Jews had now become associated in the public mind with sports, with its great symbolism and power to transfer those symbols. The irony is instructive. Before Mendoza, the Jews were molested just because they were Jewish. After Mendoza, they were left alone just because they were Jewish. Such is the other great benefit of sport: it can overcome false stereotypes and bridge barriers faster than almost any other human endeavor.

GOLDBERG'S LAW

If anything can be misconstrued about the Jews, it will be ... and has been.

Exhibit F: JEWISH POPULARITY

A JEW WAS ONCE CHOSEN AS ONE OF THE TEN MOST LOVED PEOPLE IN HISTORY—AT THE VERY SAME TIME THAT HE WAS ALSO NAMED ONE OF THE TEN MOST HATED PEOPLE IN HISTORY

Each year, Madame Tussaud's famed wax museum in London asks its thousands of visitors to list the ten people in history they most admire and the ten they most hate. In 1974, Moshe Dayan, the famed Israeli general, was selected as the fifth most loved person in history—but at the same time, he also appeared as fourth on the most hated list. No other person appeared on both lists.

VII
What About Mrs. Portnoy's Complaint?

*The truth about
the Jewish mother*

FACT: When the Inquisition began in Spain, Jewish women comprised the vast majority of those Jews who died the death of martyrs for secretly maintaining their faith.

FACT: The first woman to be appointed to a nation's highest court was a Jewish grandmother.

FACT: A Jewish barbary queen once led an army in the fight against invading Moslems.

FACT: A Chassidic male sect in Eastern Europe was headed by a young woman who gave religious teaching to her followers.

FACT: In Mexico, during the Inquisition, the spiritual leaders of the Marranos were usually the mothers.

> God could not be everywhere so He created mothers.
> —LEOPOLD KOMPERT, Austrian novelist (1822–66)

THE ATTACK on the Jewish image has been so extensive that the onslaught has even entered the Jewish home. While the Jewish male has been out in the marketplace exposed to accusations ranging from driving hard business bargains to plotting to take over the world (obviously using the time between business deals), the Jewish woman has not even been safe in the house. She has found herself the target of a growing stereotype—that she is pushy, aggressive, over-protective, and guilt-producing in her relationships with her children. She is even said to dominate her husband.

This stereotype may invade the house, but it doesn't hit home. Various elements in the image are conceivably true: Jewish mothers may exhibit some of the symptoms some of the time and undoubtedly some Jewish mothers have all of them all of the time. But it surely does not take an Abraham Lincoln (who did not have a Jewish mother) or a Solomon (who did—her name was Bathsheba) to know that the true Jewish mother could hardly recognize herself in the mirror of this incessant, widely repeated, and in many ways unfair stereotype.

Ironically, the Jewish mother is one Jewish stereotype that has been nurtured more by the Jews than by others. Jewish comedians like to put her down in countless stand-up routines; Jewish writers will liven up their works with one of her typically deadly actions.

Indeed, the image of the Jewish mother—usually drawn so broadly it seems etched by the widest-tipped Magic Marker—probably received its biggest notoriety in the best-selling novel *Portnoy's Complaint* written by Philip Roth, who is an American-born Jew. Published in 1969, this book became an instant commercial success as well as a center of controversy for its presentation of the Jewish mother. A highly talked-about book even before it was published in 1969, *Portnoy's Complaint* was excerpted in *Esquire, New American Review,* and *Partisan Review* prior to publication in book form, whereupon the novel went through numerous printings, sold close to four million copies in hardback and paperback, and eventually attained that peak of American cultural success—it was turned into a movie.

The book's portrayal of the Jewish mother is embodied in Sophie Portnoy, mother of the book's first-person narrator, thirty-three-year-old Alex Portnoy. While telling his life's story to Dr. Spielvogel, who is his analyst, Alex paints a harsh, though wildly comical, picture of growing up at the hands of what he says was a domineering, guilt-producing mother.

Not everyone, however, agreed with the book's premise about the peculiar nature of the mother to be found in all-too-many Jewish homes. Kingsley Amis, a British writer, in reviewing the book for *Harper's Magazine* in April, 1969, said that his "spirits fell" when he realized Alex Portnoy was going to go into a tirade about his mother. Why? Because, Amis stated, "even in England, where there are still quite a few Gentile authors about, it is possible to feel that one has had nearly enough of this sort of thing."

The picture evoked of life in the Jewish family was for Amis numbingly familiar. "I, the child of Protestant parents who had had a puritanical upbringing, recognize that picture. Which brings me to the point that all of us, at least most of us over the age of ten, have had to go through something like this." And as for parents giving children guilt feelings and strait jacketing them to be what parents want, he found nothing startling new or Jewish in this: It has been going on, he said, "in Western society, and probably in a lot of other societies, past and present."

In a final dismissal of the book's attempt to picture the operation of the Jewish family as somehow different than that of the non-Jewish family, Amis, a critic, poet, novelist, and graduate of Oxford (he must have made some Gentile mother happy), wrote: "Portnoy, or Mr. Roth, falls into racial/cultural provincialism by wondering what it is about specifically Jewish parents that makes them go on like this; they are just parents or, in Portnoy-Roth language, WHAT'S SO DIFFERENT WITH THE GOYIM? WE ALL KNEW ALL OF THAT ALREADY ALREADY!"

Indeed, many of the studies and books on the parent-child relationship discuss family situations that, if one were to believe the Jewish stereotype, should only be found in the Jewish home, yet are obviously universal. For instance, Dr. Wayne Dyer in his best seller *Your Erroneous Zones* makes the point that all families make the same mistakes in raising children: "The family unit nurtures, in the form of good intentions, dependence and the need for approval. Parents who don't want any harm to come to their children resolve to protect them from danger. The result, however, is the opposite of that intended."

Sociologists are not the only ones to tell us that there is more universality to the Jewish mother than meets the stereotype. The poet can be just as revealing, as was Phyllis McGinley, who in one of her poems, "The Adversary," touched on a reason why all mothers are subject to criticism by those they rear: Mothers become "hardest to forgive" because they "long to hand" the child the fruit of life—and then throughout life "relentlessly they understand" their child.

Discussions about the Jewish mother working her strong will on her family always leave me with a nagging thought I have had since publication of *Portnoy's Complaint*: throughout the book we never hear directly from Portnoy's mother. It is really a tale told by Alex Portnoy from beginning to end (only the last sentence of the book is recorded as being spoken by Dr. Spielvogel back to Alex). People forget that anything we see or learn about Portnoy's mother is through *his* remembrance of things past. What, I have always wondered, would Mrs. Portnoy have said for herself—and indeed for other Jewish mothers—if she had been allowed to speak directly to the reader?

Here is how I think this fictional woman, surely one of the best-known, if most derided, figures in literature, might respond:

MY COMPLAINT

by Alex Portnoy's Mother

I must warn you right here in the beginning. I might be a Jewish mother, but I do not write like a Jewish mother sounds.

Look son, no chicken soup. You'll find no matzoh ball stains on these pages. Tears, maybe; matzoh balls, no. Actually, most Jewish mothers do not sound like Jewish mothers. After all, isn't that why it's called the Jewish Mother Stereotype and not the Jewish Mother Fact?

Do you really believe all stereotypes are true? Of course you don't. But just the same, we all love stereotypes or else why would they be so popular? How else could the Jewish mother appear in public on so many TV shows and movie screens and in so many books and jokes? That means the stereotype not only has authors but audiences.

Take this business about Yiddish. I bet you expected to find me talking and even writing *mit an haxcent*. But even Alex knows better, as you can see in The Book where at least he doesn't make me sound like Molly Goldberg. Do you know who might sound like that? The Jewish grandmother. So there's your first clue about the Jewish mother stereotype—even if it's true, it's off by at least one generation. Now, how much can you trust something that's wrong by twenty-five years?

Yes, we Jewish mothers are not like you think. We have a lot more on the ball than our children give us credit for. After all, where do you think they get the ability to criticize and caricature us? Where, for instance, do you think my Alex got his way with words?

Which brings me to my complaint. My complaint happens to be my son Alex. He is a wonderful person, but to read his book you would think I was the cause of all his troubles except maybe pimples.

Don't get me wrong. I certainly don't mind the jokes in the book—after all, I am the first to say my Alex has quite a sense of humor (he gets that from his father), and I can still remember all the funny things he used to say whenever I asked him to help around the house.

I also don't mind the fact that Alex always said I talked too much, yet here he was talking nonstop for 274 pages. I ask you—after you listen to him going on and on for a whole book from cover to cover—*who* talks too much? Even his psychiatrist, Dr. Spielvogel, couldn't get a word in edgewise until the very last sentence. (By the way, who do you think *paid* for Alex's sessions with Dr. Spielvogel?)

No, it wasn't the jokes or the dirty language that bothered me. It wasn't even what he had to say about me, his own mother. What bothered me was the way he made it seem we Jewish mothers raise our children like we were Count Dracula in a Red Cross Blood Bank. You would think we strangle our kids with scarves, we smother them with sweaters, we drown them in steaming bowls of chicken soup, and we stuff them like geese being fattened for kosher schmaltz. Alex even says I stood over him with a knife to make him eat, and he makes it sound as though I worried about his bowels like I was Newark's Superintendent of Sanitation.

Sounds a little far-fetched the way I say it, right? But no more far-fetched than what Alex says. I'm telling you, in case you've forgotten the book, that's how he goes on and on.

As my husband always says, let's sit down and reason together. Let's see what Alex says and then see how much truth there is in it. Maybe Alex is right, but maybe not. Look, I'm not perfect. I make mistakes. But just remember one thing before I start. I love Alex and I did not *kick* Alex out of the house on his *tuschie*. What I did or did not do in raising him I did out of love, the kind of motherly feeling that Hallmark Cards would understand.

So, as Dr. Spielvogel said, we are now perhaps ready to begin.

I am willing to bet Alex his favorite meal (don't worry, Alex, we'll take you out to eat) that what he complains about with me is exactly what Italian boys, Greek boys, Mexican boys, and black boys say about *their* mothers.

Why do I say this? Because we Jewish–Italian–Greek–black mothers have to raise children who as minority children have to be protected from what other children don't have to worry about. So we worry more because we have more to worry about. And this worry, I guess, affects some children more than others—like my son, the original Worry Wart.

But isn't this also true of all mothers? Don't we all worry, for one reason or another? Years ago a writer by the name of Philip Wylie said a lot of the same things as my Alex about American mothers. Momism, he called it. He said that American men were so much under their mothers' thumbs that this was affecting America. Well, Mr. Wylie wasn't Jewish and he wasn't talking about Jewish mothers. So he must have been talking about Gentile mothers (they're the only ones left).

How could this be? How can there be such a thing as the Gentile mother? I'll tell you how. You see, the funniest joke in my Alex's book is that all his talk about Jewish mothers is part of this whole business of sons complaining about mothers, a complaint that is so old it probably started with Cain and Abel.

Now, you might say I'm just trying to get Jewish mothers off the hook by saying other mothers are the same. Not quite. In spite of Alex's complaints, I still think the Jewish mother has some wonderful things about her, as do all women who carry out their duties as mothers. If you look at Alex's complaints, you will see that many of them about me would be twice as bad if I had done just the opposite. You don't see Alex complaining about an alcoholic mother who gets drunk on Concord grape wine. You didn't hear him say he had a mother who just watched soap operas in a bubble bath, popped Barton's chocolates in her mouth, forgot even to thaw out the TV dinner, and thought that Colonel Sanders should be President of the United States. And you certainly did not see any child abuse of Alex (although Alex certainly abused himself, if you know what I mean).

And about this business of food and me forcing Alex to eat. Now, I hope you don't believe all that stuff about me standing over Alex with a knife and threatening him with it if he didn't eat. How often do you think that little scene happens with Jewish mothers? I know my Alex likes to exaggerate, but that knife business is a bit much, don't you think? And yet, I bet there are a lot of people who believed that scene. Why, here we're trying to make the child grow big and strong, yet we're supposed to use knives as threats. *Vay is mir.* I just want to remind you that the libaries I have gone into to make sure they had Alex's book (you see, no matter what a son says about his own mother, she's still proud of him)—why, every library I visited has his book in the section marked "fiction." So that ought to tell you something about how much librarians believe everything my Alex has to say. And that's why you can't believe everything *you* read.

But if you want to hear my views on this business about feeding, I would just like to say that I admit I tried to make sure Alex ate well. Food *is* tied up with love. Dr. Spielvogel and his fellow doctors are right about that at least. After all, we women literally give of our bodies to our babies. We do it inside before they're born and outside at the breast after birth. You add to this the fact that we Jews have known much poverty and starvation (no matter what the anti-Semites say about all Jews being rich), and you have the right background for being concerned about food. But we're not alone in pushing food. Napoleon is the one who said an army marches on its stomach—and Napoleon didn't even have a Jewish mother. And remember what the Pillsbury Bakery Company used to tell American mothers? "Nothing says lovin' like somethin' from the oven." And just the other day I saw a message on a box of oatmeal. It said, "The more they eat, the better you feel." Now, that oatmeal was made by the Quaker Oats Company—not the Jewish Oats Company.

There is another something else. In looking over what my Alex has to say in Mr. Roth's magnum opus, I noticed that there wasn't much shown or said about the beauty of the Jewish religion itself. There was some talk of kosher food and the Sabbath, but not much else. Now, my Alex can't fool me, his own mother. He rants and raves how not only me but the Jewish religion gave him all these guilt feelings. At one point he says, "The very first distinction I learned . . . was not night and day or hot and cold but *goyishe* and *Jewish* . . . Jew Jew Jew Jew Jew." But, except for his ranting and raving, you don't find much about Judaism itself that my Alex discusses. And isn't this Alex Portnoy's real complaint—his being Jewish?

Here is where I think I have to accept responsibility. It is really my fault that Alex was raised as a Jew without knowing very much what being a Jew is all about. As in too many Jewish families today, all he saw and learned was the negative commandments. He only heard no, no, no. He didn't learn the positive aspects of the religion, the beauty of it. This is where I fell down. (And believe me, it would have also been a lot smarter, I now realize, to have taught him at least one of the ten commandments in greater detail. You know, the one about honoring your father and mother.)

I have noticed that a lot of those Jews who criticize the Jewish mother the most either come from Jewish families in name only or come from overly strict families where all the joy has been squeezed out. But you take a person like Sam Levenson. He shows in his books a real love for his religion—and at the same time a real love for his parents. I think there is much in that connection that is more than coincidental.

You know how I think the stereotype of the Jewish mother came about? I think it was because the Jewish religion believes in the importance of three very connected items—life, children, and the future. Jewish families always realized that children were the real future. Times might be bad now, but things would get better and our children should be ready to share in it. But to do so they had to grow up healthy and strong, they had to have a good education, they had to be twice as bright as little Farnsworth IV on the other side of town if they were going to get half as far. So who was home with the child and most able to help him, encourage him, yes, even prod him? Why, surprise, surprise, it was his mother.

Look, let's face it, we mothers of all races and religions have gotten an unfair amount of criticism and misunderstanding from our sons and daughters over the centuries. But that's always the case, and I think always will be the case because of the way a child has to be raised.

It's all very logical. The child wants to run across the street but you have to stop him so he doesn't wind up with tire marks across his forehead. What happens? The child just gets mad at you—and here you've saved his life!

So I say to you Jewish women—either present or future mothers—LIBERATE YOURSELVES FROM THE STEREOTYPE OF THE JEWISH MOTHER! There's nothing wrong about caring about your child. Maybe we have cared too much—and maybe in the future we should try not to try so hard—but we can be proud that we cared. Just remember Sophie Portnoy's poem for the Jewish mother (please read with full allowance for rhyme and reason):

> From your stereotype you should liberate.
> And don't worry whether your child ate.
> Someday your love he will appreciate.
> Only for you it will probably be too late.

But we Jewish mothers do have one problem other mothers don't seem to have. Most mothers worry that their children will grow up, go away, and not call or write often enough. As you can see from my experience with Alex, the problem of the Jewish Mother is that our children grow up and, like Alex, TALK AND WRITE TOO MUCH!

The Finis of

MY COMPLAINT

by Sophie Portnoy

who reminds you that

"God could not be everywhere so He created mothers ... like me."

The Jewish woman—whether she be mother, wife, or even daughter (sometimes referred to as the Jewish princess, yet another Jewish female stereotype)—has never been correctly perceived. Her rights and obligations in Judaism and her role in Jewish life have invariably been misconstrued both by Jews and non-Jews. The feminist movement, for instance, contends that the woman's exclusion from much of the daily ritual of Judaism indicates the religion's low esteem for women. There is also the contention that over the centuries, denied the right by the Bible and Talmud to participate as fully as a man, the Jewish woman found her world narrowed into the confines of the home. The stereotypical Jewish mother is said to be the result of a female existence centered solely around her family.

Such a view of the Jewish woman, however, is based on a lack of understanding about several key tenets of Judaism. For instance, in connection with the point that women are excluded from much of the daily ritual of the faith and that Judaism denigrates the woman, critics cite the reference in a morning prayer in which a man thanks God for not making him a woman. What is not realized is that what the man is really doing by uttering this one-sentence prayer is embracing the obligation that he as a man has for performing all the commandments. He is welcoming what the rabbis call the "yoke" of the Law, and is no way expressing an antifeminist sentiment.[1] On the other hand, the woman, who has her own prayer (a reminder, often overlooked by critics, that women are required to pray), thanks God for making her according to His will. She cannot offer the same type of prayer as the man because her duties as wife and mother were seen affecting her ability to perform the many religious functions that are limited by time. The woman, called upon to nurse a child, watch a toddler, prepare a meal, ready the home for Sabbath or a holiday, cannot be expected to stop at the clearly demarcated times of day Judaism requires for prayer. As anyone who has children will readily realize, time is no longer one's own once the duties of caring for a family are involved. Judaism's exemption of women from so much of the ritual of the religion, often taken by critics for a sign of denigration of women, is really an expression of pragmatic common sense in recognition of their first time-consuming responsibility as wives and mothers. As Rabbi Hayim Halevy Donin writes in *To Be A Jew*, "While not all women have such responsibilities throughout their lives, the law cannot distinguish between those who do and those who don't—and so the leniency with regard to some observances is extended to all."

Thus, the irony and another example of Goldberg's Law: Judaism is usually attacked for being too stringent but, in the case of

---

[1] Changing the negative construction of the prayer into a positive formulation to make it clear that the prayer implies no denigration of women has been discussed in the Orthodox rabbinate. See Rabbi Joseph Hertz's prayer book commenting on this. Interestingly, the Persians and Greeks had a similar negative formula of thanks.

women, it is attacked for not being stringent enough to obligate them to the many more requirements and restrictions placed on men.

The Jewish religion's difference in attitude toward the obligations of men and women is a reminder that Judaism, a religion that traces its roots back thousands of years, reflects that long history. Until only relatively recent times, society in general saw women more attuned than men to raising the children and caring for the family. And yet, few cultures valued such a role. But Judaism espoused a remarkable concept—the veneration of the woman in her historic function. Throughout thousands of years, ever since Abraham with Sarah as his partner and helpmate began the Jewish nation, Judaism did not denigrate woman but treasured her in the traditional family role of wife, mother, and homemaker. Current fashion in life styles may support the woman in a wider range of roles. While Judaism does not deny such freedom to women, neither does it lessen its support for those interested in being mother and wife.

Indeed, the Jewish religion hallows the homemaker. According to long-standing Jewish tradition, before the Friday evening Sabbath meal, the husband is to recite from the last proverb in the book of Proverbs the Hebrew paean to the Jewish woman, who is termed "a woman of valor" whose "price is far above rubies": "The heart of her husband doth safely trust in her, and he hath no lack of gain.... Her children rise up and call her blessed; her husband also, and he praiseth her...."

This proverb is just part of the Hebrew Bible's positive view of women. The matriarchs Sarah, Rebecca, Leah, and Rachel are not shunted to the background, but are as vivid in the Biblical narrative as the patriarchs Abraham, Isaac, and Jacob.[2] Moses is saved and protected by women: the midwives are said to have braved punishment to deliver him, his sister watches him as a babe in the bulrushes, Pharaoh's daughter elects to keep him, and Moses' mother returns to raise him. One of the Judges who comes to rule over an unruly Israel is a woman, Deborah, one of seven

---

[2] One writer used the active role of the matriarchs in the Bible as evidence of the aggressive Jewish mother. For a reply to this point and an explanation of how even the Bible is often freely manipulated to distort the Jewish people, see Goldberg's Law.

prophetesses in Jewish history. Two books of the Bible are named for women: Esther, who saved the Jewish people through an act of heroism; and Ruth, who showed self-sacrificing love for her adopted faith. And while Christianity could see Eve as the temptress and the bringer of Original Sin, Judaism made no distinction in its thinking between her sin and Adam's.

This is not to say that Jewish women have not suffered exclusion and privation in a society as male-dominated as non-Jewish society. The education of Jewish girls was woeful for too long. Statements labeling women as gossipy and frivolous were frequent and derisive (although none could compare with Aristotle's definition of a woman: "Woman may be said to be an inferior man"). The legal rights of women have often been narrowly interpreted.

In spite of all this, though, Jewish women for centuries probably lived in a more supportive society than non-Jewish women: the rate of wife-beating and adultery in non-Jewish communities always far exceeded their incidence among Jews. Judaism, too, did not surround women with debilitating barriers to participating in the general life of the community, as for instance did Islam with its endorsement of the veil.

In fact, it is probably because of Judaism's open attitude about women that one can find fascinating examples in history of Jewish women involved in many endeavors far afield from the home. A catalogue of outstanding Jewish women would include a range of such unusual personages as the Jewish barbary queen, Dahiya al Kahina (Dahiya the Prophetess), who led the Jewish communities of North Africa in the fight against invading Moslems in the early 700s ... the woman zaddik who became head of a Chassidic sect in Eastern Europe, with her own following of religious male adherents whom she would teach (called the Maid of Ludomir, she lived from 1805 to 1892) ... Beruria, the wife of the great Talmudist Rabbi Meir, whose pronouncements are included in the Talmud and whose influence on her husband's career and philosophy he openly acknowledged ... Henrietta Szold, whose love of Zionism led her to help organize and in 1914 become first president of an organization to promote Jewish institutions in

Palestine; today, Hadassah is one of the world's largest women's organizations ... Israel's Prime Minister Golda Meir, one of the few women to head a nation in modern times ... Mrs. Miriam Ben Porat, who in 1977 was selected to sit on Israel's Supreme Court and thereby became the first woman in the common law world to be elevated to a nation's highest tribunal (Mrs. Justice Ben Porat, as she is called, is not only a Jewish mother but, like Golda Meir, also a Jewish grandmother) ... and Dr. Rosalyn Sussman Yalow, only the second woman to win a Nobel Prize in medicine (an observant Jew who maintains a strictly kosher home for her husband and two children, she is another Jewish mother).

This is the other dimension to the story of the Jewish woman and mother—how she has played a key role in critical periods of Jewish history, unhampered by any supposed limitations or restrictions of Judaism. In his book *History of the Marranos*, Dr. Cecil Roth, the noted historian, states that during the Inquisition, it was often the women—the mothers and wives—who held the Marrano population together. In Mexico, during the first half of the 1700s, the women presided over and inspired the Marrano community, ultimately serving as spiritual leaders. "At the earliest Inquisitional period in Spain," writes Dr. Roth, "women comprised the vast majority of the few who maintained their Judaism to the end and died the deaths of martyrs."

During the Holocaust much the same initiative was shown. Gideon Hausner, writing in *Justice in Jerusalem*, which is based on his experience prosecuting Adolf Eichmann, says that "the courage and endurance of the Jewish women in the ghetto were unbelievable." For it was the women who often were left alone with the children when the husband was jailed, deported, or killed. She had to maintain the home or what was left of it in the confines of the ghetto while also working like a man. Emmanuel Ringelblum, the chronicler of the Warsaw Ghetto, noted even the volunteer work of the women: "There are house committees where the management is exclusively in the hands of women." They also had to maintain their physical and mental health in the face of pressures that meant special burdens for women: the Nazi edicts against pregnancy, the outrages on children, the manual labor requirements for women. A Jewish gynecologist in one ghetto reported that because of the extreme tension "about eighty per cent lost their monthly cycle." And yet, said the doctor, he "always admired afresh their greatness and strength."

These women, too, were Jewish mothers.

Not only was it a Jewish woman and mother who directed the effort to save Israel during the difficult days of the Yom Kippur War (Golda Meir), but it was also in large part countless and now faceless Jewish wives and mothers who saved a large portion of world Jewry by having the fortitude—and, yes, the aggressiveness—to move their families in the early days of this century from the hole of anti-Semitic Europe to the hope of democratic America. The mass migration of more than 1,500,000 of European Jewry to the United States between 1890 and 1910—one of the largest free migrations in history—could not have been done successfully without the encouragement and strength of the wives and mothers of these families. Often the women stayed in Europe, cared for the children, and took over sole responsibility for the home while the husband went to America to earn enough money to bring over the family. This could take several years, during which time the woman functioned alone as head of her household. It may well be the residue of that earlier generation's need for aggressiveness and drive that a later Jewish generation, growing up at ease in America, saw and castigated . . . and misunderstood.

Which brings us back to *Portnoy's Complaint* and all those other examples of what has been called Jewish self-flagellation.

It is interesting that an anthropologist and historian like Dr. Raphael Patai could note that during the centuries Jewry was trapped in the ghettos of Europe the Jews rarely exhibited the self-criticism and self-hatred that so many other ethnic groups tend to show under the pressure of discrimination. Only with Jewish emancipation in Europe in the 1800s did such self-hate begin to be seen among Jews. The self-criticism seems to have surfaced in America when the children of immigrants began to grow up and the differences between an immigrant and a native-born generation began to appear. The desire of this younger generation to avoid giving cause for discrimination may have been one reason for their criticism of the older generation, but a far larger reason is the short memory if not outright ignorance one generation has for what its predecessor experienced.

Indeed, the Ignorance Factor has obscured another truth. The Jewish people have had to be tenacious, strong-willed, possibly over-bearing, probably pushy to accomplish one simple, yet spectacular goal—to survive. If Jewish mothers tend to exhibit such stereotypes in some of their actions, then it is because for centuries they have been confronted with the need to learn and practice the art of survival.

And while Jewish sons and daughters have a right to question and criticize their upbringing, one can only feel that a too-strong reaction, especially in the arena of public media, will be misconstrued by others (Goldberg's Law, remember) and will simply reinforce those negative Jewish images and stereotypes that have swirled around all Jews—child and parent alike. Jewish self-criticism is admirable, but, conducted in front of a mass audience, it is playing with the fire of centuries.

Ironically, those who stereotype the Jewish mother are themselves susceptible to being stereotyped. The self-pitying Jewish artist is now almost as much a cliché as his mother. Leon Uris, the author of such novels as *Exodus*, recently remarked to an interviewer that he was not interested in writing about how the world and his Jewishness might have done him wrong. "The market is glutted with the self-pitying prose of the Jewish writers. There is so much good about being Jewish . . . (that) I can't waste my time with that other junk."

Sophie Portnoy, I feel, would have applauded such a statement. "Leon," she would have said to Mr. Uris, "I want you to talk to Alex."

GOLDBERG'S LAW

*If anything can be misconstrued about
the Jews, it will be ... and has been.*

Exhibit G: JEWISH PRAYER SERVICES

JEWS ONCE RAN THE RISK OF BEING EXECUTED FOR SAYING A CERTAIN
PRAYER—AND A JEWISH COMMUNITY WAS ATTACKED FOR SIMPLY BLOWING
THE SHOFAR

Throughout history, Christians often believed that Jews cursed Jesus and Christianity in their prayers. For this reason, great exception was taken at times to *Alenu*, the prayer that closes the synagogue service. It was charged that the reference in this prayer to those who "bow down to vanity and emptiness and pray to a god who saveth not" was meant to disparage Jesus and his followers. To clinch this argument, attackers of the Jews who knew Hebrew pointed out that the Hebrew for "emptiness" and "Jesus" have the same numerical value. As a result, censors of the Inquisition often blacked out the passage in prayer books, Frederick I of Prussia decreed in 1703 that it was unlawful to say (and put police in the synagogues to make certain his order was followed), and Frederick II ruled (1750) that the Jews in Prussia ran the risk of being executed for saying the prayer.

To forestall any problems, Ashkenasic Jews finally deleted the reference from their prayer books, which to this day do not contain the offending passage. Ironically, the *Alenu* prayer proclaims God as King over a mankind united in His service.

Even the shofar, the ram's horn blown on Yom Kippur and Rosh Hashanoh to awaken Jews to repent their sins, has come in for misunderstanding. In Mainz, for instance, the blowing of the shofar actually had to be suspended for a time because the Christian population thought it was a signal for the Jews to revolt—and had attacked the Jewish community to prevent an uprising.

VIII
Sticks and Stones May Break Your Bones, But Names Can Kill You

*Warning: Mankind has shown
that false images
can be dangerous to life*

FACT: The legend of the Wandering Jew has been so persistent that in 1940, a man claiming to be the Wandering Jew visited the New York Public Library to do research on himself.

FACT: During the nineteenth century, a group of French psychiatrists declared that Jews psychologically were unable to settle down and had a need to wander.

FACT: Not only did Christians engage in moneylending along with the Jews during the Middle Ages, but Christian moneylenders often charged higher rates—as high as 500 percent interest.

FACT: A book claiming to show a Jewish plot to control the world has been termed as next to the Bible the most widely distributed book in the world.

FACT: Henry Ford's promotion of anti-Jewish literature so impressed Adolf Hitler that he kept a picture of Ford on his desk.

> The victor will never be asked if he told the truth.
> —ADOLF HITLER

IF ONE COULD take a voyage into the mind of the typical anti-Semite, what would one find there? I believe that among the mental cobwebs, the worn flooring of logic, the battered boxes of outdated ideas, would be found three basic images of the Jews. Flashing every so often onto the torn screen at the back of the anti-Semitic mind would be the picture of the cursed Jew as Wanderer, the cunning Jew in business accumulating money, and the secretly powerful Jew bent on gaining control of the world.

How each of these images arose, took hold, and has resisted rebuff is a fascinating look at the Ignorance Factor at work over the arching span of centuries—in which even some of history's leading figures have succumbed to the inevitability of ignorance.

The truly odd aspect about these images of the Jew is that they contradict themselves. And what adds to this Jewish paradox is that these contradictions have not diminished or lessened the persuasiveness such images seem to have had for so many people over so long a period of time.

Consider, for instance, one of the western world's most persistent legends—the legend of the Wandering Jew. By means of this story about one Jew has been conveyed the image of all Jews as cursed, bedraggled, rootless, objects of scorn. And do not be misled by the ancientness of the tale: it has had and continues to have a considerable impact, for so popular has this myth been that it is commonplace in most languages and, as a name, has also been given to a plant (which literally does wander), a card game, dice game, and a bird.

According to the legend, just before the crucifixion of Jesus a Jew had scorned Jesus and as a result had been condemned to wander the earth until the second coming. (Jesus, told by this Jew to "Go, go thou tempter and deceiver" is said to have replied, "I go, and you will await me until I come again.") No one seems to have questioned why Jesus, who taught humility in the face of persecution ("turn the other cheek," remember), should have uttered such an un-Christian curse at a man who knew not what he was doing. But the myth of the Jew forced to wander the world took tenacious hold.

It should be obvious why. The tale explained why the Jewish people were sent into exile (it was seen as punishment for rejecting Jesus as the longed-for messiah, an interesting misconception itself because the Jews had already been exiled once before and had already lost control of the land to Romans). It also offered a way to corroborate the Gospels: if a Jew really had been condemned by Jesus to walk the earth, never die and never find rest until Jesus would return, then the spotting of the Wandering Jew would be confirmation of the Christian belief.

The earliest written mention of the Wandering Jew is in a thirteenth century manuscript in which it was reported that he had been spotted. The myth became so prevalent that soon the Wandering Jew was said to have been sighted, like some medieval UFO, in such countries as England, Sweden, Denmark, Germany, Lithuania, Switzerland, and the Ukraine. People even emerged claiming to be the Wandering Jew. Some of the cities in which this occurred were Florence (1320 and 1411), Hamburg (1542), Toledo (1547), Prague (1602), Paris (1604), Brussels (1640), Leipzig (1642), Breslau (1646), Amsterdam (1700), Cambridge (1710), Munich (1721), and London (1818).

One of the more celebrated of these occurrences took place in England at the turn of the eighteenth century. As related in *Curious Myths of the Middle Ages* by Sabine Baring-Gould,[1] the man "was listened to by the ignorant and although despised by the educated," he "managed to thrust himself into the notice of the

---

[1] Baring-Gould, a pioneer British folklorist, was an unusual man. Living to the age of ninety, he wrote 140 books and the famous hymn, "Onward Christian Soldiers." *Curious Myths of the Middle Ages*, which begins with the article on the Wandering Jew, is a collection of his essays first published in two series in 1866-68. The book proved so popular that it appeared in many editions over a period of fifty years. A recent edition appeared in 1967, a hundred years after he first wrote about the myth of the Wandering Jew.

nobility, who half in jest, half in curiosity, questioned him and paid him as they might a juggler." He must have given them a good show because he declared that he had been an officer of the Sanhedrin back in the days of the crucifixion, and had struck Jesus when Jesus emerged from Pilate's judgment-hall. He said he remembered all the apostles and just to prove his point he "described their personal appearance, their clothes, and their peculiarities." He also let everybody know that he was in Rome when Nero burned it down, and knew Saladin and Tamerlane. For good measure, he could also give "minute details of the history of the Crusades."

He showed one ability that perplexed his audiences: he could speak many languages and seemed to know a lot about numerous foreign places, a certainly handy set of information for one who was asserting to have wandered over nearly all the world. As a result, "Oxford and Cambridge sent professors to question him, and to discover the imposition if any." What they found is not known, but "he shortly after appeared in Denmark, thence travelled into Sweden, and vanished." [2]

But the Wandering Jew myth was so strong that sightings of unidentified Wandering Jews continued to occur, and various people, obviously seduced by the clarion call of the legend, would come forward to claim the mantel of the eternally traveling Jew. So filled are historical accounts with these stories that Baring-Gould, writing in the 1860s, said he had intended to conclude his article "with a bibliographical account of the tracts, letters, essays, and books, written upon the Wandering Jew; but I relinquish my intention at the sight of the multitude of works which have issued from the press upon the subject. . . ." And yet, appearances of Wandering Jews have continued, even in the United States. In 1898 he was reported seen in upper New York State, and in 1940,

---

[2] Not only are there well over 100 different folk tale versions offering many variations of when the Wandering Jew appears, how he looks, what he eats, what happens when he appears (German legend had it that the Wandering Jew had given the Germans cholera and syphilis), but the name by which he was most popularly known was Ahasuerus, a cant name for the Jew through its association with the Purim story. But as anyone who knows the Purim story is fully aware, Ahasuerus is the name not of a Jew, but of the Persian king who made Esther his queen, saved the Jews in his kingdom, and thereby prevented the Jews from being killed or forced to wander. A small but interesting example of the Ignorance Factor at work.

an insurance agent appeared at the New York Public Library claiming to be the Wandering Jew. He spent time at the library reading about "himself" and, probably to make certain that everyone got the message, had a visiting card printed with his name: "T.W. Jew."

The Wandering Jew myth may seem harmless, but beneath its surface ludicrousness lurks the fostering of several disturbing Jewish stereotypes, as well as a false reading of history. Baring-Gould, in summing up his look at the many accounts of Wandering Jews, wrote: "It will be seen at once how wanting they are in all substantial evidence which could make us regard the story in any other light than myth.... But no myth is wholly without foundation, and there must be some substantial verity upon which this vast superstructure of legend has been raised. What that is I am unable to discover." But as can be seen from an understanding of the Ignorance Factor, which reminds us how the world is built on misconception, "this vast superstructure of legend" has in this case been erected on several key erroneous concepts about the Jews.

This myth enables the world to embrace the historical fallacy of the Jewish exile from the Promised Land as being timed with and a permanent result of the Jewish rejection of Jesus, to continue to place on the Jewish people the same curse as that placed on the murderer Cain—to wander—thereby linking the Jews again to the killing of Christ, and to cast a symbolic figure of the Jews as bedraggled and rootless, an object of scorn. The Wandering Jew was seen as representative of all Jews, and the legend helped perpetuate stereotypes about the Jews, who were seen as wanderers, too. In fact, toward the end of the nineteenth century, the Parisian school of French psychiatrists, under J.M. Charcot (1825–93), advocated the theory that Jews were racially disposed to the "neuropathy" of traveling and nomadism and that the Wandering Jew was simply illustrative of their "irresistible need to move around, to travel without being able to settle anywhere." Charcot even commissioned one of his aides, Henry Meige, to study the Wandering Jew phenomenon. In the doctoral thesis that resulted, Meige termed the Wandering Jew "the prototype of the neuropathic Jews wandering around the world" and wrote: "Let us not forget that they are Jews and that it is in the character of their race to move about. . . ."

Of course, what these men of psychiatry overlooked and what the legend's emphasis on wandering very nicely forgets is that the Jews have not done the wandering on their own—they've been pushed around the globe by an interesting machine of history called expulsion. England, Spain, Portugal, Russia, France, Germany—all these countries as well as others at one time or another expelled their Jewish populations. A myriad number of cities also evicted their Jewish inhabitants. What drove the Jews was not some hidden psychological delight in packing their belongings into moving vans every so often and going on their picaresque way. The Jews didn't just pull themselves up and leave. They were shoved.[3]

But if the Jews have been viewed as the bedraggled wanderers of the world, they have also quite paradoxically been seen as rich, ruthless in business, controllers of banks, and consumed with a desire for making more money. The major reason for this picture of the Jew has undoubtedly been another legacy from the Middle Ages—the medieval stereotype of the Jew as the harsh moneylender and usurer, the very Shylock that appears in Shakespeare's *Merchant of Venice* to demand his "pound of flesh" when the Christian cannot repay his loan. Such an image contains its own irony—for the Christian world had forced Jews into moneylending, and even where Jews were not involved in moneylending the stereotype continued to grow and cause the Jews great distress. Indeed, when Shakespeare wrote his play with the moneylending Jew as villain, no Jews had lived openly in England for

---

[3] The Wandering Jew myth, emphasizing as it does the supposed rootlessness of Jews, makes it all the more ironical that the one who would write the famous song about the glories of settling down—"Home, Sweet Home"—was part Jewish. John Howard Payne, the composer, was the grandson of a German Jew, named Isaacs, who converted to Christianity. On Payne's tombstone is the inscription, "An Israelite indeed in whom there was no guile."

[180]

three hundred years, and throughout Europe Christian banking houses were the principal moneylenders.[4]

Why has the moneylender image stuck to the Jews with such intensity?

We must first begin with a look at the image not of the moneylender but of money.

Mankind has always had ambivalent feelings about money. While the human being has desired wealth, his better instincts have questioned the mindless pursuit of material possessions. Christianity, especially, has emphasized this disparity between the spiritual and the mundane. "It is easier for a camel to go through the eye of a needle, than for a rich man to enter into the Kingdom of God" is just one of the sayings of Christianity that highlights its distaste for those steeped in wealth. And Paul showed his contempt for the accumulation of riches when he declared, "The love of money is the root of all evil." [5]

Thus, any group of people associated with the business of money in the early days of feudalism's transformation into capitalism ran the risk of being mistrusted and hated—and indeed we find that Christians who engaged in moneylending, such as the Lombards, were hated. But Jews had an added problem in being associated with moneylending just because they were Jewish. The Jews had already been pictured in Christian scriptures as unduly concerned with money: Jesus is said to have driven the moneychangers out of the court of the Temple; Judas informs on Jesus for pieces of silver. Sermons would use the Israelites' worship of the Golden Calf as evidence of the Jewish interest in wealth that the Christian who wished to reach Heaven should spurn.

The entrance of the Jew into moneylending, however, was brought about not by Jewish desire but Christianity's adherence to

---

[4] Here is another example of Goldberg's Law in operation. Shakespeare based his play on what was essentially a tradition in medieval tales on the continent about the usurer who demands his pound of flesh, but in the early versions of the tale the blood-thirsty moneylender is a Christian or a heathen. In several cases, a Jew is actually shown as the victim of a Christian moneylender. The source that Shakespeare utilizes, a collection of tales entitled *Il Pecorone*, marked the first time the cruel creditor appeared as a Jew.

[5] Paul's famous saying is usually erroneously stated as "money is the root of all evil." His actual statement (I Timothy 6:10) condemns the love of money rather than money itself; the fact, however, that the average person thinks the saying singles out money as the source for evil is a cogent insight into the hostility or guilt with which most people view wealth.

the Biblical teaching that usury is a sin specifically outlawed in Leviticus 25:36—"Take thou no interest of him or increase." Since Jews could lend money at interest to non-Jews ("To a foreigner you may lend [on interest]"—Deuteronomy, 12:12), during the Middle Ages the Church turned to the Jews to fill the serious commercial vacuum caused by the medieval world's steadily increasing need for loans. Vital to the economic and social revolution then occurring in feudal Europe, where a new middle class was appearing and manufacturing and international commerce was rapidly growing, were the moneylenders—the bankers of the feudal age.

That the Jew was encouraged to perform this function is surely one of the great ironies of history. For the Jewish religion was probably the one religion of ancient times to condemn usury—and here in the Middle Ages the Jews were made to practice it. Also, Jews were performing a role for Christians because Christianity was adhering to a law in the Hebrew Bible. That Jews could wind up being vilified for performing a role foisted on them by another religion following a Jewish law is a classic case study of Goldberg's Law.

The moneylending occupation was hazardous to Jewish life and limb. Rulers required Jews to pay them large portions of the profits for the right to lend money. Often, when a Jew earned any kind of wealth, most of it was taxed, fined, or taken away in the form of "contributions." Frequently, some rulers simply declared a moratorium on debts to Jewish moneylenders. The Crusaders, for instance, had the interest on their loans from "Jew-usurers" rescinded by special dispensation.

In addition, Jewish moneylenders were often imprisoned or even murdered at the request of influential debtors. As time passed, violent attacks on Jewish moneylenders grew and debtors would incite a pogrom as a way to default on loans from Jews.

Largely overlooked is that Jews were not alone as moneylenders. Although banned by the Church from moneylending during much of the Middle Ages, many Christians ignored or defied the prohibition. In fact, so many Christians were engaging in moneylending that in 1179, the Third Lateran Council had to reiterate the Church's long-standing position against the practice. Even so, enough Christians continued to operate as moneylenders that Jews actually represented a smaller and less influential group of moneylenders than the Christians. And Christian moneylenders often charged far higher interest rates, much beyond the exorbitant rates employed then because of the unusual risks of the day and many defaults (France in the fourteenth and fifteeenth centuries permitted annual interest of 40 to 50 percent). Historian Will Durant, writing in his book *Reformation* (volume six of *The Story of Civilization*), noted one of these discrepancies in loan requirements: "Jewish bankers during the Middle Ages charged an interest rate of 43 percent—but Christian moneylenders charged up to 266 percent." Actually, Christian moneylenders were known to go as high as 400 and 500 percent.

The Christian Lombards and Cahorsins were heavily involved in the lending business and were often expelled with the Jews from a country (expulsion of Jews during the Middle Ages was invariably a way for a country to rid itself of debts owed on loans).

The Jewish moneylender was actually preferred to the Christian usurer. A criticism often made of Christians involved in moneylending was that "they were worse than Jews" (a left-handed compliment to Jews, but a compliment nonetheless). It was even bemoaned that there were not more Jews to become moneylenders: "were there but Jews enough, Christians would not have to become usurers."

Jews were permitted to be the sole officially sanctioned moneylenders of Europe only until the early sixteenth century, when Christians were finally allowed to function openly as moneylenders and Jews were then shunted into less lucrative forms of lending. Pope Leo X, bowing to the ever mounting need for loans, lifted the three hundred-year ban against moneylending saying it was "holy work" because it helped the poor. But long before, St. Thomas Aquinas (1226-74), in his essays on "Usury" and "The Just Price," had recognized that Christians could charge interest, but not exact usury.

The myth of the Jew as the avaricious, heartless, cunning usurer—interested only in getting his "pound of flesh"—has proven so powerful that it is still alive today, reappearing in the supposed form of the Jew as a sharp, grasping, and greedy businessman, the possessor of wealth, the controller of banks, and—as one phone caller to a radio talk show I was on said about the Jews—the lover of the All Mighty Dollar.

Notice that the noun "Jew" has even been transformed into a verb, as in "to jew." *Webster's New World Dictionary* notes that the use of "to jew" is a colloquialism which means "to get the better of in bargaining, as by practices, or haggle with in order to get a lower price or a better bargain (usually with *down*)." Although the dictionary adds that this is a "vulgar and offensive expression, in allusion to methods attributed to Jewish merchants by anti-Semites," some dictionaries have not always referred to such a definition as "vulgar and offensive." The famed *Oxford English Dictionary*, in its second definition of Jew, states that it is used "as a name of opprobrium" and that it is "applied to a grasping or extortionate money-lender or usurer, or a trader who drives hard bargains or deals craftily." The verb form of Jew, says the great dictionary, means "to cheat or overreach, in the way attributed to Jewish traders or usurers. Hence *Jewing*," And the usury connotation of the word Jew spills over into other aspects of Judaism. According to Dagobert Runes in his book *The War Against the Jews*, the new revised edition of the dictionary of the Portuguese language published by the Brazilian Literary Academy mentions the synagogue as a "place for illegal business." [6]

This helps explain how the oft-repeated fiction could arise that Jews control the banks and "all Jews are rich." The visibility in modern times of the Rothschild family as leading bankers of Europe—and the presence of a number of German Jews as important financiers in America at the turn of the century—certainly seems to lend credence to the view that Jews are just as involved in matters of money as they were in medieval times. But again, facts do not bear out the implications of these isolated examples.

---

[6] Not only have dictionaries contributed to the bias against Jews, but so has another indispensable tool of libraries—the thesaurus. In a thesaurus, words are arranged according to the ideas that they express. It is therefore revealing to find that many thesauruses list the word "Jew" with "cunning," "lender," "rich," "extortioner," and "heretic." Contrast this with "Christian," which is associated with "charity." (See, for instance, the authorized American edition of Roget's *Thesaurus of English Words and Phrases* published by Grosset & Dunlap in 1937.)

Even when numerous Jews have had considerable wealth, far many more Jews have lived in economic distress. When Jews were the moneylenders of Europe, the overwhelming majority of Jews were wretchedly poor. Non-Jewish wealth has always far dwarfed Jewish wealth and the power it could exercise. The J.P. Morgans and the J. Paul Gettys, the H.L. Hunts and the Howard Hugheses, the Rockfellers and the Mellons have been non-Jews (indeed, most people do not even know what their religions were, but if they had been Jewish, you can be certain everyone would know).

As statistics bear out, and the personal stories of many Jews can attest, the field of commercial banking has virtually been closed to Jews. Although Jews can be found in investment houses and the operation of the stock exchanges, the figures for Jews involved in the banks of America—let alone controlling them—are shocking. In 1939, at the very time Nazis were warning about the control of Jewish financiers, B'nai B'rith surveyed the banking industry and found that out of ninety-three thousand bankers in the United States only 0.6 percent were Jewish. In the City of New York, where Jews represented 28 percent of the population, only 6 percent of banking executives were Jewish. The situation has not gotten much better over the years. In 1968, the American Jewish Committee filed an official complaint with New York City's Human Rights Commission charging that the banking industry was biased against the employment of Jews.

The most cogent comment on this, however, came from the head of the United States Senate Banking Committee, Wisconsin Senator William Proxmire. In a 1978 interview with the financial columnist for *Esquire* magazine, Senator Proxmire stated that United States banks are "controlled by the most Waspish elements ... with no Jews, no Catholics, and no blacks [running the show]. It's completely one-sided, too much Anglo-Saxon." [7]

And as for the cliché that "all Jews are rich," the vast majority of Jews are middle and upper middle class, hardly at the head of the "rich" class. It is true that Jews in general have succeeded in raising their standard of living as fast if not faster than other

---

[7] The head of the influential Senate Banking Committee made this statement in the May 9, 1978, issue of *Esquire* in the column "Full Disclosure" (page 14).

immigrant groups to America. This is something about which Jews can be proud, especially in a country that has made success part of the "American dream." Besides, what is usually forgotten is what American Jews had to overcome. It has been said that a typical Jewish immigrant family on the East Side working in the clothing industry had to sew from dawn until late into the night to earn a total family income of nine dollars a week—and ten dollars a month went just for rent.

What is also forgotten—if even known—is that many Jews today continue to live in poverty. The Metropolitan New York Coordinating Council on Jewish Poverty estimates New York City's poor Jews to total four hundred thousand—which would make it the third largest poverty group in America's largest city. In addition, there are significant pockets of Jewish poor in Miami, Chicago, Los Angeles, Philadelphia, and Baltimore, the other major American cities where Jews live.[8]

Jewish poverty was so rampant in Europe that it was one of the key motivating factors in the Zionist movement. Herzl had visualized that it would be the poor masses of Jews who would find Palestine the solution to their problem as Jews. Once Israel was established, Herzl was proved right: the impoverished Jews of Europe, Asia, and North Africa streamed into Israel. As a result, since its founding Israel has had to struggle mightily with the problem of Jewish poverty. In 1974, for instance, of the 783,000 Jewish families living in Israel, 114,479 families needed financial assistance.

Sammy Davis, Jr., the black comedian who converted to Judaism, dismissed the centuries-old fallacy of Jewish wealth in his own inimitable way: "After I decided to become a Jew, only then did I learn the Jews don't really have all the money. When I found out Rockfeller and Ford were goyim, I almost resigned."

The Church's use of Jews for moneylending has caused long

---

[8] A study by a Task Force on the Jewish Poor formed by the Jewish Federation-Council of Greater Los Angeles shocked many Jews with its 1973 report: 55,000 Jews in Greater Los Angeles—almost 13 percent of the Jewish population—were living at the poverty level (household incomes of $4,000 a year or less). Among this figure were 13,000 Jewish youngsters aged 15 to 19 living in poverty households. (*The Times of Israel and World Jewish Review*, May, 1974, "The Jewish Poor—Los Angeles Is a Shocker," pp. 55-56.)

and deep damage. For not only has it left the imprint in the public mind of the Jew associated with the unscrupulous accumulation of money, but it has led to an association of the Jew with something closely connected to money—power.

Indeed, if most people have a hangup about money, they also have one about power. It is more than coincidental, then, that we find the image of power surrounding the supposedly rich Jew, who is also, remember, seen at the same time as the poor, bedraggled, scorned Wanderer.

The specter of the powerful Jew, engaged in a secret plot to take over the world, has been a particularly vehement image ever since Jews emerged from the ghetto. Behind every turning point in the rapidly changing world of the past two hundred years has been seen by one anti-Semite or another the hand of the sinister Jew. Whether it was the French Revolution, the Russian Revolution, World War I, or World War II, whether it was inflation or the Depression, the Jews have been accused of plotting it. Even President McKinley's assassination was said to be Jewish inspired. So pervasive has been the image of Jewish power that in the days before World War II, a great American hero like Charles Lindbergh felt little compunction issuing a dire warning about the Jewish control of America. "The greatest danger of Jewish power lies in their large ownership and influence in our motion pictures, our press, our radio, and our government," he declared. That "Jewish power," however, proved oddly nonexistent just several years later when America's golden door was suddenly shut in the face of even Jewish children fleeing Nazi Europe.

Not even the Holocaust, which proved on a massive and macabre scale how impotent Jewish power really is in the world, has lessened this fiction of the powerful Jew. General George S. Brown, Chairman of the Joint Chiefs of Staff and himself a leading figure in the power structure of the United States, spoke in 1974 about "Jewish influence in this country" and how "Jews own the banks in this country (and) the newspapers," a remark that caused a storm of controversy and was so far from the truth, especially in regard to banks, that President Gerald Ford rebuked him and General Brown later openly admitted his ignorance and apologized.[9] But his statement was soon followed by that of a former Vice President of the United States, the disgraced Spiro Agnew, who to promote his first novel offered that there was too much Zionist control of America. He has not been alone. Since the founding of Israel, there has always been talk in America about a "powerful Israel lobby." [10]

How did this image emerge? How did the victimized, passive, bedraggled Jew also come to be seen as a powerful figure controlling the media and manipulating the great forces of history for eventual control of the world?

This fiction most likely started back in the days when Christianity was feuding with Judaism for adherents. The Christians accused the Jews of being in league with the Devil to stop Christianity. Jews were even said to use curses and prayers to retard the progress of Christianity. From this later emerged the Christian fear that Jews poisoned wells to try to kill Christians, that Jews secretly desecrated the host in Christian worship services, that Jews killed Christian children around Passover time to use their blood in the baking of matzoh.

The Jew was hated because he was feared, feared as a diabolical agent out to overturn Christian teachings and—as the embodiment of the anti-Christ—out to enslave, if not kill, Christians in a Jewish desire to subjugate Gentiles and rule the world.

These religion-oriented arguments against the Jews underwent a transformation in the late eighteenth century into a more secularized approach. Now, instead of being anti-Christ, Jews were seen as being anti-establishment, as desiring the overthrow of the old order (thus the French and Russian revolutions) and replacing

---

[9] At the time, some Jewish leaders questioned whether General Brown should have been criticized by President Ford and pressed to apologize. Such actions, they reasoned, would only seem to support the contention that Jews did have control of America's power structure. This viewpoint, though rejected by most Jews, was an interesting recognition of Goldberg's Law.

[10] To see how far from reality is the often repeated "powerful Israel lobby," one need only realize that never mentioned is any "powerful Arab lobby," even though Israel has only one embassy, and only one registered lobbying group represents the Jewish viewpoint, the American Israel Public Affairs Committee, while the Arabs have almost a score of embassies, several registered lobbying organizations and the support of the oil lobby. While American Jewry numbers 6 million, Arabs now living in America total a sizeable population of two and a half million.

it with their own political and social control. Instrumental in the spread of this myth was a book that may have been more disastrous for the Jews than *Mein Kampf*. It was called *The Protocols of the Elders of Zion*.[11]

First issued in 1903, *The Protocols* purported to be the transcription of twenty-four secret meetings of Jewish elders in which a Jewish plot was hatched for throwing the world into chaos to gain control of the Gentiles. The elders spelled out how the Jews would use various methods, such as democracy, socialism, communism, revolution, the press, and the arts, to replace all nations and religions with a Jewish empire.

Research soon showed that *The Protocols* was a distorted concoction using plagiarized parts of a forty-year old novel by Herman Goodsche entitled *Biarritz* and scarcely changed pieces of a fictitious dialogue found in a French political pamphlet, published in 1864 as the writing of Maurice Joly, entitled *Dialogue aux Enfers entre Montesquieu et Machiavelli* ("Dialogues in Hell"). Since it had been forbidden to criticize openly the regime of Napoleon III, Joly, a French lawyer who felt Napoleon III had ambitions of world domination, decided to present his thoughts in the form of a dialogue between Montesquieu, who would offer the case for liberalism, and Machiavelli (symbolizing Napoleon III), who would present the case for cynical despotism. Not one word of this "dialogue" mentions Jews or Judaism.

Although the author of *The Protocols* is still not known for certain, the original forgery was done in French sometime between 1894 and 1899, most probably in 1897 or 1898. This means, as Norman Cohn indicates in *Warrant for Genocide*, an in-depth study of *The Protocols*, that it was done during the anti-Semitic furor caused by the Dreyfus affair, sometime between his arrest in 1894 and his pardon in 1899. The Zion reference in the title of the *Protocols* also indicates a proximity in time to the first Zionist Congress which was held in Basle, Switzerland, in 1897. (In an example of Goldberg's Law, many anti-Semites had seen that conference, intended to restore powerless Jews to one small land

---

[11] Henry Rollin, a Frenchman and the author of one of a dozen critical studies done on *The Protocols* between 1920 and 1942, stated that after the Bible *The Protocols* was probably the most widely distributed book in the world.

in the Mideast, as a major step toward Jewish domination of the world.)

Although executed in France, the forgery, says Cohn, "is clearly the work of a Russian and oriented towards the Russian right wing." Indeed, the first appearance of *The Protocols* in 1903 was in Russia under the auspices of the Czar's secret police who wanted to use it to foment anti-Semitism. But the Czar, interestingly, dismissed the work as a hoax (he called it "vile") and *The Protocols* were not widely circulated in Russia until after the Russian Revolution.

That *The Protocols* is a forgery has been clearly and repeatedly shown. In *Warrant for Genocide*, Norman Cohn writes:

> In all, over 160 passages in *The Protocols* totalling two-fifths of the entire text, are clearly based on passages in Joly; in nine of the chapters the borrowings amount to more than half of the text, in some they amount to three-quarters, in one (Protocol VII) to almost the entire text. Moreover with less than a dozen exceptions the order of the borrowed passages remains the same as it was in Joly, as though the adaptor had worked through the Dialogue mechanically, page by page, copying straight into his "protocols" as he proceeded. Even the arrangement in chapters is much the same—the twenty-four chapters of *The Protocols* corresponding roughly with the twenty-five of the *Dialogue*. Only towards the end, where the prophecy of the Messianic Age predominates, does the adaptor allow himself any real independence of his model. It is in fact as clear a case of plagiarism—and of faking—as one could well desire.

Here, however, is another of those bitter ironies that mark the Jewish experience. For Maurice Joly's work upon which *The Protocols* is shamelessly based was actually a defense of liberalism. Joly's book was twisted by putting Machiavelli's words into the mouth of the Elder of Zion and making Montesquieu's defense of liberalism appear to be just a Jewish invention to disorganize and demoralize the Gentiles.

But even with the hoax made clear, *The Protocols* became immensely popular. Beginning in 1920, when first issued in western

Europe, this one piece of writing became, in the words of historian Salo Baron, "the most influential forgery of the twentieth century." In the years before the Second World War, translations were published in England, Spain, France, Italy, Hungary, Yugoslavia, Austria, Czechoslovakia, Poland, Belgium, Norway, Holland, Russia, Sweden, Greece, Portugal, Brazil, Japan, Germany (where the Nazis gave it wide distribution), and the United States (editions appeared in New York in 1920, Boston in 1920, and Chicago in 1934).

To show how pervasive the Ignorance Factor can be, one need only realize how much of even the intelligent world has been drawn into the orbit of *The Protocols.*

The respected *Times* of London, for instance, at first considered them possibly authentic. In 1920, after the first English edition appeared, *The Times* wrote:

> Have we been struggling these tragic years to blow up and extirpate the secret organization of German world domination only to find beneath it another, more dangerous because more secret? Have we, by straining every fibre of our national body, escaped a PAX GERMANICA only to fall into a PAX JUDAEICA?

It was not until the following year, in August, 1921, that *The Times* finally published proof—splashed across its center page on three successive days—that *The Protocols* were a lie.

Legal proceedings were also instituted against *The Protocols* so that in a court of law they could be studied impartially. Thus, in Berne, Switzerland, in 1935, a court ruled them to be "ridiculous nonsense" and "immoral."

One of the strongest believers in *The Protocols'* message of Jewry's ultimate plans was the automobile manufacturer Henry Ford. A staid individual, he worried about the changes taking place in the world and in American life and began accusing Jews of subverting traditional American ways (actually, the Model-T Ford caused as much of the changes as anything). As a result, Ford's own newspaper, *The Dearborn Independent* (circulation three hundred thousand), from May to October, 1920, published an extensive series of articles on the Jewish threat of world domination. In November, the articles were published as a book, *The International Jew: The World's Foremost Problem*. Three million copies were eventually printed and given massive promotion and distribution, especially in rural America. Eventually, *The International Jew* was translated into sixteen languages. In Germany, according to Hitler in 1923, the book was "circulated in millions," and when he heard that Ford might run for President, Hitler said, "I wish that I could send some of my shock troops to Chicago and other big American cities to help in the elections. We look to Heinrich Ford as the leader of the growing Fascist movement in America."

Hitler, who thought so highly of Ford that he put Ford's picture on his desk, even praised the businessman in *Mein Kampf* in one of Hitler's innumerable references to Jewish control: "It is Jews who govern the stock exchange forces of the American Union. Every year makes them more and more the controlling masters of the producers in a nation of one hundred and twenty millions; only a single great man, Ford, to their fury, still maintains full independence." [12]

Among the anti-Jewish charges in Ford's *The International Jew* was that "every influence that leads to lightness and looseness in Gentile youth today" was said to emanate from a Jewish source. One such result of this Jewish influence was said to be "sport clothes." Another was sex education in Russian schools, which resulted in "consequences that are too pitiable to relate." Also, all Bolsheviks were said to be Jews, and Lenin and his wife were pictured talking in Yiddish with their children—surely a model example of Goldberg's Law since Lenin and his wife were not even remotely Jewish and were, in fact, childless.[13]

---

[12] The reference to Ford can be found in the first edition of *Mein Kampf*. Interestingly, in the second edition of *Mein Kampf*, the mention of "a single great man, Ford" was changed to "only very few."

[13] Ford once even put detectives to work to see if they could uncover a secret government in the United States. One of their activities involved a great deal of effort to track down a private telephone line between the White House room where President Wilson lay seriously ill and the home of the Supreme Court Justice Brandeis, the first Jew appointed to the Court. The detectives eventually learned, after a great deal of effort, that Brandeis did not even have a telephone.

American Jewry reacted strongly to Ford's campaign. So did many prominent Americans, including President Woodrow Wilson, former president William Howard Taft, Clarence Darrow, Robert Frost, and former president Theodore Roosevelt. They were among 119 distinguished Americans who on January 16, 1921, signed a strong protest as "citizens of Gentile birth and Christian faith" that read, in part: "We regret exceedingly the publication of a number of books, pamphlets and newspapers designed to foster distrust and suspicion of our fellow citizens of Jewish ancestry and faith—distrust and suspicion of their loyalty and their patriotism."

But it took six and a half years more and the pressure of several lawsuits before Ford finally decided he had been wrong to give such publicity and backing to anti-Jewish agitation. He publicly retracted his former position and apologized to the Jewish people, saying he was "deeply mortified" that his newspaper had been the medium "for resurrecting exploded fictions, for giving currency to the so-called Protocols of the Wise Men of Zion, which have been demonstrated, as I learn, to be gross forgeries." He also apologized "for contending that the Jews have been engaged in a conspiracy to control the capital and the industries of the world...."

In November of 1927, Ford also sent a letter to the German translator and publisher of *The International Jew*, a notorious anti-Semite named Theodore Fritsch, informing him "that whatever rights you have or claim to have to publish 'The International Jew' ... are hereby revoked and terminated" and that the book's "publication, sale or other distribution" as well as "the use of the name of Henry Ford ... are hereby forbidden."

What happened in Germany? Fritsch and others simply ignored Ford's letter and went on bringing out editions of *The International Jew* with Ford's name attached to it. By 1933, the year Hitler became chancellor, twenty-nine editions of the book had been issued in Germany.

The International Jew was one of a number of writings inspired by *The Protocols*. However, *The Protocols* also had a more direct effect—causing pogroms and, in an unusual way, helping Hitler.

The pogroms that swept Eastern Europe early this century, killing tens of thousands of Jews and destroying whole communities, were fueled in large part by reaction to *The Protocols*. And Adolf Hitler was particularly influenced by the book. "I found these Protocols enormously instructive," he once said about his first exposure to the work. "I saw at once that we must copy it—in our own way of course. . . . We must beat the Jew with his own weapon. I saw that the moment I read the book." One of his early uses of the book could be seen in a 1923 speech when he publicly spoke of how Germany's escalating inflation was part of a Jewish plot. "According to the Protocols of Zion, the peoples are to be reduced to submission by hunger," he declared.

Even the widespread charges that *The Protocols* was a fraud only convinced Hitler of its validity. In *Mein Kampf*, he noted how a newspaper, the *Frankfurter Zeitung*, "moans and screams once every week" that the work is "based on a forgery." Hitler found this "the best proof that they are authentic."

But not only did Hitler find support in *The Protocols* for his anti-Jewish harangues. He actually found good advice and ideas for his own diabolical plans. He himself noted how he had profited from *The Protocols'* discussion of "political intrigue, the technique of conspiracy, revolutionary subversion, prevarication, deception, organization." In fact, so close are many of the ideas spelled out in *The Protocols* and Hitler's subsequent actions that Robert G. L. Waite, writing in his book *The Psychopathic God: Adolf Hitler*, remarks, "In reading of the alleged conspiracy of the Jews as set forth in the *Protocols* one has the feeling that one is reading descriptions of Hitler's own political ideas, plans, and techniques as set forth in his memoirs, speeches, or conversations in the 1930's or during World War II. Page after page, all one needs to do so is substitute the words 'Hitler will . . .' whenever the *Protocols* say that 'the Jews will. . . .' "

Among the examples Waite cites are how the protocols spell out that the manipulation of the people will be done through calculated terror, control of the press and education, and establishment of a Ministry of Propaganda. Also, notes Waite, "Gigantic mass meetings will be held; all those who oppose the dictatorship will have their property confiscated; civil liberties will be granted only to those who support the leader. He will be worshipped as a new god, and his 'power will excite mystical adoration.' Having crushed all domestic opposition, the leader will foment European dissension and set out on a path of conquest and domination...."

As we have seen with the development and acceptance of the Aryan race myth, despite a court case, despite public repudiation by such early advocates as Henry Ford, despite widespread dissemination of the facts about how *The Protocols* was forged, *The Protocols* gained wide audiences and, in the days before the Second World War, undoubtedly prepared many minds for a message of a total end to this "Jewish peril." But *The Protocols* have not ceased being printed—and read.

Since World War II, the printing of *The Protocols* has continued, with the Arab world one of the prime promoters, as though the 150 million Arabs in control of more than twenty nations, many of which possess huge reserves of money and oil, have to fear the power of less than 15 million Jews and one country deeply in debt. Egyptian president Gamal Abdel Nasser publicly vouched for the authenticity of *The Protocols* and his brother was publisher of one edition. Saudi Arabia's late King Faisal was said by Saudi information officials to consider it his "favorite literature" and gave copies to visiting newsmen. Muammar el-Qaddafi, ruler of Libya, who has kept a stack of them on his desk, has termed them "a most important historical document." In Beirut one year, the Arabs printed one hundred thousand copies in English and two hundred thousand in French.[14]

The myth of the Jewish world conspiracy, operating through a world-wide network of hidden agencies and organizations, controlling governments, manipulating the media, owning banks, is still very much alive—no matter what contradictory images of Jewish powerlessness and wandering imply, no matter what the

---

[14] The information on the Arabs and *The Protocols* can be found in the magazine article "Arabvertising: The New Brand of Arab Propaganda" by Jerome Bakst, head of research for the B'nai B'rith Anti-Defamation League. (See the April, 1975, cover story of *The Times of Israel and World Jewish Review*.)

Holocaust did to devastate the Jewish people and demonstrate their lack of power over governments.

Whatever names the Jews have been called—Wandering Jew, Shylock, Elders of Zion, International Banker, Money-hungry Jew—they have been a cause for hatred. And centuries of such assault on the image of the Jews had its devastating effect—it led, inexorably, to the Holocaust.

The Holocaust is the culmination of ignorance. It is the product of the long and persistent attempt to use ignorance to tarnish the Jewish image. And as we will see in the next chapter, the surprising truth is that even today, long after it ended, the Holocaust continues, in sometimes an almost imperceptible way, to damage the Jew in the minds of so many.

Let us, then, take a look at the Holocaust. Let us take a journey into the hell created by the mind of the anti-Semite.

GOLDBERG'S LAW

If anything can be misconstrued about the Jews, it will be ... and has been.

Exhibit H: THE BLOOD ACCUSATION

FOR CENTURIES, JEWS HAVE BEEN ACCUSED OF
—AND KILLED FOR—CARRYING OUT A
RELIGIOUS PRACTICE ACTUALLY OUTLAWED
BY JUDAISM

The most bizarre, yet inflammatory misconception about the Jews may be that of the Blood Accusation—that Jews kill Christian children around Passover time to use their blood in the baking of matzoh. This charge, also called the Blood Libel, has been made against the Jews in virtually every country in which Jews have resided, causing countless pogroms and untold thousands of deaths. The accusation can be found being related in Chaucer's *Canterbury Tales* (in "The Prioress's Tale"), presented in courts of law (Russia, for instance, earlier this century tried a Jew named Mendel Bellis on the charge, but he was acquitted in a case that attracted international attention), and raised as a possibility even in the United States (such as in Massena, New York, in 1928).

And yet, Jews are strictly forbidden by Mosaic law to drink blood or consume it in any shape or form. The preparation of kosher meat requires it be salted to remove as much blood as possible. An egg found to have even a drop of blood cannot be eaten.

Because of this obvious Jewish prohibition against blood, many Popes denounced the Blood Accusation. In 1247, Innocent IV issued an encyclical to protect the Jews against the charge, declaring that Jews "are falsely accused" and noting that "this, and many other fictitious pretexts" are used to "despoil them [the Jews] of their possessions." In 1272, Pope Gregory X ordered "that no Christian shall be allowed to make any allegations against the Jews on such a pretext." Martin Luther (1537), the Sultan of Turkey (1840), and the Greek Patriarch Gregory (1870), who called the charge "a disgusting prejudice," are just some of the many leaders who issued defenses of the Jews on this matter. But few were the official denunciations that stopped a mob enflamed by the ugly falsehood.

Oddly, early Christians were also accused of sacrificing children, and in later history Jesuit missionaries in China were charged with killing youngsters. But of all groups, the Jews have been exposed to this type of accusation the longest. In pre-Christian times, Apion, a well-known anti-Jewish propagandist living in Alexandria, said that Jews each year captured a Greek, fattened him up and sacrificed him, eating his entrails. The first recorded instance of Christians accusing Jews of murdering for the person's blood appeared in 1144 in Norwich, England. Several subsequent blood accusations, including one in Lincoln in 1255 where the victim, an 8-year-old boy, was later made a saint (St. Hugh), contributed to the 400-year expulsion of Jews from England in 1290.

Although unknown in the history of Islam, in 1960 the charge against the Jews finally surfaced in a Moslem paper in Daghestan: this time, though, the accusation was that religious Jews have a regular need in their rituals for Moslem blood.

IX

To Hell with Hitler: A Journey Into the Holocaust

The culmination of ignorance

FACT: While Jews were being accused of plotting Germany's severe post-World War I inflation, a non-Jew was profiting from the inflation to such an extent he amassed 25 percent of Germany's industry.

FACT: Although Hitler claimed that the Jews had made Germany lose World War I, a German Jew, who later was made Foreign Minister, offered an idea that helped Germany continue fighting the war for up to two years longer than otherwise possible.

FACT: The "Final Solution" was not decided on until eight years after Hitler came to power.

FACT: The German Army had to use more firepower to subdue the Warsaw Ghetto Uprising than to capture the entire city of Warsaw in fighting with the Polish Army at the beginning of the War.

FACT: During World War II, the United States Army's secret intelligence organization strongly advised against any attempt to assassinate Hitler.

FACT: Millions of non-Jews were also killed in concentration camps, including Catholic priests who were even subjected to some of the medical experiments used on Jews.

> If we believe absurdities, we shall commit atrocities.
> —Voltaire

THE HOLOCAUST is history's culmination of ignorance and the hatred that ignorance can arouse. The centuries of misconceptions, stereotypes and falsehoods about the Jews caused a slow, but inexorable, murder of a people's image. The Holocaust brought the vicious process to its illogical conclusion.

Indeed, we can find in the origins and operation of the Holocaust the utilization of every stereotype and fiction about the Jew—from his being labeled as inferior to his being called a usurer, from his being taunted as an avoider of military duty to his being charged as a starter of wars. And the ludicrous contradictions never stopped the Nazi onslaught. They who set out to conquer the world accused the Jews of plotting to dominate civilization; they who massacred children without compunction charged the Jews with the ritual murder of Christian youngsters; they who robbed the wealth of Europe and stole the property of Jews labeled the Jews as money hungry; they who invented the propaganda technique of the Big Lie termed the Jews unscrupulous; they who used slave labor declared the Jews to be parasites; they who called themselves the Master Race castigated the Jews for referring to themselves as the Chosen People; they who called the Jew an inferior being criticized the Jews for having too much influence over the arts and sciences of the nation.

All these accusations and more were used in a murderous assault on the image of the Jews. And in the process, truth was turned upside down. For instance:

- The Jews, charged Hitler, had made Germany lose World War I, but prominent among those who helped Germany fight as long as she did was Walter Rathenau, a German Jew who later became Foreign Minister. Rathenau had the idea for a War Raw Materials Department. This group, which consisted of Rathenau, a retired colonel, and five assistants, ensured a supply to Germany throughout the war of first metals, then chemicals, wool, rubber, cotton, and leather. Wrote Otto Friedrich in *Before the Deluge*, a book about Germany between the World Wars, "Rathenau's organization enabled Germany to continue the war at least a year, perhaps two years, longer than would otherwise have been possible."

- Even Germany's dynamic growth prior to World War I, which enabled her to wage that war, was made possible in large part by Jews. Gerson Bleichröder, the banker, provided Bismarck with the necessary credit for the Franco-Prussian War. Albert Ballin developed the maritime trade for Germany. Emil Rathenau, father of Walter Rathenau, bought the German rights to Edison's electric light, founded the German counterpart of General Electric, and helped modernize Germany through the electrification of the country. Fritz Haber freed Germany from reliance on importing nitrogen for explosives and fertilizers when he discovered the chemical process for extracting nitrogen from the air. Not only did his discovery aid the German military, but it also increased German domestic food production and better enabled Germany to feed herself in spite of the Allied blockade of 1914–19.

- Following World War I, Walter Rathenau went on to serve as Germany's Foreign Minister during the difficult days of trying to rebuild the nation. As a German, he was one of the most nationalistic of Germany's foreign ministers; as a Jew, he was one of the most highly assimilated of Jews. Yet, he was eventually assassinated by German radicals who accused him of being part of the Jewish plot to dominate the world.

- In the 1920s, the Jews were charged with creating—and benefiting from—the inflation ravaging Germany. Yet, as Stefan Lorant points out in *Sieg Heil!*, "the greatest inflation profiteer was not a Jew, but Hugo Stinnes, Germany's most prominent industrialist." In fact, at one point Stinnes owned a thousand different enterprises and enough mines, factories, and real estate that he "amassed about 25 per cent of all the nation's industry."

- Hitler always accused Jews of being parasites, of taking from Germany but not giving enough in return. And yet, by the 1930s, one fourth of all Germany's Nobel Prizes had been won by German Jews. (And of the Jews who had to flee Europe under the Nazis, another six later won the Nobel Prize in their adopted homelands.)
- While Hitler was accusing the Jews of plotting both the First and Second World Wars, the Jews were also being labeled as un-German because they wanted to outlaw war. As noted in *The 12-Year Reich*, Dr. Wilhelm Stapel, the *volkische* writer, charged in a 1932 broadcast that the Jews were corroding the nation by advocating the abolishment of war, since national-minded Germans had always acknowledged war as a creative force.
- And then, late in World War II, while European Jewry lay prostrate and most had been killed, the Nazis whipped German anti-Semitism even higher by claiming that Henry Morgenthau, Secretary of the Treasury in the United States, and Ilya Ehrenburg, a Jewish journalist in the Soviet Union, were manifestations of the Elders of Zion engaged in a conspiracy to destroy Germany.

And yet, although Nazi anti-Semitism was especially virulent, there is an eerie sameness about the discrimination Hitler visited on the Jew. A number of the Nazi-promulgated Nuremberg Laws of 1935 can be found to have their antecedents in laws passed in 1215 by the Fourth Lateran Council, an international Christian conference convened by Pope Innocent III. Here, 720 years before the Nuremberg Laws, it was decreed that Jews should be set apart from the general populace. To prevent any confusion about who was a Jew, the Council ordered that Jews should be made to dress in a way that would mark them as Jews ("such a confusion has grown up that they [the Jews] cannot be distinguished by any difference.") While this is an obvious instance of Goldberg's Law—after all, Jews have also been accused of dressing and looking too different—to add insult to Goldberg's Law, however, the Council used the Hebrew Bible as support for its order that Jews "be marked off in the eyes of the public from other peoples through the character of their dress." Said the Council: "It may be

[204]

read in the writings of Moses that this very law has been enjoined upon them."[1]

But the key factor here is that as a result of this decree, various states ordered Jews to wear a "badge of shame" on their clothing. Often, that badge was yellow, since yellow symbolized perfidy and was associated with prostitutes. Eventually, the Nazis required Jews to wear a similar badge—the yellow Star of David.

Another law handed down by the Lateran Council was that Jews could not be appointed to public offices, especially where they could impose penalties on Christians. "Since it would be altogether too absurd that a blasphemer of Christ should exercise authority over Christians ... we forbid that Jews be preferred for public offices since by pretext of some sort they manifest as much hostility to Christians as possible." (Here is a good case of Freudian projection: Christians based their hatred of Jews on the supposed Jewish hatred of Christians). This decree, which really had its antecedents in the Theodosian Code of 439 and the Third Council of Toledo in 589, persisted so long in the consciousness of Europe that such a law remained on the statute books of Poland until March, 1931—and was revived by the Nazis.

The degree to which the Nazis first sought to complete the destruction of the Jewish image before launching the destruction of the Jews themselves (the order for the "Final Solution" was not officially promulgated until 1941, eight years after Hitler became chancellor) can be seen in how the Nazis tried to pervert the innocent ignorance of children. A book of nursery rhymes published under the Nazis displayed on the first page in bold type: "The father of the Jews is the Devil." Two years after Hitler took power, *The Protocols of the Elders of Zion* was made required reading in all German schools. In 1935 in Nuremberg, one million German children swore "eternal enmity" to the Jews.

Consider a school essay written in January, 1935, and printed in

---

[1] The statement being referred to is Numbers 15:37–41, which is the law of *tzizith*, the wearing of a fringed garment. The Church law, however, said nothing about the use of fringes, but referred instead to the wearing of such non-Biblical items as badges and odd types of hats.

[205]

Der Stürmer, the anti-Semitic newspaper published in Nuremberg. The student's class had been instructed to write on the topic, "The Jews are our Misfortune." Notice how the Jew has been reduced from a human being to "vermin" (top Nazis spoke the same way for an obvious reason: it is easier to kill vermin than people).[2] Note, also, the number of centuries-old fallacies about the Jews that surface here in the mind of a youngster:

> Unfortunately many people today still say, "God created the Jews too. That is why you must respect them also." We say however, "Vermin are also animals, but we still destroy them." The Jew is a half-caste. He has inherited characteristics of Aryans, Asiatics, Negroes and Mongols. In a half-caste the worst characteristics predominate. The Jews have a wicked book of laws. It is called the Talmud. The Jews look on us as animals as well and treat us accordingly. They use cunning tricks to take away our wealth. The Jews ruled in the court of Karl of Franconia. That is why Roman law was introduced. This did not suit the German peasants; it was not a law for the Roman townsman-farmers either, but a Jewish merchant law. The Jews are also certainly guilty of the murder of Karl of Franconia.
>
> In Gelsenkirchen the Jew Gruenberg sold us rotten meat. His book of laws allows him to do that. The Jews have plotted revolts and incited war. They have led Russia into misery. In Germany they gave the Communist Party money and paid their thugs. We were at death's door. Then Adolf Hitler came. Now the Jews are abroad and stir up trouble against us. But we do not waver and we follow the *Fuehrer*. We do not buy anything

---

[2] As an insight into the Holocaust, it must be noted that as part of the destruction of the Jewish image, the Nazis had to reduce the Jew from a human to subhuman level. This was particularly important because, in truth, on a one-to-one basis, many Jews were liked by Germans. In 1943, Heinrich Himmler spoke of the problem of exterminating Jews because "each one" of "80 million worthy Germans . . . has his 'decent' Jew. Of course the others are vermin, but this one is a first-rate Jew." Among Germans who had their "decent Jew" was Hitler's mistress Eva Braun, who interceded with Hitler to rescue several of her Jewish friends. Even Hitler had a "decent Jew"—Dr. Eduard Bloch, the Hitler family doctor during his youth. With Hitler's permission, Dr. Bloch was allowed to leave Austria after the Nazis took control and go to America.

from the Jew. Every penny we give them kill one of our own people.

Heil Hitler.[3]

And it was not only children who could be affected easily by Nazi propaganda. William Shirer, a foreign correspondent in Germany during the early days of Hitler's power, writes in his monumental work, *The Rise and Fall of the Third Reich,* that he could feel himself being drawn in by the Nazi assault on the mind. Even though he had daily access to foreign newspapers and radio broadcasts from the BBC, his job necessitated his spending hours each day going through German newspapers, listening to radio reports, meeting Nazi officials and attending party meetings. "It was surprising and sometimes consternating to find that notwithstanding the opportunities I had to learn the facts and despite one's inherent distrust of what one learned from Nazi sources, a steady diet over the years of falsifications and distortions made a certain impression on one's mind and often misled it."

In Hitler's thinking, all Jewish actions became twisted. Thus, "freedom of the press" is "their (the Jews') term for poisoning and lying to the people" *(Mein Kampf,* page 245). The Jew is smart? Yes, concedes Hitler, "but his intelligence is not the result of his own development, but of visual instruction through foreigners" *(Mein Kampf,* page 300). The Jew is charitable? True, but "the Jew, despite all his love of sacrifice, naturally never becomes personally impoverished" *(Mein Kampf,* page 314).

Hitler's anti-Semitism was so deep and virulent that one psychoanalyst has noted that "never in history has there been such an anti-Semite." How to explain his anti-Semitism has also been baffling. "Is there any possible way for the historian to explain that historical fact?" asks Robert G. L. Waite in his essay on Hitler's anti-Semitism in *The Psychoanalytic Interpretation of History.* "Maybe not. There are some historical facts that defy explanation, and this may be one of them."

---

[3] See *The Yellow Star: The Persecution of the Jews in Europe 1933-1945,* where this essay is reprinted on pages 18-19. The book was compiled by Gerhard Schoenberner, a non-Jew who was born in Germany in 1931 and is today a political writer in West Germany.

[207]

Everything Adolf Hitler did in the political arena at one point or another centered around the Jews. It has been noted by many historians how Hitler's very first political speech as well as the last sentence of his last will and testament contain charges against the Jews. Even the swastika symbolized for Hitler the battle between the pure Germanic race and the inferior Semitic Jew. In writing about the Nazi flag, he said the swastika represented "the mission to struggle for the victory of the Aryan man and at the same time the victory of the idea of creative work, which is eternally anti-Semitic and always will be anti-Semitic." Albert Speer, Hitler's armaments minister, writing in *Spandau: The Secret Diaries* tells of how Hitler "was capable of tossing off quite calmly, between the soup and the vegetable course, 'I want to annihilate the Jews in Europe'" (page 25). While other top Nazis complained that Julius Streicher, the editor of the wildly anti-Semitic newspaper *Der Stürmer* had a tendency to go too far (he once actually devoted an entire issue to the discredited blood libel accusation), Hitler declared that Streicher had "idealised the Jew. The Jew is baser, fiercer, more diabolical than Streicher depicted him" *(Hitler's Secret Conversations*, page 168).

Hitler may have had his own emotional and political reasons for hating Jews, but the way in which he was able to arouse anti-Semitism in so many others showed to what extent the Ignorance Factor had already warped the European mind about the Jew. For the Jews, seen for so long as devil, deceitful, and degraded, were an alien being the populace was so used to hating that given a scientific rationale (Aryanism) and the encouragement of a government (Nazi Germany), the furies of anti-Jewish terror were unleashed in Europe as never before. Indeed, it is more than coincidental that the Holocaust came when a godless regime took control of a sovereign European nation. Although much of the dislike and distrust of the Jews had been fostered, if inadvertently, by centuries of Church policy, still the Church had not engaged in a systematic attempt to annihilate the Jewish people. Once the restraining influence of the Church was thrown aside, the stage was set for a whirlwind of prejudice stirred up easily and continuously by misinformation and misconception about a small, defenseless minority. A Hitler, arousing the passions and fears of people so long schooled to hate and fear, could therefore find a following to accept his vision of the extermination of an entire people. Because what he asked was not the murdering of Jews, but the murdering of the people's image of the Jews. Hitler aroused the populace to destroy not Jews, but usurers; not Jews, but Shylocks; not Jews, but plotters of world dominion, and international bankers, and heartless merchants, and possessors of a vindictive religion of "an eye for an eye" law, and despised cowards, and ...

It was this full-scale attack on everything and everyone Jewish, dredging up and screaming about every fiction and fallacy held about Jews for centuries, that enabled the Nazis to wreak such devastation on the Jewish people and cause such despair and destruction to so many. Indeed, the depth of the tragedy can possibly be glimpsed in a scene pictured in the book *New Lives*, which contains the reminiscences of several concentration camp survivors. One former prisoner remembered seeing "ladies who had been very spoiled, of very old, very educated Jewish families, who died as no criminal in a prison has ever died; lying on straw so foul it could not be cleaned."

But in warped Nazi thinking, these ladies were criminals—just because they were Jewish.

Ironically, the effects of the Holocaust linger on, causing in its aftermath yet another assault on the Jewish image. Not only must the Jewish people carry on without six million of their brethren (can you imagine what an additional six million Jews living today would do for the security of the Jewish people?), but decades after the Holocaust, despite having fought valiantly for their homeland in four major wars with the Arabs, the Jew is still troubled by a lingering question of the Holocaust—why didn't the Jews fight back? Why did so many of European Jewry allow themselves to be led, as the refrain goes, like lambs to the slaughter?

I believe that the very question itself is evidence of how ingrained are the stereotypes about the Jews, because it is the old image of the Jew as too cowardly or physically inept to defend himself, too much involved with intellectual concerns rather than manual labor, that enables the world—and even Jews themselves—to debate what other Jewish reaction could have been possible during the Holocaust. For a realistic examination of the Holocaust will show that the Jewish reaction could not have been different.

Most defenses of the Jews on this topic usually try to point out that Jews did try to fight back, and offer such examples as the Warsaw Ghetto Uprising. Here, during Passover of 1943, the twenty-five thousand Jewish remnants of four hundred thousand Jews stuffed into a small ghetto for several years at starvation levels rose up to battle heavily armed Nazi troops in a struggle that the Nazis thought would take three days to put down, but ran five weeks. In fact, the Jews put up such a fierce battle that the Germans had to use more firepower to subdue the Jews of the Warsaw Ghetto than to capture the entire city of Warsaw from the Polish army at the beginning of the war in 1939.

This was not the only Jewish revolt against the Nazis. There were Jewish rebellions against the Germans in the ghettos of Bendzin, Bialystok, Brody, Crackow, Czestochowa, Kovna, Lodz, Lublin, Lutzk, Lvov, Minsk, Mir, Riga, Sielce, Sosnowica, Tarnopol, Tarnov, and Vilna. Even within the extermination camps, under the most adverse of situations, Jews are on record as having fought back. Outbreaks led by Jews took place in Treblinka (August, 1943, knocking out the death factory which was not rebuilt), Auschwitz (where one of the crematoria was destroyed in October, 1944), Kruszyna (December, 1942), Krychow (August, 1943), and Sobibor (October, 1943, where four hundred inmates broke for freedom, sixty surviving to join Soviet partisans).

Such a Jewish response is even more incredible when viewed against one fact: 5,500,000 Russian prisoners of war, who were trained for combat, were knowledgable about the use of weapons and were by composition the very members of Soviet society best able to fight back, never engaged in a similar mass uprising against the Nazis in any of the concentration camps. Although they conducted individual escapes, the Soviet soldiers left no better record of survival than did the untrained civilian Jews. In fact, it is estimated that of the 5,500,000 Russian POWs, the Germans killed 4,000,000

But the truth is, as the figures about the Soviet soldiers show, that physical response to the Nazis by unarmed people was relatively rare and almost always ineffectual. The catalogue of Jewish rebellions can and should be made, but we are still left with the reality that those Jews who fought back represent little more than a handful when compared to the enormous numbers of victims. For instance, by the time twenty-five thousand Jews in the Warsaw Ghetto decided to revolt, over three hundred thousand Jews had already died in the ghetto or had been transported to their deaths. Many of the other ghetto rebellions either came too late or did little damage to the Nazis. Uprisings in the camps were staged virtually after the fact and with little or no hope of hurting the Nazi apparatus of destruction.

What, then, should be our view of Jewish actions—or lack of actions—during the Holocaust?

We must overcome the general and widespread Ignorance Factor about how the Holocaust was carried out and see just how the Nazis were able to murder more Jews in a brief span of time than had been murdered in all the years since the destruction of the Second Temple in the year 70 C.E. To do so, however, we must erase from our minds some of those archaic Jewish stereotypes and consider the reality of a people caught in the web of a ruthless modern police state.

The first thing we must realize is that for all his talk, threats, and prophecy, Hitler waited until 1941, almost a decade after he came to power, to throw the full machinery of the Reich behind a comprehensive extermination plan. Until then, the vacillations in the Nazi hierarchy, the absence of one dramatic, sustained launching of a program of genocide, coupled with the years of debilitating anti-Jewish edicts, had sapped the cohesive strength and affected the stamina of the Jewish population of Europe. Wittingly or unwittingly, the Nazis kept the Jews off guard until literally the end.[3]

With such a slow pace, the Nazis were able to capitalize on a fact of Jewish history. The outnumbered Jews had survived cen-

---

[3] For instance, not until 1939, six years after he came to power, did Hitler make the Jews wear the Star of David.

turies of persecution at the hands of a hostile majority by adopting a calculated policy of avoiding confrontation and conflict. As long as the Nazis proceeded in steps and phases, the Jews instinctively followed along—not out of cowardice, but out of a historic memory that this was the way to accommodate a vastly more numerous enemy and survive him.[4]

Our ignorance about this historic approach affects our understanding of its application by European Jewry in our own days.

Consider, for instance, the story of Masada, the fortress near the Dead Sea where after the destruction of the Second Temple the Jewish zealots held off the Roman legions for three years and then committed suicide rather than fall into Rome's hands. We glorify such a story today as evidence of Jewish courage, but what is forgotten is that enough Masadas and there would be no Jewish people today to celebrate that story. Acts of heroic national suicide make for fascinating footnotes in history books, but do not do much to keep a people in tomorrow's headlines.

Thus, the initial tendency of the Jews of the Holocaust was to adopt the same posture of accommodation that had enabled their ancestors to survive the long exile from a homeland. Such accommodation actually marks another form of courage—the ability to survive. Indeed, the rabbis have the proof of history to show they may be the world's greatest survival experts—Jews have endured while even the mightiest of their enemies have not. The Jewish strategy—to wait out the periodic storms of anti-Semitism rather than meet force with force—was suitable and logical for a small Jewry living amid a changing Gentile society. And Jews have not been alone in adopting passive response to the threat of violence.

Such great non-Jewish minds and leaders as Thoreau, Gandhi, and Martin Luther King, Jr., also saw value in nonviolence and passive resistance.

By persevering throughout a long, bitter and trying history, Jews have accomplished a physical feat of a different, but equally courageous sort—survival by utilizing a strategy of an eminently sensible nature. The mystical Jewish book, *The Zohar*, celebrated

---

[4] German Jews, even when Hitler came to power, continued to offer the Sabbath synagogue prayer for the welfare of the Government.

this other form of courage: "Jews are strong. Despite heathen blandishment and oppression, they adhere to their laws and customs like lions and lionesses." And Emma Lazarus, the Jewish poetess of Statue of Liberty fame, admired this kind of courage, too. As she wrote in 1882:

> Coward? Not he, who faces death,
> Who singly against the world has fought,
> For what? A name he may not breathe,
> For liberty of prayer and thought.

This was the type of physical courage that could be effective in a world that had not yet come to learn the bitter truth in Mao Tsetung's philosophy that "power begins at the end of a gun barrel."

European Jewry in the first half of the twentieth century, as indeed the world itself, was not yet prepared to deal with a nation such as Nazi Germany bent on using all the ruthless force, savage terror, and diabolic guile at the disposal of a modern state for one gruesome priority above all others—the total destruction of a people.

While the Nazi hatred for the Jew was obvious, what also fooled the Jews, in addition to Hitler's start and stop tactics, was that not since the days of Haman had an empire tried to snuff out the physical lives of all the Jews within its realm. The Jew was prepared to suffer, but like any other human being, by nature he was not prepared to die willingly. Understanding this, the Nazis, once they finally launched their extermination program, set up elaborate plans to hide the truth until virtually the moment the doors of the gas chambers clanged shut. This is where the misreading of the seeming passivity of the Jews during the Holocaust comes in. We tend to concentrate on Nazi terror in the telling of the Holocaust, but it was the calculated Nazi guile that also minimized Jewish rebellion. However, because of an erroneous stereotype of the Jew as passive victim, since the Holocaust Jews and non-Jews alike have tended to see the inactions of the Jew but not the actions of the Nazi.

Here, for instance, are just some of the ways the Germans tried to shield the awesome truth from the Jews.

The first was to keep the populace as ignorant as possible about the ultimate Nazi aim of genocide. (Note that the term "Final Solution" is itself ambiguous and was often referred to in even hazier language by the top Nazis.)

When Germany invaded Russia, for instance, the Russian Jews did not realize they were being singled out for liquidation since the first victims included not only Jews, but partisans, Russian functionaries, Gypsies, the asocial, and the insane. As even Hannah Arendt, who raised the issue of Jewish passivity in her book about the Eichmann trial, has written in that work, "Jews were included as 'potential enemies,' and, unfortunately, it was months before the Russian Jews came to understand this, and then it was too late to scatter."

And then in a clear case of the Ignorance Factor at work at its most diabolical, Arendt goes on to show how sheer lack of knowledge helped seal the doom of many Russian Jews: "The older generation remembered the First World War, when the German Army had been greeted as liberators; neither the young nor the old had heard anything about 'how Jews were treated in Germany, or, for that matter, in Warsaw'; they were 'remarkably ill-informed,' as the German Intelligence service reported from White Russia." [5]

Another irony: "More remarkable, occasionally German Jews arrived in these regions who were under the illusion they had been sent here as 'pioneers' for the Third Reich."

The crowding of Jews into ghettos was another tactic to keep the Jews off guard. By herding the Jews together, the Nazis were able to control the populace's movement, restrict their ability to rebel by cutting them off from food and weapons, and make more

---

[5] Compounding the problem for Russia's Jews was their leader, Josef Stalin, who purposely kept quiet about atrocities being committed against Jews by the advancing German army and the SS mobile killing squads, further preventing Jews from fleeing—or marshaling the resources to fight back. Since this type of behavior was shown not only by Stalin but by many Russians, Poles, Ukranians, Rumanians, and Hungarians during the war, it should be realized that European Jewry not only had to worry about the Germans, but much of the rest of Europe, too. Jews who escaped ghettos or concentration camps were often killed or reported to the Nazis by those living in the area. This is another reason why resistance or rebellion was so difficult during the Holocaust. The Jews had nowhere to go once they did rebel. For instance, of the three thousand Jews who one day fled to the forests near Tuczyn, only fifteen survived. The Ukrainians, with only some help from the Germans, had killed or captured the rest.

orderly the eventual transportation of the Jews to the death camps. In the Warsaw Ghetto, for instance, the Nazis carefully controlled supplies, restricting rations per person to 800 calories a day. As a result, starvation was rampant and typhus raged, killing tens of thousands of hunger-ravaged victims. "The inhabitants, reduced to living skeletons, slowly died and were left lying in the street where they fell," writes Paul Borchsenius in *And It Was Morning*. "The bodies of those who died in the houses were laid naked on the pavement, their clothes having been taken by the survivors." Gideon Hausner, in *Justice in Jerusalem*, says that in Warsaw "had it not been for the smuggling of food, which was punishable with instant death, the ghetto prisoner would not have survived even until the deportations." When viewed against this situation, the Warsaw Ghetto revolt becomes astonishing.

Perhaps the most subtle of all the Nazi techniques for silent extermination lay in their invention of the institution called the Jewish Council or *Judenrat*. In all the ghettos involved throughout occupied eastern Europe, the first step taken by the Nazis was to place the actual internal government of the ghetto in the hands of Jews. The Judenrat was usually composed of the sort of men who were most likely to enjoy the respect of the Jewish populace. These included the most prominent local rabbi, physicians, lawyers, merchants, and professors. The Judenrat was served by a police force composed of Jews.

Although the councils and the Jewish police received various forms of preferential treatment, the Nazis led them to believe they were performing a vital function for the Jewish community. The members of the Judenrat in turn could feel that they made the lot of the ordinary Jews easier by acting as intermediaries with the Nazis. Also, when the councils were given quotas to fill for the drafts of work volunteers being "relocated," there was some truth to the Nazi claim that Jews might improve their lot by volunteering to labor outside the ghetto. A percentage of these volunteers was indeed sent to work in factories.

The councils, however, were quite ignorant, until it was too late, of the fact that most of the drafted and volunteer laborers had been sent to the gas chambers. Even after the suspicions of Jewish Council members and policemen began to grow, most of them could be kept in line by the threat that if they did not cooperate in filling the quotas of labor transports, they or their families would have to fill the deficits.

The transportation of the Jews to the death camps was invariably accompanied by the greatest subterfuge of all. The Nazis, who could have adopted this as a moment of glory, instead went out of their way to assure the Jews they were being sent away to work or be resettled. In *Fighting Auschwitz*, Josef Garlinski, a non-Jew in the Polish underground captured by the Nazis and interned in Auschwitz for two years, shows how the Nazis camouflaged their intentions: "In the countries from which Jews were sent to Auschwitz, they were told that they were going to labor camps in the East and should therefore take as many of their valuables as they could carry. Doctors should take their instruments with them, dentists their chairs, musicians their violins. In Greece people even signed contracts with the German authorities for the purchase of lots and shops in the Ukraine."

Once on the trains, the Jews were subjected to another ruse. The German soldiers would make an elaborate display of counting the number of people in each boxcar and then select one person in each car to be responsible for any escapes. The occupants were told that if anyone were missing at the end of the trip this person would be shot. But it was all a sham. At the death camps, the Nazis, who usually loved to keep records, did not count the arriving cargo by boxcar.

To further curtail rebellion during the transportation phase of the extermination process, the Nazis sealed the boxcars shut, bolting them on the outside; inside, the passengers were packed so tightly that people could not lie down. "In summer it would be insufferably hot, in winter perishingly cold," relates *And It Was Morning* of the conditions on these train trips, which could last days, sometimes weeks. "It was not often they had latrine pails and the passengers would have to stand in their own dirt.... When the trains finally arrived at their destination and the doors were opened, there might be five or six corpses among the passengers; or perhaps a woman would have given birth to a baby."

Upon arrival at the death camps, the Jews were hardly in any condition to fight. During the previous several years, they had been subjected to continual harassment and deprivation. During the previous days, they had been subjected to the physical abuse and energy draining conditions of the locked and crowded cattle cars.

And yet, as they spilled out of the trains and into the camps, the Jews were exposed to further deceptions. A band of Jewish musicians often played music. Flowers could be seen growing in the camp. And the announcement was made that before being settled in a work area, as a health measure the people would have to take a shower in the camp's bathhouse to be disinfected. The Jews were then given bars of soap, told to take off their clothing which would be returned to them (they were even told to fold the clothes neatly and leave identification on them so they would be sure to get them back), and in a naked state (which further precluded rebellion or flight) were then herded into the gas chambers, which were built with false shower nozzles and even false drains to simulate bathhouses.[7]

Thus, as the doors to the gas chambers were swung shut, the Nazis concluded a carefully thought out, cunningly devised scheme years in the making. It was so cunning that it not only fooled their victims but years later, even today, continues to fool others. The ones who are being fooled now are those who do not see the draconian actions of the Nazis, only the apparent passivity of their victims as making the destruction of so many people possible without their putting up a substantial fight.

Besides, I have always felt that those who persist in asking why the Jews did not fight back—as if they, themselves, would have done battle in such a situation—are simply exhibiting the courage of the armchair.

At what point in this machinery of the Holocaust, for instance, should the Jews have fought back? At the beginning in 1933? But German Jewry, which numbered only 500,000, did react: many began to leave and by 1938, when emigration was no longer possi-

---

[7] To further insure secrecy, the SS men who supervised this macabre procedure had to sign a special declaration swearing silence: "About all the actions necessary in the evacuation of Jews, I must keep absolutely silent even among my comrades." Note, even in this SS declaration, the euphemism about "evacuation."

ble, almost half of German Jewry had emigrated. In 1938? Not until 1940 did the vast majority of European Jewry even live under the Nazis. Should the Jews have fought back in 1942 when the Final Solution was in full swing? But even in 1942 the German plans were secret and the Jews, while realizing that Nazi tyranny was opposed to Judaism, could believe like everyone else at the time that the Germans were a civilized nation that would stop short of total barbarism. Says Gideon Hausner in *Justice in Jerusalem*, "The systematic Nazi disavowal of their real objectives coincided with a rationalist inability to believe in them." Wrote a survivor, Nathan Eck, "The possibility of a devilish scheme to destroy us all, to the last man, did not occur in September 1942 even to the greatest pessimist."

Once the machinery of the Final Solution went into furious operation in 1942 (the first deportation from the Warsaw Ghetto began in July, 1942) it proved too late or too unrealistic for any widespread revolt by an unarmed civilian population which—remember—consisted to a large part of women, children, and the aged. The Nazi tactic of brutal revenge—it was standard procedure for the Nazis to execute ten people at random in reprisal for the death of one German—made any single display of violence against the Nazis foolhardy. In 1943, a chronicler for the Polish underground recorded in his diary for October 19 of that year how eleven non-Jewish Poles had been shot in retaliation for a German shot at the railway station, and kidnappings and more shootings by the Nazis continued thereafter. "People's reactions? Everybody talks of the executions with horror. ... Some people put down candles, sacred pictures and flowers there. ... Beyond such gestures, there is obviously no other manifestation of resistance, because there can be none. Horror rules."

The tactic obviously worked. In the case of the Poles, Hans Frank, Nazi Governor-General of Poland, was able to report to Berlin on December 14, 1943, that while two hundred Germans had been killed in June "the number went down following the measures we took, and it is now no more than ten, twenty or thirty casualties per month. We shall therefore certainly proceed with our method."

Also, because of the Nazi propensity for inflicting the harshest torture on an individual who fought back, acts of personal retaliation, even in the face of certain death, were not always reasonable. If the rationale we apply today is that more doomed Jews should have tried to kill at least one Nazi since this would have meant more dignity in death, one needs to wonder—after reading as I have done the cases of torture meted out to those who would so much as strike a German—if there is more dignity and rationality in going into a gas chamber than submitting to the indignity of a tortured death.

Fighting back as a group? Consider what happened when, in 1942, a transport of fifteen hundred Polish Jews was being led to the gas chambers. Panic broke out after a Jew working nearby told them they were going to their death. The Polish Jews turned on their SS guards, but with little effect. All of the Jews were murdered on the spot.

What about a group trying to escape once the truth was known? On the evening of May 25, 1944, a contingent of Hungarian Jews, sensing something as they were being led to the crematorium building, scattered into nearby woods. The SS merely trained their searchlights on the woods and machinegunned the Jews to death. A similar episode three days later resulted in the same carnage. As the author of *Fighting Auschwitz* remarks, "Attempts at unorganized escape at the last minute always ended in a massacre."

And what of the idea of each doomed Jew trying to kill one Nazi? In an incident that has become famous, a Jewess arriving with a transport in Auschwitz on October 23, 1943, managed to take the pistol of *Rapportführer* Josef Schillinger and shoot him to death. What was the result? The infuriated SS guards did not go through the selection process for the labor camp (which would have saved some lives, even if just temporarily), nor did they wait to march the Jews to the gas chamber, but beat and bludgeoned the entire transport to death on the railway ramp.

Even planned escapes by prisoners incarcerated as laborers in a concentration camp were not always the logical action to take. Until early 1942, when the German authorities ruled otherwise, the collective responsibility of prisoners for individual escapes was the rule in concentration camps. This meant that not only did a person take his own life in his hands when trying to escape, but literally the lives of other inmates, who would be subjected to the cruelest punishment for any camp escape. For this reason, notes Garlinski, until the policy shift in 1942, "the draconian punishment meted out in reprisal was such that the underground movement not only did not organize escapes but even forbade them."

Consider even the symbolic responses available to the Jews.

• *Assassinate a high-ranking Nazi as revenge?* In November, 1938, Herschel Grynszpan, a seventeen-year-old German Jew residing in France, became enraged after learning that his parents living in Germany had been deported to Poland. On November 7, he went to the German embassy in Paris and, in revenge for Nazi treatment of his parents and other Jews, killed the first member of the embassy he encountered—a low ranking official named Ernst vom Rath. The Nazis simply used Rath's death as pretext for the first massive assault on the Jews of Germany—a savage attack on November 9, 1938, that has been called *Kristallnacht* (Crystal Night or Night of the Broken Glass) for the great amount of damage done to Jewish shops and homes, not to mention the many Jews killed and imprisoned. The irony here is that Rath, whom Grynszpan picked at random, had never shown any anti-Semitic feelings and was actually being shadowed by the Gestapo for his anti-Nazi attitude (see the *Rise and Fall of the Third Reich*, page 430). Thus, assassination of any one person can hardly change the course of events and can be counter-productive.

In fact, when Czech partisans tried the same thing and assassinated SS leader Reinhard Heydrich, the Nazis retaliated by burning to the ground the entire Czechoslovakian town of Lidice, massacring all its men and transporting all women and children to concentration camps where few survived. The Nazi actions effectively curtailed Czech partisan activities for the rest of the war.

• *Assassinate Adolf Hitler?* This possibility was explored by the United States wartime intelligence agency—and rejected as harmful, especially if carried out by Jews. In *The Mind of Adolf Hitler*, in which is published the agency's secret psychological report on

Hitler in 1943 to assess his future actions, the author of the study, Walter C. Langer, is shown to have considered this possible end to Hitler and assessed what it would mean. Assassination of Hitler, he wrote, "would be undesirable from our point of view inasmuch as it would make a martyr of him and strengthen the legend." But then he considered what it would mean if a Jew killed Hitler. "It would be even more undesirable if the assassin were a Jew, for this would convince the German people of Hitler's infallibility and strengthen the fanaticism of the German troops and people." In addition to helping Germany's war effort, a Jewish assassination of Hitler would have simply speeded up the Holocaust. Wrote Langer, "Needless to say, it would be followed by the complete extermination of all Jews in Germany and the occupied territories."

Thus, all the tools of fighting back—clear indication of an opponent's strategy and goals, weapons, food, stamina, means of escape, logical and practical objectives for physical response—were systematically denied to the Jews.

Besides, who were these six million who, by their sheer numbers, were supposed to be able to overwhelm their oppressors—or at the very least cripple the Nazis by fighting back? Of the six million, at least one million were children. (Nora Levin in *The Holocaust* puts the figure at one-and-a-half million.) It is safe to assume, then, that another one million were elderly. Of the remaining four million, at least 2 million were women. Among the two million men surely half were unable for various reasons to take up arms—disabled, sick, chronically ill, physically unprepared (after all, the most daring and able men fled or went to fight with the partisans). This leaves approximately one million Jews who could be considered any physical threat to the Germans. This is hardly a statistically significant force, spread out as it was over the face of Europe, arrayed against a German armed force that with its Fascist allies in Europe totaled approximately twenty million.[8]

It took all the might and energy of the United States, Russia,

---

[8] Germany alone suffered three million military deaths. Altogether, the Axis powers lost six million soldiers.

Britain, France, and others over a span of six years to defeat such a force, a whirlwind of terror and destruction that so tore up Europe that upward of thirty million non-Jewish civilians also perished. And yet, Jews are still being forced today to wonder how many of those six million Jews could have been saved by acting on their own, without outside assistance from the Allied forces.

I submit that it is the lingering effects of the myth about Jewish passivity and the false stereotype of the Jew as the shirker of military duty that is at the root of the issue, for how else can we explain the deep psychological hurt Jews feel—and the openly questioning attitude of non-Jews—about the supposed inactions of Jews during the Holocaust when the doubts and the questions are being raised about a totally civilian population—most of whom were women, children, and the aged—caught in an insidious web by surely the cruelest, most satanic force of armed might in history.

This instance of the erroneous concept of the Jew, however, has had its positive effects. It can be seen in the actions of the Israeli armed forces, where Jews who were not even alive in the days of the Holocaust have fought in the Israel-Arab wars with a tenaciousness that has astonished the military experts and amazed the world. It can be seen in the famed Entebbe rescue, where the Israeli government was obviously motivated by a desire to ensure that Jews need never again feel alone, abandoned, and powerless.

Ego and pride explain much about why a person does what he does. But ego and pride are equally great motivating factors in the psyche of a nation and its people. The great irony of Jewish history may be that the desire to destroy an image, a false image to begin with—the Jew as passive and cowardly—may have helped more than any other single force to propel the Jews out of the ashes of Auschwitz and into the establishment and successful defense of their own homeland. Those Israeli jets that swooped down on Egypt and destroyed the Arab airfields at the beginning of the Six Day War were propelled, after all, by a secret weapon—the memory of the Holocaust.

But if the Jewish experience in history teaches anything, it warns that what happens to the Jews soon happens to other minorities, for all minorities can fall victim to ignorance. Thus, the first to be killed by Hitler's extermination policy were not the Jews, but actually the Germans. The Nazis tested out their gassing operation on retarded Germans in mental hospitals. In addition to the Jews, the Nazis sought to massacre such other groups as the Gypsies, Poles, Serbs, Croats, and Slavs. And then the anti-Semitism spilled over into vicious attacks on Catholics.

Hitler, born and raised as a Catholic, often spoke of his hatred of Christianity. "The heaviest blow that ever struck humanity was the coming of Christianity," he said in 1941. And he declared that the ancient world had been free of "two great scourges: the pox and Christianity." Martin Bormann, an especially close assistant to Hitler, sent an order to the Gauleiters in June, 1941, in which he discussed the Nazi position toward the Christian religion: "The concepts of National Socialism and Christianity are irreconcilable. . . . Our National Socialist ideology is far loftier than the concepts of Christianity, which in their essential points have been taken over from Jewry. For this reason also we have no need of Christianity."

And so we find, in the official transcripts of the Nuremberg Trials of war criminals, eyewitness testimony about how the Nazis destroyed churches and tortured and killed priests. "The monument of Jesus at Poznan was blown up. They destroyed the stone chapelets with dynamite; the crosses were torn down and chopped to bits; churches were destroyed or converted into theatres, concert halls (e.g., the cathedral in Gniezno), dance halls or storage places for ordnance supplies."

In numerous Polish dioceses, the Germans exported "all the Polish priests that they could get their hands on" to concentration camps where they were placed with criminals; "in very many countries they were all murdered." On September 24, 1941, the priests imprisoned in Dachau were forced to work building crematories and gas chambers: "Those priests who died were removed on wheelbarrows. The priests labored in the blazing heat and during inclement weather with no food and insufficient dress. SS troops gave the guards strict orders to use the clergy on the most difficult and hazardous jobs. Punishment was very severe for the slightest offense."

At Dachau, the Catholic priests, as did the Jews, lived in intolerable conditions. Of 1,646 priests interred in the camp, 846 died from torture. They were even used for the notorious medical experiments that took many Jewish lives. Reverend Stanislaw Wolak, who was imprisoned at Dachau for 5½ years, stated, "Of the twenty of us who were taken for experimental purposes, seven died a horrible death. Others remained crippled for the rest of their lives."

Clergymen were also put into Auschwitz, where they were used as slave laborers for road building: "The steam roller used for pressing down gravel was tended and pulled by Catholic priests only. They were whipped with clubs until they fell unconscious, and then the steam roller rolled over them and crushed them." [9]

The Holocaust, then, represents not just for Jews, but for everyone, the devastation awaiting a world in which ignorance is allowed to fester and enflame. The Jews have been history's victim until now, but does another minority now await their own Holocaust? Indeed, the question usually posed is—can the Holocaust happen again to the Jews? But now that the Holocaust has happened to the Jews, the real question, in view of the continuing turmoil in the world, is—when will the Holocaust happen to some other group?

And what about what has been lost to the world through ignorance? After all, Hitler, whose Reich Chancellory used dinnerware stolen from a Jew, robbed not only the Jewish people, but in essence all people. For the world cannot lose six million people and not feel their absence and the absence of their progeny. We have seen how among Jewish refugees who escaped the Nazis six went on to win the Nobel Prize. Among those who had been forced to leave earlier was the towering figure of Albert Einstein, who through his genius in science helped usher in the atomic age.

But Jews are also noted for their interests and abilities in medicine. What about those now nameless and faceless Jewish doctors and medical researchers who were not able to escape the

---

[9] These reports on the abuse of Catholic priests and churches can be found on pages 1074–1075 of Volume V of *Trials of War Criminals Before the Nuremberg Military Tribunals Under Control Council Law No. 10* issued by the United States Government Printing Office in Washington in 1950.

hell of the Holocaust? What about those Jewish students who would have gone into medicine, but whose careers were snuffed out with their lives? Ad what about those million Jewish children, and the children they would have had, now reduced to nothingness for the eternity of this world? Would they not have made some great contribution to the world, now lost? For as can be seen in the achievements of those Jews who escaped, the Jews of the Holocaust era possibly represented one of the world's largest pools of achievers in the arts, sciences, and medicine.

The loss of such a highly able group of people—indeed, the death of any population that numbers in the millions—must have an effect on our world, leaving us not only with a void as to their presence but as to their possible contributions.

The question must then be asked, especially since in recent decades Jews have made such great medical contributions as the polio vaccine: did the cure for cancer go up in smoke at Auschwitz?

GOLDBERG'S LAW

If anything can be misconstrued about the Jews, it will be ... and has been.

Exhibit I: TOLERATION

A WIDELY HAILED ACT OF TOLERANCE DECREED THE DEATH PENALTY FOR JEWS

The Holocaust was not the only time when being a Jew was made a capital offense. It also occurred in America—where an official governmental body passed a law calling for the death of Jews.

In 1649, the Maryland Legislature enacted the first religious liberty act to be passed by an established legislature in the New World. Called the Act Concerning Religion (Tolerance), it was widely hailed in its day for its expression of religious freedoms.

The Act, however, had one defect. While it ordered toleration for all who proposed faith in Jsus Christ and subscribed to the orthodox interpretation of the Trinity, America's first Toleration Act decreed the death penalty for certain Christian heretics, atheists, and Jews.

A Jew was actually arrested under this law. In 1658, Jacob Lumbrozo was imprisoned and was saved only by an amnesty proclaimed while he awaited trial.

X
Hath a Jew Eyes?

In conclusion . . .

FACT: Josef Stalin once planned a massive expulsion of all Russian Jews to Siberia.

FACT: Almost 80% of Americans polled in 1945 following World War II said that learning about the mass killings of Jewish people in the war had not changed their previous attitude toward Jews.

FACT: More than 15,000,000 pages of evidence about the Holocaust exist in German and Jewish sources alone—and yet the charge has been made, even by university professors, that the Holocaust never happened.

FACT: The Arabs boycotted the Walt Disney film *Snow White and the Seven Dwarfs* because a horse in the movie had the name of a Jewish Biblical hero.

FACT: Shylock's speech in Shakespeare's *Merchant of Venice* has been called a "majestic vindication of Judaism"—and yet the speech contains no mention of the Jewish religion.

> Anti-Semitism is not to be overcome by getting people to forget us, but to know us.
>
> —Meyer Levin

> Knowledge is ruin to my young men.
> —Adolf Hitler

But it did not stop with the Holocaust.

On July 4, 1946, pogroms broke out in Poland, where more than two million Jews had already perished.

On May 14, 1948, the Arabs attacked Israel—a new nation which included within its population three hundred thousand survivors of concentration camps.

In the early 1950s, Josef Stalin charged Jewish doctors with a plot to poison him and planned a massive forced movement of Russia's post-Holocaust Jewish population to Siberia. Only the dictator's sudden death from a stroke on March 5, 1953, prevented implementation of the plan, which was scheduled for March 9.

In the years since Hitler, the assault on the Jewish image—and on Jews—has continued. Yet, anti-Semitism has also undergone a transformation. Following the death of Stalin, anti-Semitism became less blatant. Instead of attacks against Jews, it became attacks against "Zionists." "Anti-Zionism" was said to be opposed to the establishment of a Jewish state in Palestine and was not supposed to be an expression of "anti-Semitism," although the objects of both were the same—Jews.

The Arabs, for instance, mount an economic boycott said to be directed only against Israel, but in reality the boycott involves all Jews everywhere—and anything that smacks of Jewishness (a ludicrous example, amply documented: the Walt Disney film *Snow White and the Seven Dwarfs* was denied entry into Arab lands because a horse in the movie was named "Samson").

The Soviet Union, cracking down harder on the practice of Judaism than on other religions, conducts periodic campaigns against its Jewish citizens, singling them out for "economic crimes" (a carryover of the Shylock image?), closing down all but a few show-place synagogues, harassing Jews in their desire to emigrate (one way has been to draft Jewish youths into the army as soon as they are of age, then later deny them the opportunity to emigrate because they now had military secrets), and moving to eradicate Jewish achievements and emphasize Jewish failings (starting in the 1950s, Soviet encyclopedias have virtually erased all earlier mentions of successful Jews).

And yet, even with all this, the level of anti-Semitism has not been the shrill kind found in the pre-Holocaust and Holocaust periods. It was as though mankind had covered its face in embarrassment and guilt at what the Nazis had done and what, by implication, others had done or not done to help make possible the deaths of so many.

But could the hiatus now be ending?

On November 10, 1975, little more than two decades after Stalin and three decades after Hitler, the United Nations voted to label Zionism, which is nothing more than the embodiment of the Jewish aspiration for a homeland, as "a form of racism and racial discrimination." Since that vote, many Third World countries and other minorities, who had previously showed support of Israel or expressed sympathy for Jewish causes, have cooled in their commitment. And Russia has seemingly increased its anti-Jewish attacks. For instance, between 1975 and 1978 more than twenty anti-Jewish books were issued in the Soviet Union. Most were in editions of one hundred thousand to two hundred thousand and were couched as anti-Israeli or anti-Zionist studies. One of the recurring themes in these books provides another example of Goldberg's Law—the charge that Zionists collaborated with Nazis during the war to insure the eventual creation of a Jewish state.

There has also been a slow, but perceptible growth in neo-Nazism in various countries. Glimmers of this can be seen in West Germany where, even though outlawed, expressions of support for Nazis have increased. Nazi groups have sprouted up in Argentina, where the Jewish community has been subjected to growing abuses. Even the United States has witnessed a petty Nazi rebirth. And the spate of books and films about Hitler and the Nazi era have been received with a morbid fascination.

Indeed, the pull of the Holocaust on humanity's conscience has weakened as the Holocaust itself has dimmed in memory. Now, one generation later, with mankind having passed through an unusual period of support for the Jews, could the reversal back to past form be taking place?

One indication that this may be happening is the recent assertion by some, including several university professors, that the Holocaust never even took place—or that the number of Jews killed amounted to no more than several hundred thousand (as though this figure were acceptable). Pamphlets have been published in a variety of languages (the title of one: *Did Six Million Really Die? The Truth at Last*) warning that it is just Jewish propaganda that refers to "German atrocities." French author Paul Rassinier has talked of "the lie of Auschwitz." Northwest University professor Arthur Butz has labeled the Holocaust "the hoax of the century." Robert Faurisson, Sorbonne professor, has claimed that no Jew was ever gassed.[1]

The issue of whether the Holocaust happened—raised not centuries later, but within decades of its occurrence—is a disheartening, grotesque example of Goldberg's Law, of how even the greatest of Jewish tragedies can be used to try to tarnish the Jewish image. For those who question the existence of the Holocaust are really out to imply that once again the Jews are engaged in an effort to dupe the world. Even the public discussion of this ludicrous issue, an attempt to rob Jewish victims even in their death, is indicative of the insensitivity and ignorance the Jews face.

To question the existence of the Holocaust is to fly in the face of every accepted method we have for overcoming our ignorance and arriving at the truth. After all, by what process do we know that anything has happened in the world outside of our field of vision

---

[1] That Jewish victims of persecution would be pursued even after death in order to erase the world's memory of them is not new. No monument to Jewish dead exists at Babi Yar, and until recently none existed at Auschwitz. Also, an ambassador at the United Nations once called *The Diary of Anne Frank* a forgery.

and before we were born? (For instance, as a classroom assignment, prove that the American Revolution really occurred.) The answer is that we must rely on others—in the form of eyewitness accounts, diaries, letters, newspaper accounts, films, photographs, the testimony of participants, and the evaluations and conclusions of reputable historians sifting the evidence created by these forms of proof.

By every one of these criteria, the extermination of millions of European Jews in a massive program of genocide can be proved. The existence of the concentration camps? We have the eyewitness accounts of soldiers from the armies of four nations who liberated these camps (including a future president of the United States, General Dwight David Eisenhower). The atrocities? We have the photographs and films taken not by Jews but by the Nazis themselves.

We have the records of deportations, confiscation of property, camp internments, and deaths that the Germans kept so meticulously. We have the testimony of survivors. We have diaries, letters, and drawings left by those who did not survive. We have a meticulous record-keeping center at Yad Vashem in Jerusalem. And we have the findings of the most impartial apparatus developed by mankind for the pursuit of truth—courts of law. In the extensive war crimes trials conducted over a period of years by the Allies in Nuremberg, and in later trials, evidence has been accepted and judgment has been rendered by impartial judges and juries.

As a result of these trials, and the documentation amassed and printed in the many volumes covering the Nuremberg War Trials and maintained in the National Archives of the United States and at the Library of Congress, the Holocaust has been called one of the most documented of all crimes. In fact, it has been estimated that German and Jewish documentation alone runs to 15,000,000 pages. And the conclusion from all this evidence and research—a conclusion reached not by Jews, but by others—is that at least 4,194,000 and as many as 5,721,000 Jews were murdered during the Holocaust (see *Documents on Nazism 1919-1945* edited by Jeremy Noakes and Geoffrey Pridham, page 493).

But ignorance and insensitivity about the Holocaust are apparent in other forms and guises. The rise of Neo-Nazism among German youth has been said to be the result of their lack of knowledge about the Holocaust: it is not taught in German schools. In *New Lives*, a concentration camp survivor recalls how a person spotted the camp number tattoed on her arm and asked why she was wearing her "laundry numbers." Was it some sort of decoration, he inquired. In disgust she told him it was her telephone number. The questioner was the dean of a law school.

And as for the impact of the Holocaust on the conscience of the non-Jew, the evidence is that many were unmoved by the Jewish tragedy. In 1945 following the war, pollsters in the United States asked people if learning about the mass killings of Jews in Europe had caused a change in their attitude to Jews. Of those polled, 79 percent replied that it had not. Only 12 percent said that it had made them more sympathetic to Jews—and 2 percent actually said it had caused them to be less.[2]

Why, it has often been asked, has there been so much anti-Semitism? Numerous theories have been offered. One theory is that the myth of the Jewish world conspiracy is at the root of much distrust and hatred for Jews *(Warrant for Genocide* by Norman Cohn). Another theory is that the early Christian teaching that Jews were evil and doing the devil's work debased the Jew and made him an object of scorn and fear in the eyes of the non-Jew *(The Devil and the Jews* by Joshua Trachtenberg). Yet another explanation offered is that Jews in the Diaspora have been unnaturally urbanized and must become more rural-oriented to lessen hostility of non-Jews, who have always been more rural *(How Odd of God* by Lewis Browne). Even such famous figures as Sigmund Freud and Jean-Paul Sartre have advanced their own theories: Christians hate Jews because they brought prohibitions of Christianity to a Gentile world (Freud) . . . anti-Semites and not the Semites cause anti-Semitism for their own personal reasons

---

[2] The results of these polls can be found in *Jews in the Mind of America* by Charles Herbert Stember and others. Another survey also conducted in 1945 found that 26 percent of the respondents actually became less friendly to Jews during the war.

(Sartre). Another recent theory: Jewish achievements are so outstanding that Jews are envied—and then hated—for their accomplishments.

All of this is reminiscent of the story of the blind men touching parts of an elephant and relating a description of the entire animal based on the part they feel. So, too, with theorizing about anti-Semitism. Each of these reasons is probably true, but only in part. All touch an aspect of the hulking beast of anti-Semitism. Yet anti-Semitism has proven too vast, complex, changing in scope and intensity, altering in form to fit a new country, century, or conditions, to easily fit one theory for all time.

One commonality about anti-Semitism, however, may be found in its implementation. Invariably, it has been a few leaders at the head of an anti-Semitic movement or at the top of a government who build on the people's general ignorance about Jews to whip up anti-Semitism for their own personal reasons—either of opportunism, greed, personal hatred or distorted religious fervor.

Thus, anti-Semitism appears to have two levels—that exhibited by the leadership of a movement who use anti-Semitism and that shown by the masses whose feelings must be aroused to make the movement work. The top leaders may very well know the truth about their accusations against the Jews. Attempts to dissuade such individuals by appealing to them with the facts would accomplish nothing more than give them pause for laughter. But the general populace has usually shown signs of being fully within the grip of the Ignorance Factor and therefore susceptible both to the misconceptions and falsehoods fed to them by their leaders and to the truth. It is with the average person, then, that efforts to overcome the Ignorance Factor can have results in the battle to combat anti-Semitism.

Of course, the existence and persistence of so much anti-Semitism makes one wonder even what the truth could do to alleviate what is so easily aroused by unscrupulous leaders. The Blood Libel, for instance, so easily debunked, so far from based on a shred of evidence, so repudiated by Popes, has had a long and virulent life. But as Meyer Levin, the novelist, has said, "Anti-Semitism is not to be overcome by getting people to forget us, but to know us." Elie Wiesel had a succinct view of this problem, once writing: "Is silence the answer? It never was."

Indeed, the answer is obvious—Jews really have no choice. The attempt must be made to tell the truth, to replace ignorance with information, because to do otherwise would invite further and even more dangerous ignorance.

The Ignorance Factor has led to another problem—the insensitivity about sullying the Jewish image. This insensitivity, which has long been in the world in subtle ways, may be as significant a problem as open acts of anti-Semitism.

Consider that area of our lives which is supposed to reflect the most shining pursuit of mankind—the arts. Yet, here we find instances of a particularly damaging anti-Jewish bias.

Great works of literature, for example, contain demonstrations of ignorant insensitivity to the Jewish people that can lay the seeds of anti-Semitism for generations. And while the point may be made that these writers are only reflecting the bias of their times, the perpetual reminder of that bias keeps it alive for our times. The towering figures of English and American literature—Chaucer, Marlowe, Shakespeare, Dickens, Eliot, Pound, Fitzgerald, Hemingway, Mencken—all offer characters or sentiments decidedly antagonistic to Jews. And that antagonism often reappears, if only by way of insensitive use, in modern dress. Dickens, searching for a villain, creates Fagin, the evil Jew. Years later, *Time* magazine, casting about for a way to subtly indicate its hostility to Israeli leader Menachem Begin, tells its readers that the pronunciation of Begin "rhymes with Fagin."

To see how a literary classic by even the world's most acclaimed author can perpetuate ignorance and insensitivity about the Jewish people, let us look closely at William Shakespeare's *Merchant of Venice*.

This is a play about a mercenary, vengeful Jewish moneylender named Shylock, who so hates a Christian merchant for insulting him that he literally seeks "a pound of flesh" of the merchant as repayment for a defaulted loan. At the end of the play, the Jew is outwitted and loses his money, his daughter (she marries a Christian), and his religion (he is forced to convert). The *World Book*

Encyclopedia, terming the play "a vivid study of greed and hatred," calls it "one of Shakespeare's most popular."

The Shakespearian creation of Shylock has dogged the Jewish people since the English dramatist wrote his play four hundred years ago. *Jews in the Mind of America* devotes a special section to what it calls the "Shylock image," noting that "the tenacious belief that Jews as a group are mercenary, unscrupulous or dishonest" is "perhaps the most significant of central images" of the Jew. And what makes *The Merchant of Venice* damaging in a subtle way is that, in addition to still being widely performed, it has been one of the favorite works of Shakespeare to be taught in the schools. It was required reading in many school systems in English-speaking countries for generations. Up through the 1950s, it was often the standard Shakespearian play taught in many of the 9th and 10th grades in America.

One can only wonder why, with so many Shakespearian plays from which to select, schools would choose *The Merchant of Venice,* knowing not only that it keeps alive one of the most damaging stereotypes of the Jews, but demands of the student a more than superficial knowledge of medieval history. Even a teacher's attempt to explain the rationale behind the play and to place it in the perspective of history so that modern day Jews are not harmed poses the very real possibility of arousing a host of other negative Jewish images. After all, we have Goldberg's Law to worry about.

In fact, this is precisely what has happened. Take an important classroom edition of the play—the Arden Shakespeare series— published by D.C. Heath and Company, one of the larger school textbook publishers in the United States. I came across a fresh printing of this edition, which was first issued in 1916, when I taught English in a Baltimore public high school in 1963 and found the book still in use. Employed by many other school systems and even colleges for decades in the teaching of *The Merchant of Venice,* the Arden Shakespeare edition tries to explain to the student the play's anti-Jewish bias, but the explanations simply lead to further problems. For instance, in informing the student why the Jews appear miserly and squalid in the play, the book's introduction offers that Jews had to fear exhibiting riches, then adds: "But this unlovely hardness of life was only assumed by compulsion. In reality, Jews have always been fond of a rich and even luxurious style of living."

As for the conflict between the Christian and Jewish religions demonstrated in the play, this is explained by an interesting rummaging of ancient history: "It must also be remembered that religious intolerance was, in the 'ages of conflict,' almost universal and was displayed by the Jews themselves on a great scale during that short period of their history when they had the power of the sword over aliens in race and religion." As if that were not enough, the point is then made that "some of the beliefs and rites of medieval Christianity appeared to Jews to be idolatrous and blasphemous" and therefore for Jews "it was lawful and right in their eyes to feel a 'lodged hate' and 'a loathing' " against Christians.

Concludes the introductory essay, explaining why Shylock was hated (italics are mine):

> Shylock was thus one of a body who in religion and in society kept themselves aloof in *repulsive* isolation, who not only declined but *abhorred* the religious beliefs of their neighbors, and who, while taught by persecution not to show signs of wealth, were at the same time accumulating precious metals, and *obtaining a great hold* over individual Christians by their system of loans.

Thus, *The Merchant of Venice*, no matter what its intrinsic literary merit, is a vehicle, if not for prejudice then for unwitting offense.

The insensitivity about tarnishing the Jewish image can well be seen in the actions of the schools in selecting this play so widely. I don't think the selection has been anti-Semitic in motivation. Instead, I believe the play has been taught so often because unimaginative educators felt here was at least one Shakespearian play even dull-witted students could be interested in: it had an easily recognizable and boo-able villain (Shylock has every attribute of the bad guy except the black hat—and if it were done in modern dress, he would have that, too).

The historic ignorance and insensitivity that Jews face can be found, ironically, in Shylock's famous speech in defense of being a Jew. This oration, coming in Act III, Scene 1, is often cited by defenders of the play to show how the great playwright provided Shylock with human feelings and the Jews with a sense of humanity rarely seen in other literary works of Shakespeare's time or before. But does the speech do that? Or is it itself symbolic of the gap between non-Jew and Jew?

Let us first look at Shylock's speech. It comes in response to taunts by his Christian adversaries:

> I am a Jew
> Hath not a Jew eyes? hath not a Jew hands, organs, dimensions, senses, affections, passions? fed with the same food, hurt with the same weapons, subject to the same diseases, healed by the same means, warmed and cooled by the same winter and summer, as a Christian is?
> If you prick us, do we not bleed? If you tickle us, do we not laugh? If you poison us, do we not die? and if you wrong us, shall we not revenge?

Notice that Shakespeare's writing here is marked by a very unusual aspect—a curious overuse of the same point. Critics have noted that Shylock is hated in the play for four main reasons—his race, religion, way of life, and manner of doing business. Although elsewhere in the play Shakespeare has Shylock react briefly to some of these points, here in Shylock's major speech Shakespeare offers only a superficial perspective on the Jews. In essence, Shylock's defense is a plea for tolerance based on the fact that he is physically the same as the non-Jew and that he therefore should be treated as a human being like all other people. This may be an advancement in thinking for an age in which the Jew was seen as an incarnation of the devil, but that is only one of the many misconceptions and stereotypes held about the Jews and only one of the criticisms made of Shylock in the play. What the Jew-hater bases his hatred on is his debased view of the Jew's religion, social practices, occupations. A defense of those images is glaringly absent here. Shakespeare, with his great insight into human nature, has given Shylock the opportunity to show the other side of his nature, but all we see is the physical side, not the moral, spiritual, *Jewish* side.[3]

Shylock's speech is one of the great pieces of evidence of how the non-Jewish world has for so long been ignorant of the Jew. Shakespeare, who may never have even seen an openly practicing Jew—since Jews were not officially readmitted into England until a half century after he died—had to base his Jewish villain not on his own personal contact or knowledge of Jews, but on what he had read or been told. Shylock, then, is the product of anti-Jewish propaganda in its most basic form—the rumor, gossip, and talebearing that hurt Jews back in the days of Rome, that harmed them in the days of Shakespeare, and that threaten to continue to damage the Jews in our days.

Indeed, the only thing that will lessen the perpetual anti-Semitism of the ages is a lessening of the persistent ignorance about the Jew. All hatred against the Jew cannot be erased, any more than hatred itself will ever disappear between people. But what must be eradicated is the continuous attempt, in whatever guise it appears, to tarnish the image of the Jew and thereby enable an unscrupulous few to build on the ignorance of many.

If future Holocausts are not to occur, the world must awaken to its ignorance—and resulting insensitivity—and rethink its ancient attitude toward people they have persecuted and condemned for so long. Shylock's speech could have helped open the world's eyes about the Jews. His words could have served as the Jewish message to the world—if but the power of Shakespeare's language would have been combined with a knowledge of the Jew.

Here, for instance, is Shylock's speech as it might have emerged had Shakespeare written it with a true understanding of the Jewish soul:

> I am a Jew.
> Hath not a Jew a noble heritage? hath not a Jew ethics,

---

[3] The D.C. Heath edition quotes F. S. Bons, in *Shakespeare and His Predecessors*, as saying that the speech is a "majestic vindication of Judaism." Where? How? There is no mention of religion anywhere in these remarks. Only in our wistful thinking about what a great writer should have done with the speech do these "vindications" appear.

morals, scruples? fed with the same Bible, hurt with the same weapons against faith, subject to the same Ten Commandments, healed by the same Almighty, warmed by the same ideals of peace and goodwill, as a Christian is?

If you prick our flesh, do we not bleed? if you mock our religion, do we not weep? if you poison our good name, do we not suffer? and if you slander us, shall we not resist lest we die?

Chapter Sources

ALTHOUGH THE Ignorance Factor indicates that to err is not only human, it is inevitable, every effort was made to insure the accuracy of facts by securing the most reliable sources on a given topic and rechecking their statements in other works and with people knowledgeable in the appropriate field. What follows, listed by chapter and exhibit, are only those sources, culled from many others, that either directly contributed information or provided supporting material or documentation. At the conclusion of the chapter listings are those encyclopedias and other reference works also consulted throughout the preparation of *The Jewish Paradox*.

CHAPTER I

Burnam, Tom. *Dictionary of Misinformation*. New York: Thomas Y. Crowell, 1975.
Friederich, Otto. *Before the Deluge*. New York: Harper & Row, 1972.
Hoover, Calvin. *Germany Enters the Third Reich*. New York: The Macmillan Company, 1933.
Massing, Paul W. *Rehearsal for Destruction: A Study of Political Anti-Semitism in Imperial Germany*. New York: Howard Fertig, 1967
McCullough, David. *The Path Between the Seas*. New York: Simon & Schuster, 1977.
Montagu, Ashley and Darling, Edward. *The Prevalence of Nonsense*. New York: Harper & Row, 1967.
Payne, Robert. *The Life and Death of Adolf Hitler*. New York: Praeger Publishers, 1973.
Poliakov, Leon. *The Aryan Myth*. New York: Basic Books, 1974.
Shirer, William L. *The Rise and Fall of the Third Reich*. New York: Simon & Schuster, 1960.

Toland, John. *Adolf Hitler.* Garden City, New York: Doubleday, 1976.
Twersky, Isadore (ed.). *A Maimonides Reader.* New York: Behrman House, 1972.
United States v. Bhagat Singh Thind. 43 Supreme Court Reporter 338, United States Supreme Court Decisions. October Term, 1922 (Argued Jan. 11, 12, 1923. Decided Feb. 19, 1923). St. Paul: West Publishing, 1924.

Exhibit A

Dimont, Max. *Jews, God and History.* New York: Simon & Schuster, 1962.
Newman, Louis Israel. *Jewish Influence on Christian Reform Movements.* New York: Columbia University Press/Columbia University Oriental Studies, Vol. XX. AMS Press, 1966.

CHAPTER II

Bean, Robert Bennet. "The Nose of the Jew and the Quadratus Labii Superioris Muscle." *American Anthropologist,* November, 15, 1913, pp. 106–108.
Evans, Bergen. *Natural History of Nonsense.* New York: Alfred A. Knopf, 1946.
Fishberg, Maurice. *The Jews: A Study of Race and Environment.* New York: The Walter Scott Publishing Co., Ltd., Charles Scribner's Sons, 1911.
Mencken, H. L. *A New Dictionary of Quotations.* New York: Alfred A. Knopf, 1942.
Oroy, Homer. *Our Will Rogers.* New York: Duell, Sloan and Pearce, 1953.
Parkes, James. *Antisemitism.* Chicago: Quadrangle Books, 1963.
Partridge, Eric. *Dictionary of Effective Speech.* New York: Grosset & Dunlap, 1942.
Patai, Raphael. *The Jewish Mind.* New York: Charles Scribner's Sons, 1977.
Patai, Raphael and Wing, Jennifer P. *The Myth of the Jewish Race.* New York: Charles Scribner's Sons, 1975.
Stember, Charles Herbert and others. *Jews in the Mind of America.* New York: Basic Books, 1966.
Taft, Kendall B.; McDermott, John Francis; and Jensen, Dana O. (eds.). *College Readings in Contemporary Thought.* Boston: Houghton Mifflin Company, 1929.

Trachtenberg, Joshua. *The Devil and the Jews*. New Haven: Yale University Press, 1941.

Exhibit B

Gunther, John. *Inside Asia*. New York: Harper & Brothers, 1939.
Sartre, Jean-Paul. *Anti-Semite and Jew*. New York: Schocken Books, 1948.
Shirer, William L. *Berlin Diary*. New York: Alfred A. Knopf, 1941.

CHAPTER III

Birnbaum, Philip. *Prayer Book for Sabbath and Festivals*. New York: Hebrew Publishing Company, 1965.
Burnam, Tom. *Dictionary of Misinformation*. New York: Thomas Y. Crowell, 1975.
Daube, D. *The New Testament and Rabbinic Judaism*. London: University of London, 1956.
"Fish." *New York Magazine*, April 10, 1978, p. 44.
Fleming, Alice. *Alcohol: The Delightful Poison (A History)*. New York: Delacorte Press, 1975.
Fluegel, Maurice. *Israel, The Biblical People*. Baltimore: H. Fluegel & Company, 1899.
Golden, Harry. *The Golden Book of Jewish Humor*. New York: G. P. Putnam's Sons, 1972.
Graham, Billy. "My Answer." *The Baltimore Sun*, February 1, 1978.
Grant, Michael. *Jesus: An Historian's Review of the Gospels*. New York: Charles Scribner's Sons, 1977.
Herman, Nolan B. (ed.). *The Interpreter's Bible, Vols. 1-12*. New York: Abingdon Press, 1952.
Hertz, Joseph H. *The Authorized Daily Prayer Book*. New York: Bloch Publishing Co., 1960.
Hitler, Adolf. *Mein Kampf*. (Translated by Ralph Manheim.) Boston: Houghton Mifflin Co., Sentry Edition, 1943.
Isaac, Jules. *Jesus and Israel*. New York: Holt Rinehart and Winston, 1971.
Leon, Harry J. *The Jews of Ancient Rome*. Philadelphia: Jewish Publication Society, 1960.
Marcus, Jacob R. *The Jew in the Medieval World*. New York: Harper Torchbooks, 1965.
Mayer, Jean. "Trichinosis Remains a Risk." *The Sun*, Baltimore: May 6, 1976, p. Dl.

[244]

Mencken, H. L. *A New Dictionary of Quotations*. New York: Alfred A. Knopf, 1942.

Noveck, Simon (ed.). *Great Jewish Personalities*. B'nai B'rith Great Book Series, 1959, Vol. 1.

"The Papacy: Reluctant Revolutionary." *Time* magazine, September 24, 1965, pp. 62-68.

Parkes, James. *Antisemitism*. Chicago: Quadrangle Books, 1963.

Postal, Bernard and Koppman, Lionel. *A Jewish Tourist's Guide to the U.S.* Philadelphia: Jewish Publication Society, 1954.

Roth, Cecil. *History of the Marranos*. Philadelphia: Jewish Publication Society, 1959.

Rynne, Xavier. *The Fourth Session: The Debates and Decrees of Vatican Council II, September 14 to December 8, 1965.* New York: Farrar, Straus and Giroux, 1966.

Trachtenberg, Joshua. *The Devil and the Jews*. New Haven: Yale University Press, 1941.

Westermarck, Edward. *The Origin and Development of the Moral Ideas*. New York: Johnson Reprint Corp., 1912, 1917.

Zangwill, Israel. *Chosen Peoples*. London: George Allen & Unwin Ltd., 1918.

Exhibit C

Herman, Nolan B. (ed.). *The Interpreter's Bible*, Vols. 1-12. New York: Abingdon Press, 1952.

Hertz, Joseph H. (ed.) *The Pentateuch and Haftorahs*. London: The Soncino Press, 1961.

Wallechinsky, David and Wallace, Irving and Wallace, Amy. *The Book of Lists*. New York: William Morrow, 1977.

CHAPTER IV

Ausubel, Nathan. *A Treasury of Jewish Folklore*. New York: Crown Publishers, 1948.

Boudet, J. (ed.). *Jerusalem: A History*. New York: G. P. Putnam's Sons, 1967.

Corddry, Charles W. "The Yom Kippur War, 1973—Lessons New and Old." *National Defense Magazine*, May-June, 1974.

Croche, Florence. "An Authentic 'Judas Maccabeus.'" *The Sunday Sun*, Baltimore: February 5, 1978, p. N6.

Durant, Will, and Durant, Ariel. *Age of Voltaire (Story of Civilization*, Vol. 9). New York: Simon & Schuster, 1965.
Edelman, Lily. "Arabs, Jews and the New Antisemitism." *The National Jewish Monthly*, February, 1976, pp. 30-33.
Fredman, J. George and Falk, Louis A. *Jews in American Wars.* Washington: The Jewish War Veterans of the United States of America, 1963.
Friederich, Otto. *Before the Deluge.* New York: Harper & Row, 1972.
Gilbert, Martin. *Jewish History Atlas.* New York: Collier Books, 1969.
Goldberg, M. Hirsh. *The Jewish Connection.* New York: Stein and Day, 1976.
Golden, Harry. *For 2¢ Plain.* New York: Permabook, 1960.
Grumberger, Richard. *The 12-Year Reich.* New York: Holt, Rinehart and Winston, 1971.
Howe, Pete. "Here's Howe." *Baltimore American Sunday Pictorial Review*, January 16, 1955.
Kaufman, I. *American Jews in World War II.* New York: Dial Press, 1947.
Kumpa, Peter J. "The Torment Continues for the Jews in Russia." *The Sunday Sun*, Baltimore: February 22, 1976, p. K-1.
Levitan, Tina. *The Firsts of American Jewish History.* Brooklyn: Charuth Press, 1957.
Litvinoff, Barnet. *A Peculiar People.* New York: Waybright and Talley, 1969.
Manners, Ande. *Poor Cousins.* New York: Coward, McCann & Geoghegan, 1972.
Mencken, H. L. *A New Dictionary of Quotations.* New York: Alfred A. Knopf, 1942.
Neider, Charles. *The Complete Essays of Mark Twain.* New York: Doubleday, 1963.
Postal, Bernard and Koppman, Lionel. *American Jewish Landmarks: A Travel Guide and History.* Vol. 1. New York: Fleet Press, 1977.
Rabinowitz, Major Lewis. *Soldiers From Judea.* London: American Zionist Emergency Council by Arrangement with Victor Gollancz, Ltd., 1945.
Roth, Cecil. *Personalities and Events in Jewish History.* Philadelphia: Jewish Publication Society, 1953.
Rubin, E. *140 Jewish Marshalls, Generals & Admirals.* London: DeVero Books, 1952.
Sampson, Anthony. *The Arms Bazaar.* New York: The Viking Press, 1977.
Segal, Charles. *Fascinating Facts About American Jewish History.* New York· Twayne Publishers, 1955.

[246]

Shecter, Alan. "The Truth About the Yom Kippur War." *The Times of Israel and World Jewish Review*, October, 1974, pp. 26–29.
St. John, Robert. *Jews, Justice and Judaism.* Garden City, New York: Doubleday, 1969.
Singer, Howard. *Bring Forth the Mighty Men.* New York: Funk & Wagnalls, 1969.
Szajkowski, Zosa. *Jews and the French Foreign Legion.* New York: Ktav Publishing House, 1975.
Twersky, Isadore (ed.). *A Maimonides Reader.* New York: Behrman House, 1972.
Werbell, Rabbi Frederick E. "Where Nazis Accepted Jews." *The Jewish Week–American Examiner*, April 24, 1977.

Exhibit D
Narkiss, Bezalel (ed.). *Picture History of Jewish Civilization.* New York: Harry N. Abrams, 1970.

CHAPTER V

Altman, Richard with Kaufman, Merwyn. *The Making of a Musical.* New York: Crown Publishers, 1971.
Ausubel, Nathan. *A Treasury of Jewish Folklore.* New York: Crown Publishers, 1948.
Barch, Joan Rubinstein. *Jewish Egg Farmers in New Jersey.* Unpublished Master's Degree in Department of Geographic and Environmental Studies in Northeastern Illinois University, Chicago, Fall, 1976.
Christopher, Milbourne. *Houdini—A Pictorial Life.* New York: Thomas Y. Crowell, 1976.
"Creator of MIG is Dead." *The Canadian Jewish News*, December 10, 1976, p. 10.
Davis, Mac. *They All Are Jews.* New York: Jordan Publishing Company, 1937.
"Good Guys Emerge Triumphant in Battle Over Rights to Superman." *The Canadian Jewish News*, March 5, 1976, p. 4.
Gresham, William Lindsay. *Houdini: The Man Who Walked Through Walls.* New York: Holt, Rinehart and Winston, 1959.
Gross, Nachum (ed.). *Economic History of the Jews.* New York: Schocken Books, 1975.
Hitler, Adolf. *Mein Kampf.* (Translated by Ralph Manheim.) Boston: Houghton Mifflin, Sentry Edition. 1943.

"Israel Shows the World How." *The Canadian Jewish News*, Friday, May 20, 1977, p. 2.

Jeal, Tim. *Livingstone*. East Rutherford, New Jersey: G. P. Putnam's, 1973.

Manchester, P. W. (ed.). *The Dance Encyclopedia*. New York: Simon & Schuster, 1967.

Miller, Charles. *The Lunatic Express*. New York: Macmillan, 1971.

Postal, Bernard and Koppman, Lionel. *American Jewish Landmarks (Vol. 1— The Northeast)*. New York: Fleet Press, 1977.

Sampson, Anthony. *The Arms Bazaar*. New York: The Viking Press, 1977.

Schecter, Joel. *Desert Research in Israel*. Kidman–Israel Journal of Development, Vol. 1, No. 1, 1973.

Schweitzer, George. *Emin Pasha: His Life and Work*. Westminster: Archibald Constable and Company, 1898.

Stanley, Henry M. *In Darkest Africa*. New York: Charles Scribner's Sons, 1891.

Stember, Charles Herbert and others. *Jews in the Mind of America*. New York: Basic Books, 1966.

"Strength and Longevity." *The New York Times*, October 16, 1925, editorial page.

"Superman Creators Live on Comic-Book Memories, Pennies," *The Baltimore Sun*, December 9, 1975, p. B6.

Tobias, Andrew. *Fire and Ice*. New York: William Morrow and Company, 1976.

Tyler, Karen. *Something You Always Wanted to Know About Almost Everything*. New York: Popular Library, 1964.

Wallechinsky, David and Wallace, Irving and Wallace, Amy. *The Book of Lists*. New York: William Morrow, 1977.

Weisinger, Mort. "I Flew with Superman." *Parade Magazine*, October 23, 1977.

Exhibit E

Gross, Nachum (ed.) *Economic History of the Jews*. New York: Schocken Books, 1975.

CHAPTER VI

Ausubel, Nathan, (ed.). *A Treasury of Jewish Folklore*. New York: Crown Publishers, 1948.

Bermant, Chaim. *The Jews.* New York: Quadrangle, The New York Times Book Co., 1977.
Cohen, Abraham. *Everyman's Talmud.* New York: Schocken Books, 1975.
Elkin, Michael. "Baseball's Most Valuable Player (Rod Carew) and Judaism." *The Jewish Digest,* February, 1978, pp. 18-19.
Franklin, Sidney. *Bullfighter from Brooklyn.* New York: Prentice-Hall, 1952.
Hemingway, Ernest. *The Sun Also Rises.* New York: Charles Scribner's Sons, 1926.
———*Death in the Afternoon.* New York: Charles Scribner's Sons, 1932.
Hertz, Joseph H. (ed.). *The Pentateuch and Haftorahs.* London: The Soncino Press, 1961.
Lachman, Dr. Frederick. "Sports Traditionally Shunned by Jews." *The Buffalo Jewish Review,* July 25, 1975, p. 9.
Menke, Frank G. (ed.). *The Encyclopedia of Sports.* Cranbury, New Jersey: A. S. Barnes & Co., 1975.
National Baseball Hall of Fame and Museum. Cooperstown, New York, 1975.
Postal, Bernard; Silver, Jesse, and Silver, Roy. *Encyclopedia of Jews in Sports.* New York: Bloch Publishing Company, 1965.
Ribalow, Harold U. *The Jew in American Sports.* New York: Bloch Publishing Company, 1966.
Yee, Min S. (ed.). *The Sports Book.* New York: Holt, Rinehart and Winston, 1975.

Exhibit F

Wallechinsky, David and Wallace, Irving. *The People's Almanac.* New York: Doubleday & Company, 1975.

CHAPTER VII

Alter, Robert. "Defaming the Jews." *Commentary,* January, 1973, pp. 77-82.
Amis, Kingsley. "Waxing Wroth." *Harper's Magazine,* April, 1969, pp. 104-07.
Banks, Lynn Reid. "Self-flagellation in Anglo-Jewish Writing." *Congress Monthly,* October, 1977, pp. 15-17.
Bready, James H. "The Battle Cries of Leon Uris." *The Sunday Sun,* Baltimore: April 16, 1978.

Brine, Ruth. "Women's Lib: Beyond Sexual Politics." *Time* magazine, July 26, 1971, pp. 36–37.
Donin, Rabbi Hayim Halevy. *To Be A Jew*. New York: Basic Books, 1972.
Dyer, Wayne. *Your Erroneous Zones*. New York: Funk & Wagnalls, 1976.
Gittelsohn, Roland B. "Women's Lib and Judaism." *Midstream*, October, 1971, pp. 51–58.
Gordis, Robert. "Sex in Judaism." *Congress Monthly*, January, 1978, pp. 10–13.
Hacohen, Devora and Hacohen, Menahem. *One People: The Story of the Eastern Jews*. New York: Sabra Books, Funk & Wagnalls, 1969.
Hausner, Gideon. *Justice in Jerusalem*. New York: Harper & Row, 1966.
Hertz, Joseph H. *The Authorized Daily Prayer Book*. New York: Bloch Publishing Company, 1961.
Lerner, Annie Lapidus. "How the Jewish Feminist Movement Was Born." *Jewish Digest*, 1977, pp. 35–38.
Noveck, Simon (ed.) *Great Jewish Personalities*. B'nai B'rith Great Book Series, Vol. 1, 1959.
Oliver, Rose. "The 'Jewish Mother.' " *Congress Monthly*, September, 1977, pp. 15–18.
Patai, Raphael. *The Jewish Mind*. New York: Charles Scribner's Sons, 1977.
Petersen, Clarence. *The Bantam Story*. New York: Bantam Books, 1977.
Postal, Bernard. "A Nobel Laureate and Her Kosher Kitchen." *Jewish Digest*, 1978, pp. 7–8.
Priesand, Sally. *Judaism and the New Woman*. New York: Behrman House, 1975.
Roth, Cecil. *History of the Marranos*. Philadelphia: Jewish Publication Society, 1959.
Roth, Philip. *Portnoy's Complaint*. New York: Random House, 1969.
Swidler, Leonard. "Beruria: The First Jewish Feminist." *Jewish Digest*, 1978, pp. 60–64.
Wylie, Philip. *Generation of Vipers*. New York: Farrar, Straus, 1942.
Zaharoff, Howard. "The Jewish Mother, Without Shmaltz." *Baltimore Jewish Times*, May 6, 1977.

Exhibit G

Ausubel, Nathan. *The Book of Jewish Knowledge*. New York: Crown Publishers, 1964.
Birnbaum, Philip. *A Book of Jewish Concepts*. New York: Hebrew Publishing Company, 1964.

CHAPTER VIII

Bakst, Jerome. " 'Arab-vertizing': The New Brand of Arab Propaganda." *The Times of Israel and World Jewish Review,* April, 1975, p. 15–23.

Baring-Gould, Sabine. *Curious Myths of the Middle Ages.* New Hyde Park, New York: University Books, 1967.

Bernstein, Herman. *The Truth About "The Protocols of Zion."* New York: Ktav Publishing House, 1971.

Cohn, Norman. *Warrant for Genocide.* New York: Harper & Row, 1967.

Dorfman, Dan. "Full Disclosure." *Esquire Magazine,* May 9, 1978, p. 13.

Dreher, Carl. *Sarnoff, an American Success.* New York: Quadrangle, The New York Times Book Co., 1977.

Durant, Will. *Reformation (Story of Civilization,* Vol. 6). New York: Simon & Schuster, 1953.

Gallob, Ben. "Distribution of Anti-poverty Funds Hurts New York's Jewish Poor." *The Buffalo Jewish Review,* January 6, 1978, p. 12.

Gilbert, Martin. *Jewish History Atlas.* New York: Collier Books, 1969.

Greenberg, Harold I. and Nadler, Samuel. *Poverty in Israel: Economic Realities and the Promise of Social Justice.* New York: Praeger Publishers, 1977.

Gross, Nachum (ed). *Economic History of the Jews.* New York: Schocken Books, 1975.

Hitler, Adolf. *Mein Kampf.* (Translated by Ralph Manheim.) Boston: Houghton Mifflin, Sentry Edition 1943.

Jacobs, Joseph. *Jewish Contribution to Civilization.* Philadelphia: Jewish Publication Society, 1919.

The Oxford English Dictionary. London: Oxford University Press, 1961.

Parkes, James. *Antisemitism.* Chicago: Quadrangle Books, 1963.

Poliakov, Leon. *The Aryan Myth.* New York: Basic Books, 1974.

Roget, Peter Mark. *Thesaurus of English Words and Phrases.* New York: Grosset & Dunlap, 1937.

Runes, Dagobert D. *The War Against the Jew.* New York: Philosophical Library, 1968.

Trachtenberg, Joshua. *The Devil and the Jews.* New Haven: Yale University Press, 1941.

Trubo, Richard. "The Jewish Poor—Los Angeles is a Shocker." *The Times of Israel and World Jewish Reviews,* May, 1974, pp. 55–56.

Waite, Robert G. L. *The Psychopathic God Adolf Hitler.* New York: Basic Books, 1977.

Webster's New World Dictionary of the American Language. Cleveland: The World Publishing Company, 1964.

Exhibit H

Roth, Cecil (ed.). *The Ritual Murder Libel and the Jew.* The Report by Cardinal Lorenzo Ganganelli (Pope Clement XIV). London: The Woburn Press, 1940.
Trachtenberg, Joshua. *The Devil and the Jews.* New Haven: Yale University Press, 1941.

CHAPTER IX

Arendt, Hannah. *Eichmann in Jerusalem: A Report on the Banality of Evil.* New York: The Viking Press, 1963.
Bauer, Yehuda. "When the Jews Fought Back." *Jewish Digest,* April, 1977.
Borchsenius, Paul. *And It Was Morning.* London: George Allen & Unwin, 1962.
Dubnov, Simon. *History of the Jews.* New York: Thomas Yoseloff, 1973.
Friedrich, Otto. *Before the Deluge: A Portrait of Berlin in the 1920s.* New York: Avon Books, 1973.
Garlinski, Jozef. *Fighting Auschwitz.* New York: Fawcett Crest, 1975.
Hausner, Gideon. *Justice in Jerusalem.* New York: Harper & Row, 1966.
Hillel, Marc and Henry, Clarissa. *Of Pure Blood.* New York: McGraw-Hill Book Company, 1976.
Hitler, Adolf. *Mein Kampf.* (Translated by Ralph Manheim.) Boston: Houghton Mifflin, Sentry Edition, 1943.
Hitler's Secret Conversations. New York: Signet Books, 1961.
Infield, Glenn B. *Eva and Adolf.* New York: Grosset & Dunlap, 1974.
Langer, Walter C. *The Mind of Adolf Hitler.* New York: Basic Books, 1972.
Levin, Nora. *The Holocaust: The Destruction of European Jewry 1933–1945.* New York: Schocken Books, 1973.
Litvinoff, Barnet. *A Peculiar People.* New York: Weybright and Talley, 1969.
Lorant, Stefan. *Sieg Heil!* New York: W. W. Norton & Co., 1974.
Marcus, Jacob R. *The Rise and Destiny of the German Jew.* Cincinnati: Union of American Hebrew Congregations, 1934.
Massing, Paul W. *Rehearsal for Destruction: A Study of Political Anti-Semitism in Imperial Germany.* New York: Howard Fertig, 1967.
Meltzer, Milton. *Never to Forget: The Jews of the Holocaust.* New York: Harper & Row, 1976.
Noakes, Jeremy and Pridham, Geoffrey (eds.). *Documents on Nazism 1919–1945.* New York: The Viking Press, 1975.

Payne, Robert. *The Life and Death of Adolf Hitler.* New York: Praeger Publishers, 1973.

Rabinowitz, Dorothy. *New Lives: Survivors of the Holocaust Living in America.* New York: Alfred A. Knopf, 1976.

Schoenberner, Gerhard. *The Yellow Star: The Persecution of the Jews in Europe, 1933–1945.* New York: Bantam Books, 1973.

Shirer, William L. *The Rise and Fall of the Third Reich.* New York: Simon & Schuster, 1960.

Speer, Albert. *Spandau—The Secret Diaries.* New York: Pocket Books, 1977.

Trachtenberg, Joshua. *The Devil and the Jews.* New Haven: Yale University Press, 1941.

Waite, Roger G. L. *The Psychopathic God Adolf Hitler.* New York: Basic Books, 1977.

Wolman, Benjamin B. (ed.). *The Psychoanalytic Interpretation of History.* New York: Basic Books, 1971.

Exhibit I

De Hass, Jacob (ed.). *The Encyclopedia of Jewish Knowledge.* New York: Behrman's Jewish Book House, 1949.

The Encyclopaedia Judaica. Jerusalem: Keter Publishing House, 1971.

CHAPTER X

Baron, Joseph L. *A Treasury of Jewish Quotations.* New York: Crown Publishers, 1956.

Browne, Lewis. *How Odd of God.* New York: The Macmillan Company, 1934.

Busi, Frederick. "Anti-Semitism and Anti-Zionism." *The American Zionist,* December, 1973.

Cohn, Norman. *Warrant for Genocide.* New York: Harper & Row, 1967.

Einbinder, Harvey. *The Myth of the Britannica.* New York: Grove Press, 1964.

Gallob, Ben. "Teachers Warned to be Aware of Anti-Semitism in 'Classics'." *The Buffalo Jewish Review,* April 1, 1977.

Harrison, G.B. (ed.). *Shakespeare's Major Plays and Sonnets.* New York: Harcourt, Brace and Company, 1948.

Morrison, Theodore (ed.). *The Portable Chaucer.* New York: The Viking Press, 1975.

Noakes, Jeremy and Pridham, Geoffrey (eds.). *Documents on Nazism, 1919–1945.* New York: The Viking Press, 1975.

Rabinowitz, Dorothy. *New Lives: Survivors of the Holocaust Living in America*. New York: Alfred A. Knopf, 1976.
Runes, Dagobert D. *The War Against the Jew*. New York: Philosophical Library, 1968.
Sartre, Jean-Paul. *Anti-Semite and Jew*. New York: Schocken Books, 1948.
"Stalin Latter Day Haman." *Update—News and Analysis Newsletter*. National Zionist Affairs Department of Hadassah, October 17, 1977.
Stember, Charles Herbert and Others. *Jews in the Mind of America*. New York: Basic Books, 1966.
Stern, David. "Imagining the Holocaust." *Commentary*, July, 1976, p. 46.
Weisel, Eli. "The Holocaust—Some Say it Didn't Happen." *The Canadian Jewish News*, November 18, 1977.
Withers, H.L. (ed.). *The Merchant of Venice* (The Arden Shakespeare Edition). Boston: D.C. Heath and Company, 1916.

ENCYCLOPEDIAS AND OTHER BASIC REFERENCES

Ausubel, Nathan. *The Book of Jewish Knowledge*. New York: Crown Publishers, 1964.
Ausubel, Nathan. *Pictorial History of the Jewish People*. New York: Crown Publishers, 1958.
Baron, Joseph. *A Treasury of Jewish Quotations*. New York: Crown Publishers, 1956.
De Haas, Jacob (ed.). *The Encyclopedia of Jewish Knowledge*. New York: Behrman's Jewish Book House, 1949.
The Encyclopaedia Britannica (15th ed.). Chicago: Encyclopaedia Britannica, 1974.
Encyclopaedia Judaica. Jerusalem: Keter Publishing House, 1971.
The Jewish Encyclopedia. New York and London: Funk and Wagnalls, 1901.
The New Catholic Encyclopedia. New York: McGraw-Hill, 1967.
Peters, Laurence J. *Peter's Quotations*. New York: William Morrow and Company, 1977.
The Soncino Books of the Bible. 14 Volumes. London: The Soncino Press, 1970.
The World Book Encyclopedia. Chicago: Field Enterprises Educational Corporation, 1975.

ACKNOWLEDGMENTS

I have many people to thank for helping make this work possible. The thousands of hours of research and writing that went into this could not have been done—nor could it have borne the fruit now called a book—without many other hands.

Once again my wife, Barbara, helped make this book not only possible, but better. She was my best critic, adding appreciably to the final work with her insight and sensitivity and with suggestions that improved it greatly. But she also made my labors easier by taking upon herself that many more of the family responsibilities. I am eternally grateful; I just hope she is not eternally exhausted.

In this regard, I must also acknowledge the burden borne by my children—Aviva, Stuart, and Seth—who waited patiently while the work proceeded at all hours of day and night. I was especially encouraged by my daughter Aviva's pride in this work and by my son Stuart's eagerness to help with the research. Two-year-old Seth helped by sleeping late in the mornings.

There are others who played an important role in this book. I wish to thank Michaela Hamilton, who worked so closely with me as editor of my first book and contributed significantly to the thrust of this one. I also thank Patricia Day for being such a perceptive editor and keeping me always on the right—and succinct—path. And I extend my gratitude to Sol Stein, whose direction and counsel have been paramount in the creation of this work.

For reading parts of the manuscript, clarifying facts, and supplying me with important analysis of the work in progress, I am grateful to Rhoda Weyr, George Gipe, Bernard Postal, Robert St. John, Rabbi Israel Goldberg, Miriam Goldberg, Mark Reches, Rabbi Alvin Kass, Eileen Prescott, and my brother, Victor Goldberg. In this regard, I especially want to extend my appreciation to Dr. Arnold Blumberg, professor of history at Towson State University, for bringing his considerable scholarship to bear on a review of the entire work. He not only checked for errors, but aided me by pointing out additional sources for information. However, the responsibility for any lapses or inaccuracies that may exist in the final work is mine.

For typing the manuscript with such care, I thank Anne Marder, who also provided much beneficial feedback. Thanks also to typists Myra Satisky, Shirley Cornblatt, and Natalie Ettlin.

For being of aid in my research, I am grateful to the staffs of the Enoch Pratt Free Library System of Baltimore, the Randallstown Branch of the Baltimore County Library System, the Bard Library at the Community College of Baltimore, and the Joseph Meyerhoff Library of the Baltimore Hebrew College. I am especially appreciative to Dr. Rosy Bodenheimer and Betty K. Sachs of the Baltimore Hebrew College Library, both of whom went out of their busy ways to be of service. Dale Kessler once again aided me in the tracking down of hard to get research materials.

In closing, I want to extend special appreciation to my parents—to my mother, Ida, for her encouragement and interest not only in this book but throughout my writing career and to my father, Herman, for once again being so helpful in so many ways with ideas, suggestions, and his ever meticulous research.

M. Hirsh Goldberg

Randallstown, Maryland
August 4, 1978

Index

Aaron, Henry, 145
Action Comics, 118
Adelung, Johann Christoph, 7
Agnew, Spiro, 187
Alcohol: the Delightful Poison (A History), 48
Alexander the Great, 80, 83
Ali, Muhammad, 149
Alston, Walter, 146-47
American Jewish Committee, 184
American Jewish Joint Distribution Committee, 89
American Legion, 86
American Revolution, 86
Amin, Idi, 80
Amis, Kingsley, 156
And It Was Morning, 214, 215
Anti-Catholic activities, Nazi, 222-23
Anti-Semite and Jew, 40-41
Anti-Semitic League, 12
Anti-Semitism, 4, 9, 11, 12, 225, 229; anti-Zionism, transformation to, 229, 230; combating, 234-35, 239-40; continuing, 229-34; German, 201-08; Hitler's, 206-08; implementation of, 234, 239; persistent false images leading to, 175-95; theories of, 233-34
Anti-Semitism, 51, 55, 69
Apion, 70, 197

Arendt, Hannah, 213
Aristotle, 166
Arms Bazaar, The, 75, 124
Arnold, Henry A. "Hap," 122
Arthur, King, 83
Aryan myth, 2, 5, 6-15, 64
Aryan Myth, The, 7-8, 11
Attas, Nissum, 94
Attell, Abe, 138
Auerbach, Arnold Jacob "Red," 140
Aviation Week and Space Technology, 95

Ballin, Albert, 202
Bar Kochba, 79, 84
Baring-Gould, Sabine, 176-77, 178
Baron, Salo, 190
Barsimson, Jacob, 86
Baseball Hall of Fame, 145, 146
Basketball Hall of Fame, 140
Bean, Robert Bennett, 30-31
Before the Deluge, 92, 202
Ben Porat, Mrs. Miriam, 167
Berlin Diary, The, 40
Biarritz, 188
Birnbaum, Dr. Philip, 67
Bismarck, Otto von, 20, 34-35, 202
Bleichröder, Gerson, 202
Bloch, Adolph, 123

[257]

Blood Accusation (Libel), 196-97, 207, 234
Blumenberg, Leopold, 87
B'nai B'rith, 184
Book of Jewish Knowledge, 46
Book of Lists, 116
Bormann, Martin, 222
Borchsenius, Paul, 214
Boxing Hall of Fame, 138
Boykoff, Harry, 141
Breitbart, Sigmund, 115-16
Bring Forth the Mighty Men, 76
Brown, Gen. George S., 186-87
Browne, Lewis, 233
Butz, Arthur, 231

Caesar, Julius, 80, 83
Canterbury Tales, "The Prioress's Tale," 196
Capp, Al, 118
Carter, Jimmy, 81
Castro, Fidel, 80
Catholic Diet of Cracow, Poland, 111
Catholic War Veterans, 86
Chamberlain, Houston Stewart, 12
Chamberlin, Clarence, 123
Charcot, J. M., 178
Charlemagne, 80, 83
Chaucer, Geoffrey, 196, 235
Chiang Kai-shek, 89
Civil War, 86, 87-88
Cohen, Louis, 89
Cohen, Morris Abraham, 89-90
Cohen, Robert, 138
Cohn, Norman, 188-89, 233
College Football Hall of Fame, 141, 142
"Concerning the Jews," 77
Curious Myths of the Middle Ages, 176-77
Czarist Russia and twelve-year-old Jewish soldiers, 98-99

Dahiya al Kahina (Dahiya the Prophetess), 166
Dassault, Marcel, 123-24
David, King, 82, 83, 84
Davis, Sammy, Jr., 185
de Gaulle, Charles, 124
Dearborn Independent, The, 190-91
Death in the Afternoon, 132
Declaration on the Relationship of the Church to Non-Christian Religions, 57
Devil and the Jews, The, 29, 233
Dialogue aux Enfers entre Montesquieu et Machiavelli ("Dialogues in Hell"), 188, 189
Diaspora, 33, 56, 78-79, 135, 233
Dictionary of Misinformation, 49
Did Six Million Really Die? The Truth at Last, 231
DiMaggio, Joe, 145, 149
Dinter, Arthur, 12
Disabled American Veterans, 86
Documents on Nazism, 232
Domenechino, 120
Donin, Rabbi Hayim Halevy, 164
Dreben, Sam, 89
Dreyfus, Alfred, 82
Dreyfus Affair, 12, 82, 188
Drucker, Norman, 140
Drumont, Edouard, 12
Duffus, Robert L., 24
Durant, Will: *Age of Voltaire*, 83; *Reformation*, 182
Dutch West India Company, 86
Dyer, Dr. Wayne, 157

Ebreo de Pesaro, Guglielmo, 120
Eck, Nathan, 217
Ehrenburg, Ilya, 203
Eichmann, Adolf, 167, 213
Einstein, Albert, 115, 223
Einstein, Max, 87
Eisenhower, Dwight David, 81, 232

Elias, Samuel ("Dutch Sam"), 138
Emin Pasha (Effendi). *See* Schnitzer, Eduard
Encyclopaedia Britannica, 13
Encyclopaedia Judaica, 92
Enemy of the People: Antisemitism, An, 69
Entebbe rescue, 221
Epstein, Moses Henry, 141
Esquire magazine, 184
Essay on the Inequality of the Human Race, 10
Essay on the Language and Wisdom of the Indians, 8
Evans, Bergen, 31
"Eye for an eye, an," 44, 57-63

Fairbanks, Douglas, Sr., 118
Faisal, King, 194
Farming and landowning by Jews, 110-15; in America, 112-14; in Israel, 114-15
Faurisson, Robert, 231
Fighting Auschwitz, 215, 218
"Final Solution," 200, 204, 212-21
Finnish-Russian war (1939-40), 94
Finot, Jean, 12
Fishberg, Dr. Maurice, 31-32, 35
Fleming, Alice, 48
Flowers, Sir Newman, 83
Ford, Gerald, 186
Ford, Henry, 174, 190-92, 194; anti-Ford protest, 192
Foundations of the Nineteenth Century, 12
Fourth Lateran Council (1215), 203-04
Foxx, Jimmy, 144, 145
France Juive, La (Jewish France), 12
Frank, Hans, 217
Frankfurter Zeitung, 193
Franklin, Sidney, 131-33
Frauenthal (Fronthal), Max, 87

Frederick I and II of Prussia, 170
French Revolution, 90, 108m, 186, 187
Freud, Sigmund, 134, 233
Friedman, Benny, 141-42
Friedrich, Otto, 202
Fritsch, Theodore, 192

Gandhi, Mohandas K., 211
Garfield, James, 81
Garlinski, Josef, 215, 218, 219
Gilbert, W. S., 30
Gobineau, Count Joseph Arthur de, 10
Godfrey de Bouillon, 83
Goebbels, Josef, 121
Goldberg, Marshall, 141, 142
Goldberg, Rube, 118
Goldbergian Institute: Jewish Athletes Hall of Fame, 137, 138, 140-41, 147; military exhibit, 85-97
Goldberg's Law, 16, 27, 28, 36, 37, 39, 56, 63, 68, 80, 107, 135, 164-65, 169, 181, 188, 191, 203, 230, 231, 236; specific instances of, 16-17, 40-41, 71, 98-99, 127, 152, 170-71, 196-97, 225
Golden Rule, 51
Goodsche, Herman, 188
Gordon, Aharon David, 114
Gordon, Gen. Charles G., 104
Grant, Michael, 51
Grant, Ulysses S., 81, 87
Greenberg, Hank, 144-45
Gregory X, Pope, 197
Grynszpan, Herschel, 219
Gunther, John, 40
Gurevich, Mikhail, 124-25
Guttmann, Hugo, 92

Haber, Fritz, 202
Hammurabi, Code of, 59, 62

Handel, George Frederick, 83-84
Harper's Monthly (Magazine), 24, 77, 156
Harrison, William Henry, 81
Hart, Abraham, 87
Hassan, Vita, 105
Hausner, Gideon, 167, 214, 217
Hays, Jacob, 121-22
Hays, Moses Judah, 121
Hecht, Ben, 92
Hector, 83
Heidrich, Reinhard, 219
Hemingway, Ernest, 130, 132, 235
Hertz, Dr. Joseph H., 61, 66, 107
Herzl, Theodor, 21, 30, 40, 112, 185
Heyman, Arthur, 139
Hilchoth Melachim, 85
Hillel the Elder, 107
Hindenburg, Paul von, 5
Hirsch, Baron Maurice de, 112
History of the Marranos, 167
Hitler, Adolf, 2, 4, 5-7, 12, 13, 14-15, 20, 30, 33, 63-64, 80, 92, 93, 107, 121, 123, 150, 174, 191, 192-93, 200, 201, 203, 204, 205, 206-08, 210, 219-20, 222, 223, 229, 231
Hitler's Secret Conversations, 207
Hollandersky, Abe, "the Newsboy," 139
Holocaust, 2, 5, 15, 26, 79, 167, 186, 195, 201-24, 225, 228, 229; attempts to refute, 231-32; erasing memory of, 221; Jewish acquiescence during, 210-21; Jewish resistance and uprisings during, 208-10, 216-20; Nazi extermination techniques, 212-16; world loss from, 223-24
Holocaust, The, 33-34, 220
Houdini, Harry, 116-18, 123
How Odd of God, 233
Howard, Maj.-Gen. O. O., 88
Human Rights Commission, New York City, 184

Ignorance: effects of, 3-5, 13, 15, 201; and Jews, 4-5, 13, 15, 26-27, 36-39, 67-69, 170-71, 195
Ignorance Factor, 3-5, 11, 13-14, 26, 29, 36, 38, 39, 49, 68, 69, 77, 82, 93, 108, 110, 115, 143, 168, 178, 190, 207, 210, 213, 234, 235
Immaculate Conception, 49
In Darkest Africa, 105
Indo-European languages, 7
Innocent III, Pope, 203
Innocent IV, Pope, 196-97
Inquisition and the Jews, 16-17, 48, 167
Inside Asia, 40
International and interfaith prejudices, 23-25
International Jew: The World's Foremost Problem, The, 191, 192
Isaiah, 84-85

Jabotinsky, Vladimir, 88
Jachman, Isador, 94
Jackson, Andrew, 81
Jacobi, Dr. Roland, 147
Jerusalem—A History, 79
Jesus: An Historian's Review of the Gospels, 51
"Jew as a Soldier, The," *Harper's Monthly*, 77
Jew in American Sports, The, 137-38
Jewish Colonization Association, 112
Jewish Connection, The, 4, 85
Jewish Councils, 214-15
Jewish image, insensitivity to tarnishing, 235-40
Jewish "Look," The, 40-41
Jewish Mind, The, 33
Jewish mother stereotype, 115-69
Jewish popularity, 152
Jewish prayer services, 170-71
Jewish State, The, 21
Jewish War Veterans, 86

Jewish Week-American Examiner, The, 94
Jewish women, role of, 163-68, 169
Jews: and ability to survive, 210-12; in aviation, 122-25; as Chosen People, 63-67; definition of, 32-34; and eating pork, 45-49; and "an eye for an eye," 44, 57-63; farming and landowning by, 110-15, 127; as fighters, 75-97; ghetto existence of, 108-11; ignorance and, 4-5, 13, 15, 26-27, 36-39, 67-69, 170-71, 195; involvement in garment industries by, 109-10; as killers of Christ, 54-57; literary bias against, 235-40; and moneylender image, 179-85; Nazi tactics of delusion used against, 212-16; noses of, 30-32; and posture of accommodation, 210-12; poverty of, 184-85; as power manipulators, 185-95; religious misconceptions about, 45-70, 170-71, 196-97; role of, 69-70; self-criticism among, 168-69; in sports, 130-51; stereotype-breakers among, 103-26; stereotypic misconceptions about, 21-22, 25-36, 178-95, 201; three persistent false images about, 175-95; work and occupations among, 105-25

Jews: A Study of Race and Environment, The, 31-32

Jews in the Mind of America, 28, 236
Joachimsen, Philip J., 87
John XXIII, Pope, 57
Johnson, Jack, 149, 150
Joly, Maurice, 188, 189
Jones, William, 7
Joshua, 82, 83, 84
Judaism and athletics, 133-36
Judaism in music, 12

Judas Maccabaeus (Handel), 83
Judenrat. See Jewish Councils
Justice in Jerusalem, 167, 214, 217

Kennedy, John F., 81
Khadaffi, Muammar, 194
Kibbutzim, 114
King, Martin Luther, Jr., 211
Kling, Johnny, 143
Knefler, Frederick, 87
Kol Nidre, 116
Kosciusko, Gen. Tadeusz, 90
Koufax, Sanford (Sandy), 145-47
Kristallnacht (Crystal Night or Night of the Broken Glass), 219

Lachman, Charles, 119
Langer, Walter C., 220
Lapouge, Georges Vacher de, 15
Lazarus, Emma, 212
Lenin, 40, 191
Leo X, Pope, 182
Leonard, Benny, 138-39
Levenson, Sam, 162
Levin, Meyer, 229, 234-35
Levin, Nora, 33-34, 220
Levine, Charles, 123
Levy, Asser, 86
Levy, Edward Laurence, 147
Levy, Uriah Phillips, 81-82
Lidice, massacre at, 219
Life magazine, 75-76
Lilienthal, Otto, 122
Lincoln, Abraham, 87, 155
Lindbergh, Charles, 122, 123, 186
Lipsner, Capt. Benjamin, 123
Liuzzi, Giorgio and Guido, 90
Livingstone, Dr. David, 103, 105
London Times, 91. See also *Times, The* (London)
Lorant, Stefan, 202
Louis, Joe, 150
Luckman, Sid, 141, 142
Lueger, Karl, 32, 92
Luther, Martin, 197

Maccabee, Judah, 82-83, 84
Maccabiah international games, 136, 149
McGraw, John, 143-44
Maimonides, 85
Mannerheim, Field Marshal, 94
Mantle, Mickey, 145
Mao Tse-tung, 80, 212
Maris, Roger, 144
Marr, William, 11-12
Mathewson, Christy, 146
Mayer, Dr. Jean, 47
Mayer, Erskine, 143
Mays, Willie, 145
Meige, Henry, 178-79
Mein Kampf, 6-7, 64, 107, 188, 191, 193, 206
Meir, Golda, 167, 168
Mencken, H. L., 85, 235
Mendelssohn, Moses, 13
Mendoza, Daniel, 138, 150-51
Merchant of Venice, 179, 228, 235-40
Metropolitan New York Coordinating Council on Jewish Poverty, 185
Michelangelo, 29
Mikoyan, Anastas, 125
Mikoyan, Artem, 125
Miley, Gen. Henry A., Jr., 96
Mind of Adolf Hitler, The, 219-220
Minorities, 22-23, 37, 38-39, 221-22
Monash, Lt. Gen. Sir John, 92-93
Morgenthau, Henry, 203
Moses and Monotheism, 134
Müller, Prof. Friedrich Max, 10-11
Mussolini, Benito, 80
Myth of the Jewish Race, The, 35-36

Napoleon, 80, 89, 91
Napoleon III, 188
Nasser, Gamal Abdel, 194

National Basketball Association, 139
National Football Foundation, 142
National Security Industrial Association (Washington), 96
Natural History of Nonsense, The, 31, 36
Naturalization Law (British; 1753), 150
Nazi extermination techniques, 212-16
New Dictionary of Quotations, 85
New Lives, 208, 233
New York Times, The, 116, 123
Newman, Leopold C., 87
Nicholas I, Czar, 98
Nicholas II, Czar, 80
Nixon, Richard M., 25
Nobel Prizes, 103, 223
Nordau, Max, 135
"Nose of the Jew and the Quadratus Labii Superioris Muscle, The," *American Anthropologist*, 30-31
Nuremberg Laws (1935), 203
Nuremberg Trials, 222, 232

Old Testament vs. New, 50-53
Origin and Development of the Moral Ideas, The, 53-54
Oroy, Homer, 37-38
Our Will Rogers, 37-38
Oxford English Dictionary, 183

Panov, Yuri, 119
Parkes, James, 51, 55, 69
Patai, Dr. Raphael, 33, 35-36, 168
Pershing, Gen. John J., 89
Pierce, Franklin, 87
Pike, Lipman E. (Lip), 143
Pilate, Pontius, 55
Place, Francis, 150-51
Podoloff, Maurice, 139
Poliakov, Leon, 7-8, 9, 10,11

[263]

Portnoy's Complaint, 155-57, 168
"Portnoy's Complaint," Mrs. Sophie, 157-63
Prayer Book for Sabbath and Festivals, published by the Hebrew Publishing Company of New York, 67
Professional Football Hall of Fame, 142
Protocols of the Elders of Zion, The, 188-94, 204
Proxmire, William, 184
Psychoanalytic Interpretation of History, The, 206
Psychopathic God: Adolf Hitler, The, 193-94

Rabinowitz, Maj. Lewis, 93-94
Rashi, 58, 111
Rassinier, Paul, 231
Rath, Ernst vom, 219
Rathenau, Emil, 202
Rathenau, Walter, 201-02
Renan, Ernest, 10
Revson (family), 119
Ribalow, Harold, 137
Rice, Grantland, 143
Ringelblum, Emmanuel, 167-68
Rise and Fall of the Third Reich, The, 206
Rogers, Will, 22-23, 37-39
Roosevelt, Theodore, 81, 192
Rose, Maj. Gen. Maurice, 89
Rosen, Al, 144
Rosenbloom, Maxie, 138
Rosenbluth, Len, 139
Ross, Barney, 137-38
Roth, Dr. Cecil, 167
Roth, Philip, 155, 156
Rubinstein, Helena, 119
Rudolph, Mendy, 140
Runes, Dagobert, 183
Russian Revolution, 186, 187, 189
Ruth, Babe, 143-44

Sabbath, 70
St. Thomas Aquinas, 182
Sampson, Anthony, 75, 124
Saperstein, Abe, 141
Sartre, Jean-Paul, 40-41, 233-34
Schayes, Adolph (Dolph), 140
Schlegel, August Wilhelm von, 9
Schlegel, Karl W. Friedrich von, 7-9, 11, 13
Schmeling, Max, 150
Schnitzer, Eduard, 103-05
Seddon, John, 87
Seneca, 70
Shakespeare, William, 179, 228, 235, 236, 238-39
Shatnes, law of, 109
Sherman, Gen. William T., 87
Sherrill, Gen. Charles H., 131, 149
Shirer, William, 40, 206
Shomrim Society, 121
Shuster, Joe, 118-19
Sieg Heil!, 202
Siegel, Jerry, 118-19
Singer, Howard, 76
Sirica, Judge John, 25
Six Day War, 75-76, 95, 221
Smushkevich, Gen. Jacob, 78
Soldiers from Judea, 93
Solomon, Edward, 87
Solomon, King, 84, 155
Solomon, Moses, 144
Sorell, Walter, 120-21
Spandau: The Secret Diaries, 207
Speer, Albert, 207
Spitz, Mark, 148
Sports Book, The, 146
Stahel, General, 88
Stalin, Josef, 28, 78, 80, 228, 229
Stanley, Henry Morton, 103-04, 105
Stapel, Dr. Wilhelm, 203
Steinberg, Paul "Twister," 139
Stern, Daniel, 147
Stinnes, Hugo, 202

Stone, George, 143
Streicher, Julius, 207
Studies of Religious History, 10
Sturmer, Der, 205, 207
Stuyvesant, Peter, 86
Sun Also Rises, The, 133
Sun Yat-sen, 89
Sunde wider das Blut, Die, 12
Superman, 102, 118-19
Supreme Court, U.S., 14
Szold, Henrietta, 166-67

Talmud, 60, 62-63, 107, 112, 163
Taylor, Zachary, 81
Ten Commandments, 70-71, 84
Third Reich, 5
Thoreau, Henry David, 211
Time magazine, 235
Times, The (London), 190. See also *London Times*
To Be a Jew, 164
Tobey, David, 140
Torah, 60-61, 62, 66, 69, 85, 107
Trachtenberg, Joshua, 29, 233
"Trichinosis remains a risk," 47
Trumpeldor, Joseph, 88-89
Twain, Mark, 77-78
12-Year Reich, The, 203

United States vs. Bhagat Sing Thind, 14
Uris, Leon, 169

Vatican Ecumenical Council, Second, 57
Veterans of Foreign Wars, 86
Victory of Judaism over Germandom, 11-12
Vietnam War, 58, 86

Voltaire, 45, 53, 54
Volynov, Lt.-Col. Boris, 123

Wagner, Richard, 12
Waite, Robert G. L., 193-94, 206
Wall Street Journal, 50
Wandering Jew, legend of, 175-79
War Against the Jews, The, 183
Warrant for Genocide, 188-89, 233
Warsaw Ghetto, 167-68, 200, 209, 210, 214, 217
Washington, George, 80
Webster's New World Dictionary, 13-14, 183
Weiss, Dr. Bernhard, 121
Weiss, Erich. *See* Houdini, Harry
Weizmann, Chaim, 40
Wellington, Duke of, 91
Welsh, Arthur, 122
Werbell, Frederick E., 94
Westermarck, Dr. Edward, 53-54
"Where Do We Get Our Prejudices?," *Harper's Magazine*, 24
Wiesel, Elie, 235
Wilhelm II, Kaiser, 12, 64
Williams, Ted, 145
Wolak, Rev. Stanislaw, 223
World Book Encyclopedia, 14, 235-36
World Maccabi Union, 135-36
Wright brothers, 122, 123

Yalow, Dr. Rosalyn Sussman, 167
Yom Kippur War, 95-96
Yoselovich, Berek, 90, 91
Yoselovich, Yossel, 90-91
Your Erroneous Zones, 157

Zam, Zvi Herz, 82
Zionism, 229, 230
Zohar, The, 211-12
Zunser, Eliakim, 112

ABOUT THE AUTHOR

M. Hirsh Goldberg is the author of three other books—*The Jewish Connection*, *The Blunder Book* and *The Book of Lies*—and more than 450 columns and articles in numerous magazines and newspapers. He has lectured widely in the United States and Canada, and has appeared on such national television shows as "Good Morning America."

Mr. Goldberg is a graduate of The Johns Hopkins University, with a bachelor's degree in English and a master's degree in teaching. A public relations executive accredited by the Public Relations Society of America, he was press secretary to the Mayor of Baltimore at the age of twenty-four (he was then the youngest press secretary to the mayor of a major American city). He has also served as the press secretary to the Governor of Maryland and as speech writer and public relations advisor for two of Maryland's Attorneys General. He is presently head of a Baltimore-based public relations agency.

Cited for excellence in Jewish journalism by the national Boris Smolar Award committee, Mr. Goldberg wrote a weekly freelance column for the *Baltimore Jewish Times* for nine years and served as editor of the *Times of Israel and World Jewish Review*. He contributes frequently to the editorial pages of the Baltimore *Sunpapers*.

Mr. Goldberg, who was born in Baltimore, Md., lives with his family in a suburb of Baltimore.